CASES IN CRITICAL CROSS-CULTURAL MANAGEMENT

This book is a collection of 16 empirical cases in critical Cross-Cultural Management (CCM). All cases approach culture in CCM beyond national cultures, and all examine power as an integrative part of any cross-cultural situation. The cases also consider diversity in the sense of culturally or historically learned categorizations of difference (such as gender, race, ethnicity, religion and class), and acknowledge how diversity categories might differ across cultures. Furthermore, each case suggests a specific method or concept for improving upon the situation. Out of this approach, novel insights emerge: we can see how culture, power and diversity categories are inseparable, and we can understand exactly how this is the case. The uses and benefits of this book are thus both conceptual and methodological; they emerge at the intersections of Critical CCM and diversity studies. All cases also discuss implications for practitioners and are suitable for teaching.

Mainstream CCM often limits itself to comparative models or cultural dimensions. This approach is widely critiqued for its simplicity but is equally used for the exact same reason. Often, academics teach this approach whilst cautioning students against implementing it, and this might be simply due to a lack of alternatives. Through means of rich empirical cases, this book offers such an alternative.

Considering the intersections of culture, diversity and power enables students, researchers and practitioners alike to see 'more' or 'different' things in the situation, and then to come up with novel approaches and solutions that do justice to the realities of culture and diversity in today's (and the future's) management and organizations. The chapters of this book thus offer concepts and methods to approach cross-cultural situations: the conceptual gain lies in bringing together CCM and (critical) diversity studies in an easily accessible manner. As a methodological contribution, the cases in this book offer the concise tools and methods for implementing an intersectional approach to culture.

Jasmin Mahadevan is Professor of International and Cross-Cultural Management at Pforzheim University, Germany. She is interested in studying culturally complex contexts by means of various approaches.

Henriett Primecz is a Professor at Corvinus University of Budapest, Hungary. Her research interest is cross-cultural management, gender and diversity and organizational theory.

Laurence Romani is Associate Professor at the Stockholm School of Economics, Sweden. Her work focuses on issues of representation and interaction with the cultural Other in respectful and enriching ways.

ROUTLEDGE STUDIES IN INTERNATIONAL BUSINESS AND THE WORLD ECONOMY

Expatriate Managers
The Paradoxes of Living and Working Abroad
Anna Spiegel, Ursula Mense-Petermann, and Bastian Bredenkötter

The International Business Environment and National Identity
Tatiana Gladkikh

European Born Globals
Job Creation in Young International Businesses
Edited by Irene Mandl and Valentina Patrini

Management Research
European Perspectives
Edited by Sabina Siebert

Global Business Intelligence
Edited by J. Mark Munoz

Confucianism, Discipline and Competitiveness
Chris Baumann, Hume Winzar, and Doris Viengkham

Cases in Critical Cross-Cultural Management
An Intersectional Approach to Culture
Edited by Jasmin Mahadevan, Henriett Primecz, and Laurence Romani

For more information about this series, please visit: www.routledge.com/ Routledge-Studies-in-International-Business-and-the-World-Economy/ book-series/SE0358

CASES IN CRITICAL CROSS-CULTURAL MANAGEMENT

An Intersectional Approach to Culture

Edited by Jasmin Mahadevan, Henriett Primecz, and Laurence Romani

NEW YORK AND LONDON

First published 2020
by Routledge
52 Vanderbilt Avenue, New York, NY 10017

and by Routledge
2 Park Square, Milton Park, Abingdon, Oxon, OX14 4RN

Routledge is an imprint of the Taylor & Francis Group, an informa business

© 2020 Taylor & Francis

The right of Jasmin Mahadevan, Henriett Primecz, and Laurence
Romani to be identified as the authors of the editorial material,
and of the authors for their individual chapters, has been asserted in
accordance with sections 77 and 78 of the Copyright, Designs and
Patents Act 1988.

Library of Congress Cataloging-in-Publication Data
Names: Mahadevan, Jasmin, editor. | Primecz, Henriett, editor. |
    Romani, Laurence, editor.
Title: Cases in critical cross-cultural management : an intersectional
    approach to culture / edited by Jasmin Mahadevan, Henriett
    Primecz, and Laurence Romani.
Description: New York : Routledge, 2019. | Series: Routledge
    international studies in business history | Includes bibliographical
    references and index.
Identifiers: LCCN 2019044879 | ISBN 9780815383482 (hardback) |
    ISBN 9780815359340 (paperback) | ISBN 9781351121064 (ebook)
Subjects: LCSH: Management—Cross-cultural studies. | Diversity in
    the workplace—Management. | Intercultural communication.
Classification: LCC HD62.4 .C3667 2019 | DDC 658.3008—dc23
LC record available at https://lccn.loc.gov/2019044879

ISBN: 978-0-8153-8348-2 (hbk)
ISBN: 978-0-8153-5934-0 (pbk)
ISBN: 978-1-351-12106-4 (ebk)

Typeset in Bembo
by Apex CoVantage, LLC

Printed in the United Kingdom
by Henry Ling Limited

CONTENTS

CONTRIBUTORS

Sa'ad Ali

Dr. Sa'ad Ali is a lecturer in Human Resource Management at the University of Worcester, United Kingdom. He has worked and taught in several countries, including Jordan, the United Kingdom and China. He is interested in cross-cultural Human Resource Management research, particularly, in how social networks impact business conduct in the Arab world and in China.

Esra Cetinkaya

Esra Cetinkaya received her BSc in International Management and Engineering from Pforzheim University, Germany. She specialized in International Industrial Engineering and International Technical Sales.

Sébastien Chehaitly

Sébastien Chehaitly is a Master of Social Work candidate at Université de Montréal, Canada, and is working as a researcher on the LGBT Muslims in Canada project. He is currently working as a liaison officer with LGBT racialized communities for the Research Chair on Homophobia at the Université du Québec à Montréal. He has been involved in Muslim and Arabic community groups, doing community action with them for the past 10 years.

Linda Cohen

Linda Cohen is a specialist in managing cultural and linguistic diversity in organizations. She chaired the department of Language and Culture at ESCP Europe, Paris Campus. Her current research areas include the use of English as a working language in international business and managing language diversity in organizations. She is a founding member of GEM&L, an international research group on management and language, and currently consults on managing diversity in organizations.

Helena Fornstedt

Helena Fornstedt is a doctoral student at the department of Industrial Engineering and Management at Uppsala University, Sweden. In addition to her interest in critical cross-cultural management, her research focus on critical as well as mainstream innovation diffusion studies. She has previously published in the *Scandinavian Journal of Management* and in *Energy Policy*.

Hamid Foroughi

Hamid Foroughi is Senior Lecturer in organization studies at the University of Portsmouth, United Kingdom. His PhD thesis from Henley Business School, on collective memory and mnemonic politics, received the best critical dissertation award of the 2015 Academy of Management meeting in Vancouver. His research interests encompass ethnographic and narrative approaches to change, social memory and politics of knowledge production. He co-edited a special issue on 'Leadership narratives in a post-truth era' (*Leadership*) and has published, for example, on 'collective forgetting in a changing organization' (*Organization Studies*).

Emanuela Girei

Emanuela Girei is a lecturer in Organisation Studies at the University of Sheffield Management School, United Kingdom. Her main area of research is management, politics and social change, focusing in particular on whether and how management theory and practice can contribute to making organizations, institutions and societies more just, equitable and sustainable. She also is interested in qualitative and critical research methodologies and processes and in strategies to decolonize research and knowledge.

François Goxe

François Goxe is an associate professor at the University of Versailles (Paris-Saclay), France. He received his PhD in management from Paris-Dauphine University. He also holds an MBA from Queensland University of Technology, Australia, and a BA from Shanghai Jiaotong University, China. Before joining graduate school, he worked as a consultant for various firms including PwC in Australia and China. His research focusses on social relations, power, domination and identities among international entrepreneurs and managers.

Anna Laura Hidegh

Anna Laura Hidegh is an associate professor at Budapest Business School in Hungary. She wrote her dissertation in Critical Human Resource Management, analysing corporate Christmas from a Habermasian perspective. Her main research interest is Critical Management Studies, but she also took part in research projects on career change, responsible management education, diversity at the workplace and human resource management in small- and medium-sized companies.

Elin Hunger

Elin Hunger holds a MSc in Business and Management and a BSc in Business and Economics from the Stockholm School of Economics in Sweden, where she specialized in Organization studies and (language-oriented) qualitative research methods. In her master's thesis, she employed critical discourse analysis to unpack taken-for-granted ideas about (working) age, conceptualized as 'chrononormativity in the workplace'. Elin also holds a BA in Gender Research from Uppsala University in Sweden.

Iuliana Ancuța Ilie

Iuliana Ancuța Ilie is a research assistant at Pforzheim University, Germany. She supports tertiary education and publication projects in the areas of cross-cultural management, international human resource management and management accounting. She holds a BA in Romanian and English Language and Literature, a BA in International Business Administration and Intercultural Studies, and a MA in Medieval Studies. Her research interests include cross-cultural management, diversity management and the mobility of ideas, and she has published on these themes in academic journals and books.

Qahraman Kakar

Qahraman Kakar was born and raised in Pakistan. He earned a BSc in political science and economics from Forman Christian College, Lahore, Pakistan, and completed his MSc in development economics and international project management at University Paris-Est Créteil, France. He is a PhD candidate in economics at University of Paris-Est Marne-la-Vallée, France. His research focuses on the inequality of the access to education in developing countries. His research interests include cross-cultural management, conflicts and social fragmentation.

Jane Kassis-Henderson

Jane Kassis-Henderson is Emeritus Professor at ESCP Europe Business School, Paris Campus. Her research interests focus on language-related factors in international management and academic contexts. Her publications include studies of language diversity in international management teams and the implications of language boundaries on the development of trust in teams. She is a founding member of GEM&L, an international research group on management and language.

Anders Klitmøller

Anders Klitmøller is Associate Professor at the Department of Language and Communication, University of Southern Denmark. Taking an ethnographic approach, his current research applies a practice perspective on reflexivity and power in organizations. He has published in outlets such as *Organization Studies, Journal of World Business* and *Critical Perspectives on International Business*.

Heidrun Knorr

Heidrun Knorr is an assistant professor of organizational leadership and intercultural competence in the Organization and Leadership Stream at the School of Culture and Global Studies, Aalborg University, Denmark. She received her PhD from Aalborg University. Her research interests include diversity management, leadership development, intersectionality, trust, practice theory, and intercultural competence and cultural intelligence.

Jasmin Mahadevan

Jasmin Mahadevan is Professor of International and Cross-Cultural Management at Pforzheim University, Germany. Stemming from an interdisciplinary background in international business, cultural anthropology, and languages and area studies, her research, publications and editorial work span critical cross-cultural and human resource management. Prior to her academic career, she worked as an intercultural consultant. Her *Very Short, Fairly Interesting and Reasonably Cheap Book about Cross-Cultural Management* was published by Sage (2017).

Mohammed Mohsen

Mohammed Mohsen works as Head of Communication and Fundraising at Islamic Relief Sweden. As part of this role, he works with projects and policy that seek to enhance religious literacy among stakeholders in the aid sector, in order to improve the efficiency and impact of humanitarian and development aid policies. He holds a BSc in Business and Economics from Stockholm School of Economics, Sweden.

Miguel Morillas

Miguel Morillas is a PhD candidate in Business Administration at the Center for Advanced Studies in Leadership, Stockholm School of Economics, Sweden. Focusing on highly skilled migrant integration, his dissertation analyzes the intersection of class and ethnicity in inclusive organizations. His further research interests include organizational theory, diversity management, migrant integration, skilled migrants, cultural capital and class. He holds a MPhil in Public Policy, a MA in Political Science, and a BA in Sociology.

Beáta Nagy

Prof. Beáta Nagy works at the Institute of Sociology and Social Policy at Corvinus University of Budapest, Hungary. Her main research field is gender and work. She is the co-director of the Gender and Cultural Centre at her university. She published a book on the lack of female students in IT and technology and has published articles in journals such as *Gender in Management: An International Journal* and *Gender, Work and Organization*.

Loice Natukunda

Loice Natukunda is a lecturer of Organisational Studies at the College of Humanities and Social Sciences, Makerere University, Kampala, Uganda. She obtained her PhD from the University of Sheffield, United Kingdom, wherein she explored the integration of Western-designed models of management into the African cultural context. She has explored the cross-cultural implications of conducting field research in rural Africa, examining the opportunities and challenges faced by insider as well as outsider researchers during data collection, management and analysis.

Simon Cedrick Nunka Dikuba

Simon Cedrick Nunka Dikuba received his BSc in International Management and Engineering from Pforzheim University, Germany, specializing in International Industrial Engineering and International Technical Sales. His interests include Intercultural Management, Supply Chain Management, Enterprise Resource Planning, Accounting and Entrepreneurship in Africa.

Dilara Özer

Dilara Özer received her BSc in International Management and Engineering from Pforzheim University, Germany. She specialized in International Industrial Engineering and International Technical Sales.

Henriett Primecz

Henriett Primecz is a professor at Corvinus University of Budapest, Hungary. Her research interest is cross-cultural management, gender and diversity, and organizational theory. She published papers in *Organizational Research Methods*, *International Journal of Cross Cultural Management* and *International Studies in*

Management & Organization. She edited *Cross-Cultural Management in Practice: Culture and Negotiated Meaning* with Laurence Romani and Sonja Sackmann.

Momin Rahman

Momin Rahman is a Professor of Sociology at Trent University in Canada and is leading a funded project on LGBT Muslims in Canada. He has published over 25 chapters and articles and three books: *Homosexualities, Muslim Cultures and Modernity,* (2014, Palgrave Macmillan), *Gender and Sexuality* (2010, with Stevi Jackson, Polity), and *Sexuality and Democracy* (2000, Edinburgh University Press).

Laurence Romani

Laurence Romani is Associate Professor at the Stockholm School of Economics (Sweden). Her work focuses on issues of representation and interaction with the cultural Other in respectful and enriching ways. She considers contributions from critical management, feminist and postcolonial organization studies to further cross-cultural management research. She has published articles in journals such as *Organization, Journal of Business Ethics,* the *International Journal of Cross-Cultural Management* and multiple book chapters in international handbooks.

Chidozie Umeh

Chidozie Umeh completed his PhD in Human Resource Management and Organisational Behaviour from Queen Mary University of London. He has over 10 years of prior work experience in the Nigerian banking sector. Currently he is a Teaching Associate at Queen Mary University of London. His research centres around cross-cultural studies and managing diversity and identity in the Global South. He recently co-authored a publication on diversity which was launched in the British House of Commons in 2017.

Mounia Utzeri

Mounia Utzeri completed her doctoral dissertation at Corvinus University of Budapest (Institute of Sociology and Social Policy). Her main research fields are gender, diversity and organisation. She holds an MBA in International Trade and Asian Studies. Working for the automotive industry in China and across Europe, she carries on investigations on organisational initiatives in terms of gender diversity within the European motor vehicle sector.

David Weir

David Weir is Professor of Intercultural Management at York St John University, United Kingdom, and has held chairs at several universities, including

Glasgow, Bradford, Northumbria, Suffolk, SKEMA and Liverpool Hope. He has researched and published extensively on management in the Arab Middle East and has consulted with many leading organizations. He is a regular presenter at major international and regional economic conferences, including the GCC summit, and hosted the Arab Management conferences at Bradford University.

PREFACE

This book is a collection of 16 empirical cases in Critical Cross-Cultural Management (CCM). All cases approach culture in CCM beyond national cultures, and all examine power as an integrative part of any cross-cultural situation. The cases also consider diversity in the sense of culturally or historically learned categorizations of difference (such as gender, race, ethnicity, religion and class), and acknowledge how diversity categories might differ across cultures. Furthermore, each case suggests a specific method or concept for improving upon the situation. Out of this approach, novel insights emerge: we can see how culture, power and diversity categories are inseparable, and we can understand exactly how this is the case. The uses and benefits of this book are thus both conceptual and methodological; they emerge at the intersections of Critical CCM and diversity studies. All cases also discuss implications for practitioners and are suitable for teaching.

Unique Contributions of This Book: Culture in Intersection With Power

Models simplify reality, and this both facilitates and limits their applicability. The obvious CCM example for this phenomenon is 'the Hofstedian approach' to culture: widely critiqued for its simplicity, but equally used for the exact same reason. Often, academics teach 'the Hofstedian approach' whilst cautioning students against implementing it, and this might be simply due to a lack of alternatives. By means of rich empirical cases, this book offers such an alternative.

Considering the intersections of culture, diversity and power enables students, researchers and practitioners alike to see 'more' or 'different' things in the situation and then to come up with novel approaches and solutions that do justice to the realities of culture and diversity in today's (and the future's) management and organizations. The chapters of this book thus offer concepts and methods to approach cross-cultural situations: The conceptual gain lies in bringing together CCM and (critical) diversity studies in an easily accessible manner. As a methodological contribution, the cases in this book offer concise tools and methods for implementing an intersectional approach to culture.

How This Book Came Into Being

We, the three editors of this volume, work within and across differences in academic fields and cultures, but all of us position themselves firmly within a Critical CCM. With this, we refer to the understanding that power and culture are intertwined, as are culture, identity and diversity. We have come to realize that students, researchers and practitioners wishing to actually implement Critical CCM lack the material and tools for doing so. Out of this insight originated the call for contributions to this book. It first took shape during the International Critical Management Studies Conference in Liverpool in 2017, where we convened a track on Critical CCM together. With an open call for chapters and committed authors, our idea to create a book of short, easily accessible and nonetheless 'sharp' empirical cases has materialized in this volume which can be used in undergraduate and graduate teaching and which also offers practical tools for managers in organizations.

Jasmin Mahadevan, Laurence Romani and Henriett Primecz
September 2019

INTRODUCTION

Why Study CCM in Intersection?

*Jasmin Mahadevan, Laurence Romani
and Henriett Primecz*

An African American lawyer from the United States comes to Paris for work purposes. She embraces the culture, learns French and receives positive feedback from the locals for doing so. Yet, as her language fluency improves to a near-native level, and after she has successfully immersed herself into French culture, she notices that French people treat her differently and seem to hold more negative opinions about her in their minds. She switches back to an American accent and, suddenly, things are back to normal. How could being versed in both languages and cultures lead to negative encounters? How can we understand this puzzling cross-cultural experience?

The Limitations of Mainstream CCM

Mainstream cross-cultural management (CCM), with its two main sub-fields of comparative CCM and intercultural interactions (see Mahadevan, 2017), does not provide a satisfying explanation to this case.

Comparative CCM aims to identify objective cultural differences between national and societal macro-cultures. This is done via comparing selected aspects of culture which are assumed to exist in all cultures, so-called cultural dimensions or cultural value orientation. The American lawyer has integrated into French culture—thus, she should not experience cross-cultural difficulties of such kinds.

Alternatively, there are CCM theories and models focusing on how cross-cultural differences are experienced in the micro-context of intercultural interactions and communication. These stress the need to change perspective, to learn from experience and to apply skills, to increase language and intercultural competencies or to develop role flexibility. The American lawyer does all of this—thus, she should experience less, not more, difficulties in intercultural interactions and communication.

Both approaches are of limited help in solving this case, because we do not find an answer as to *why* the reality (or its perception) becomes more negative as the American lawyer 'performs better' from the perspective of mainstream CCM. The first reason is that intercultural encounters involve individuals who are diverse not only in terms of culture, as considered by mainstream CCM, but also in terms of other diversity categories (such as ethnicity, gender, race, ability, class, religion/worldview and more). The second reason is that culture and diversity markers result in power effects which then influence intercultural encounters. In this case, we do not know how exactly cross-cultural differences and established notions about race, class and other diversity markers come together in the protagonist's experience. However, we must assume that all of these factors intersect: being black with an American accent seems to be perceived as 'better' than being 'French' black. We therefore need a new framework to analyse and solve this situation.

Understanding Culture

In this book, we understand culture broadly, as "that complex whole" (Tylor, 1871: 1) which involves all aspects of social life and the material world, as well as the technologies with which humans interact. We also consider culture as socialisation, namely as 'any learned and social way of how one is expected to do or perceive things' (our own words). Thus, cultural differences in the sense of this book might also arise, for instance, from interactions between professional, ethnic, religious or organizational groups, or might involve diversity categories such as gender, age, tenure or others.

The Need for an Intersectional Approach to Culture

We suggest that the study of cross-cultural differences will gain from approaching culture in intersection, namely as involving the interrelated facets of culture, power and diversity. If this is done, we can then ask where categorizations of difference come from, how they have emerged, whose interests they serve, and whether, to whom, and how exactly they might be problematic. On a methodological level, this requires a critical reflexivity regarding what constitutes culture and cultural differences, and how to study them in CCM, with ensuing implications for researchers' role and involvement.

When going back to our introductory case, we now can see that, for instance, historically learned notions of race and presently held ideas about French people of colour influence how the (white?) French majority perceives the African American lawyer. The problem is that she is perceived as a specific *type* of French person (involving negative notions of race and class) as soon as she has fully integrated in terms of language and culture, and this is why 'perfect French' is to her disadvantage. For a white person, the story would have been otherwise, as Jane Kassis-Henderson and Linda Cohen show in Chapter 1 of this book.

Situations involving cultural differences are thus to be studied in intersection. To understand these situations, we need to approach culture as intersecting with power, crystalized into differences and hierarchies around, for example, race and social status.

What Is 'CCM in Intersection'?

CCM is not power-free, and diversity studies are not free of culture. If combined, these two premises bring about an intersectional approach to culture: the realization that power, culture and diversity categories are inseparable, and that we need to investigate whether and how exactly they intersect in universal or culture-specific ways or both.

When speaking of diversity, we refer to those categories of difference which are thought of as relevant for achieving societal or organizational inclusion. In this context, gender, race, ethnicity, age, sexual orientation, ability and religion/worldview are often mentioned, with the argument that these emerged out of struggles against unfair discrimination (Prasad et al., 2006). Yet there is no universal definition as to which diversity categories need to be considered (Klarsfeld et al., 2014). This tells us that the meaning and perceived relevance of 'diversity categories', too, are historically and socially learned, and might thus be culture-specific. For instance, race is a much more prominent diversity category in North America than in Europe, where perceived differences are often explained in terms of ethnicity or culture (Lentin, 2008). In this book, we thus do not understand diversity categories as universally applicable 'realities' but as yet another aspect shaping the power effects in cross-cultural situations.

In a nutshell, we can thus understand 'CCM in intersection' as a diversity-conscious and power-sensitive approach to 'culture' and 'difference' in the contemporary world. With power, we refer to the interrelated aspects of discourse (how people view the world and talk about it, thereby shaping material practices and structures), structure (systems of inequalities), rules of practice (how things are normally done), agency (the power to enable oneself, and to resist and change systems of inequalities) and history. We assume that all of these aspects together shape actual power effects in CCM (see Primecz et al., 2016; Mahadevan, 2017). This also means that CCM in intersection needs to move beyond a merely interpersonal or organizational approach to power, and needs to consider power on historical or geopolitical levels as well.

Diversity, Culture and Identity at the Crossroads

Intersectionality theory, as informing our approach, stems from Black Feminism (Crenshaw, 1989) and has since then influenced (critical) diversity studies. It is rooted in the insight that there is no 'universal female life experience', as early feminism tended to assume, but that the ways in which black women experience gender differ fundamentally from the ways in which white women experience the same diversity category, as do the structural boundary conditions of those experiences.

As a term, intersectionality was coined by African American lawyer Kimberle Crenshaw (1989). She used the crossroads metaphor to explain how an intersectional approach might change our ideas of who is disadvantaged and exactly why and how. Visualizing discrimination 'at the crossroads', Crenshaw (1989: 149) writes:

> Discrimination . . . may flow in one direction, and it may flow in another. If an accident happens in an intersection, it can be caused by cars traveling from any number of directions and, sometimes, from all of them.

An intersectional approach thus wishes to understand *how exactly* exclusion and inclusion and advantage and disadvantage are brought about at the crossroads of multiple diversity categories. Thus it is not only useful for specific diversity categories but for understanding how certain boundary conditions and processes of culture, diversity and identity come together in the contemporary managerial and societal world *in general*, and for shedding light onto the ideas, structures and practices underpinning these interrelations. This potential, as exemplified by the cases in this book, has not yet been fully considered by CCM.

For instance, Simon Cedrick Nunka Dikuba and Jasmin Mahadevan (Chapter 2) narrate the cross-cultural life experiences of a German student of Cameroonian descent who identifies as black African. She has experienced race in three national contexts—Germany, Cameroon and Romania—and across all these contexts, race matters, but it matters differently. We can also see how she can influence perceptions of race by cultural versatility and via pursuing a high-status education and occupation; out of this, we can understand how different aspects of power come together (e.g., individual agency, and historically learned hierarchies and ideas about the world), and how diversity categories such as 'race' play out differently in different cultural contexts.

The contribution of this book lies in applying intersectionality theory as a lens to CCM, thereby not only making intersectionality accessible to CCM scholars, students and practitioners, but also extending the CCM body of knowledge. For instance, Momin Rahman and Sébastien Chehaitly (Chapter 3) ask what CCM might learn from the lived realities of LGBT (lesbian, gay, bisexual and transgender) Muslim minority individuals in Canada. Through their intersectional approach, the authors show that it is a combination of homophobia, racism and Islamophobia that creates inequalities for LGBT Muslims. Providing alternative angles, the authors also highlight how Islam has a stronger tradition of embracing homosexuality than the West. Furthermore, this case suggests that LGBT Muslim minority individuals employ successful 'bridging' and 'boundary-spanning' strategies, these being key elements of a successful management across cultures. Thus, this case also highlights the need to consider previously 'invisible' groups for the creation of CCM knowledge.

Challenging What Seems 'Normal' and Acknowledging Multiple Standpoints

Intersectionality theory also points to the perspectivity of our lived realities, meaning that our lived realities are bound to the 'standpoints' from which we experience them, and that those not sharing these experiences (because their standpoints differ) might not necessarily be able to comprehend them (Collins, 2000). Out of this follows the need to reflect upon taken-for-granted CCM perspectives, concepts and practices, and to suggest alternative angles from which to reconsider them.

For example, religion has emerged as a prominent theme in CCM and international business (Peltonen, forthcoming). However, it is often the religious practices and beliefs of 'non-Western' others, such as Muslim minorities in the West, which are examined,. Shedding light onto this implicit perspectivity of CCM, Anna Laura Hidegh and Henriett Primecz (Chapter 4) investigate the 'seemingly normal' annual corporate Christmas party of a Western multinational in Hungary. They raise the question *why* corporate Christmas is not challenged as a religious and potentially exclusive event in an allegedly secular corporate life. The authors argue that this cultural blindness toward Christmas is a symptom of the power asymmetry inherent in the concept of the secular workplace, which favours atheism and Christianity over alternative beliefs. They also suggest that those practicing alternative beliefs face cultural disadvantages at work.

Sa'ad Ali and David Weir (Chapter 5) examine the concept of *wasta* in Jordanian banking from an inside (emic) perspective: how the concept is perceived by those practicing it. *Wasta* involves ideas of networking and reciprocity and rests upon powerful intermediaries who can provide access to certain networks. In outside (etic) terms, it often is reported negatively, as nepotism. Conversely, this case sheds light on the positive and negative effects of *wasta* solely in emic terms, without putting an external scale of judgement first. Out of this examination emerge, for instance, unexpected connections between concepts from different cultural regions, such as *guanxi* in Greater China and *wasta*, and we can better understand the emic meaning as well as the negative emic consequences of the practice and idea of *wasta*.

Considering Power on Multiple Levels

Personal Interests and Agendas

In CCM situations, the interests and agendas which individuals might pursue often remain hidden. Yet, as a closer examination of individual power positions and motifs suggests, these interests and agendas are always there. For instance, François Goxe (Chapter 6) highlights how a French consultant 'preparing' a French delegation for doing business in China pursues his own interests when doing so. The author also shows how the picture which the consultant paints of China does not correspond to the experiences of the French delegation while it is there. Out of this case emerge questions of ethics and the need for a more power-sensitive approach to culture in CCM that considers the strategic interests and standpoints of those involved, one that investigates how these individual agendas underpin organizational structures and practices.

Historical and Geopolitical Power Effects

History is intertwined with power because, often, contemporary power relations are rooted in actual historical developments. Furthermore, history has created economic and political disparities between countries which are intertwined with how these historical developments are interpreted—another geopolitical implication of power. For example, Qahraman Kakar and Jasmin Mahadevan (Chapter 7) investigate the operations of a Chinese mining consortium in Pakistan. They show how this cooperation also exemplifies the effects of 19th century European colonialism and imperialism, and U.S. hegemony after World War II. Out of these actual historical developments, the Anglo-American world became the historically learned centre of world business, with English, and not, for example, Mandarin Chinese the lingua franca of the business world. This suggests that some (neo-) colonial relations (e.g., Anglo-American multinational corporations investing in other parts of the world) have become more 'normalized' than others; they are now 'taken for granted' by most and are rarely perceived as problematic. In the given case, the Chinese, not being the 'old' and 'normalized' rulers, are less accepted in their claims to power for simply being 'Chinese', and they themselves also perceive the Pakistani as being 'too influenced' by their former colonizers. As a result, experiences of difference are culturalized—that is, explained and rationalized in terms of national culture—by those involved. Yet the conflict is actually rooted in the historically learned hierarchies of world business. In such a way, an intersectional approach to culture enables us to see how power is part of today's world order and how organizational and individual perspectives on difference often reflect such hierarchies, without those involved being aware of perpetuating these hierarchies.

Events such as colonialism or imperialism help us understand present ideas about 'high-status' and 'low-status' countries of origin, and how these views have an impact on the appreciation of people's work. For instance, history has resulted in certain learned categorizations of the world, such as (modern, developed) 'West' and (traditional, underdeveloped) 'non-West'. Helena Fornstedt (Chapter 8) investigates how Swedish consultants talk about the Indian offshore site with which they collaborate. Again, this case shows that certain cultural images are attached to certain locations, and that these images reflect historically learned ideas of who is part of the 'developed West' and who is not, and also which culture is 'more developed' or 'modern'. This way, we can see how macrostructural boundary conditions, meso-organizational structures and practices, and micro-individual sensemaking come together in portraying Indian IT consultants as less capable and 'modern' than their Swedish counterparts.

Ethnicity and Culture as Interconnected CCM Phenomena

Power positions in cross-cultural interactions touch upon how difference is constructed and when CCM talks about culture, ethnicity is clearly and strongly interconnected. For instance, as Eriksen (2010 [1993]) suggests, the dominant ethnic group or groups in any given society are not assigned an 'ethnicity'—this is reserved only for those who are thought of as marginal or a minority. Likewise, even in multiethnic countries, there are dominant ideas of national belonging, in the sense of an 'imagined nationality' which is always more simplified than the variety of actual 'lived (ethnic) identities' in any given country (Hall, 1990). In other words, CCM literature on national management practices or value orientations is likely to have considered only the ethnic majority or the 'imagined national identity' of a given country, and to have neglected the perspective of ethnic minorities or marginal national identities. This means that what CCM thinks of as 'national' management practices or value orientations are not representative of the whole range of national cultural possibilities. Moreover, what is seen as 'cultural' is actually rooted in ethnicity, or at least in dominant ideas about ethnicity.

Furthermore, as Barth (1969) states, ethnicity is mainly a boundary mechanism: from this perspective, there is no factual or homogeneous content to any ethnicity because as soon as groups of people migrate or come in contact with each other, the content of their 'ethnicity' or 'culture' will change. Thus it is relevant to CCM to study these processes of transference and integration in order to grasp national culture. The question that needs to be asked is *why* second- or third-generation migrants living in a certain country are still perceived as 'ethnically' or 'culturally' different or construct themselves as such, despite having grown up and being socialized in the same society as those perceived as the 'majority' or as fitting the 'national image'?

To this end, Jasmin Mahadevan, Esra Cetinkaya and Dilara Özer narrate the life stories of two 'Turkish' women who migrated to Germany as young adults (Chapter 9). The authors show how the subjects' lived ethnicities differ from each other and from the dominant ethnic image attached to them.

Moving the analysis to the organizational level, Heidrun Knorr (Chapter 10) sheds light onto how ethnic 'Turkish' employees are perceived in a Danish company. She shows how the majority ('the Danes') take their ethnicity for granted and as the implicit norm of how employees should act and 'be'. This way, they construct employees of Turkish descent as negatively different and simplify what 'Turkish ethnicity' involves.

Chidozie Umeh (Chapter 11) investigates ethnicity in the multiethnic national context of Nigeria. He shows that Nigerian bankers *use* ethnicity—both at the level of ethnic image and lived ethnicity—to position themselves in relation to others, to strengthen loyalties and to achieve certain goals. Out of this follows that no individual is clearly 'ethnic' in certain ways: rather, we tend to have options of how we wish to position ourselves and of how we want to be seen; this varies from context to context and depends on the goals and interests of those involved.

These cases thus highlight how ethnicity is not a factual reality but constructed in certain ways: first, there is the ethnic image that overshadows the multiple realities of lived ethnicity. Second, ethnicity emerges as something malleable, something to be used and played with to serve different purposes and interests. Out of this, we can see that ethnicity, just like (national) culture, is constructed and that this phenomenon is not power-free, because the construction of 'the other' is (always) to the advantage of the one doing the construction.

Intersecting Implications

Ethnicity, like culture, is intertwined with multiple diversity categories. For instance, Elin Hunger, Miguel Morillas, Laurence Romani and Mohammed Mohsen (Chapter 12) examine the labour market integration of high-skilled migrants in Sweden. They show how the idea of how to 'see' and 'prove' integration is underpinned by ideas of 'Swedishness' which are specific to a certain class and ethnic image. This way, a certain class and ethnic group is advantaged over the equally skilled migrants who do not fit this picture.

Intersecting disadvantages not only harm the individuals concerned but also create organizational blind spots. Mounia Utzeri, Béata Nagy and Iuliana Ancuța Ilie (Chapter 13) highlight this for two automotive companies in Germany and France. Both companies have gender-diversity policies in place; however, via these policies, the companies actually promote one diversity category (gender) over others, such as country of origin. As a result, the companies fail to see, for instance, the alternative strategies by which women managers from other countries of origin (besides France and Germany) resist and navigate a double 'minority image' (gender and nationality). Seeing and considering these strategies would enrich organizational policies and practices aiming at higher acceptance and at the promotion of minority individuals. Thus, this case also shows that it might not be enough to 'study minorities' just to point out how they are disadvantaged, but that we also need to highlight the ways in which minority individuals' knowledge and experiences can be an asset to and a resource for CCM.

Reflexivity in CCM Knowledge Production

This brings about critical questions as to how CCM knowledge is produced in theory and practice. An intersectional approach to culture thus also asks what can be learned beyond what is presently 'known' or considered relevant by the majority or those in power. It is underpinned by the idea that a plurality of perspectives and standpoints is helpful for getting 'the full picture' of any CCM context or situation.

To reach this goal, an intersectional approach to culture invites us to be reflexive regarding how CCM knowledge is produced. For instance, most CCM theories and methods originate from 'the West' or from the countries of the 'Global North' (developed countries, mainly on the Northern hemisphere), with the implicit idea that this knowledge is more relevant than knowledge from the 'non-West' or the 'Global South' (developing countries, mainly on the Southern hemisphere). As Hamid Foroughi (Chapter 14) shows, for a research consortium in the international development sector, these underlying hierarchies even underpin the knowledge that is produced in order to overcome them, in this case: research on how the development of the Global South should be achieved. This happens *despite* individuals and organizations in international development working toward the opposite goal.

Thus, we must assume that the same mechanisms limit the knowledge that is produced in CCM (even if we intend otherwise). To solve this dilemma, Emanuela Girei and Loice Natukunda (Chapter 15) reflect upon the limitations and possibilities of insider–outsider ethnographic research in sub-Saharan Africa. They suggest that we need an intersectional approach to 'who we are' (as researchers or practitioners) in relation to any given CCM field.

This then suggests that researchers and practitioners alike need to pay attention to the processes by which they navigate CCM situations. To this end, Anders Klitmøller (Chapter 16) reflects upon how he, as an academic consultant, contributed to reproducing and legitimizing certain hierarchies which underpinned corporate language policy strategies. Out of this follows the need for a reflexive CCM practice and the requirement to examine our own standpoints-in-action, in order to understand and manage the power effects of how we, too, influence the situation and are influenced by it.

Methodological Contributions: Puzzling With Culture in Context

The starting point of 'doing' an intersectional approach to culture is the insight that CCM requires us to 'puzzle with culture in context'. This means that we should not depart from established notions of 'culture' or 'difference' but should investigate why, how, under which boundary conditions, in whose interests and to what ends they emerge in context. To do so, we need to act as a 'cultural detective' who engages in the process of shuffling the pieces of the cultural puzzle (Mahadevan, 2017). Some of these pieces might be objective cross-cultural differences (as comparative CCM proposes), some might be rooted in multiple perceptions of cross-cultural differences (as the intercultural interactions perspective proposes), some are historically learned and some are linked to power and diversity.

Studying CCM in intersection thus unravels the meanings and realities of 'culture' and 'difference' from the context itself. When employing this approach, it does not matter whether difference is real or perceived: as social constructivism and sense-making informs us, the consequences of how individuals perceive the social world are *real* in any case. For instance, the ethnic image of the subordinated Turkish women wearing a headscarf, which is projected upon a high-skilled Turkish-German woman seeking employment in Germany, has real implications on the subject's ability to work as a dental assistant (Chapter 9). In this way, an intersectional approach to culture integrates objectivist and interpretive perspectives of mainstream CCM and adds power, diversity and reflexivity as complementary angles from which to approach—and potentially change—the situation.

An intersectional approach to culture also requires us to acknowledge culture as more than selected and immaterial aspects of culture such as values (comparative CCM) or communication (intercultural interactions); namely, as 'that complex whole' (Tylor, 1871: 1). This involves, for instance, phenomenology (how we experience the world via our senses), as episodes in several cases (Chapters 4, 7, 8, 10 and 14) show. Embodiment (how we inhabit our body and how it is perceived) is also an aspect to be considered, as Chapters 1 and 2 suggest, narrating the experiences of two black women experiencing racialization differently across cultures. Furthermore, embodied capitals and habitus (fine social distinctions, such as regarding social class) deserve attention in how we construct differences, as they play a role in how non-Swedish migrants are perceived as suitable or not suitable employees (Chapter 12). Finally, material culture (how humans interact with and perceive objects and technology), and the materiality of places and their heritage, must be part of our investigations—as we can see from the reactions triggered by an international project meeting taking place in a former colonial venue (see Chapter 14). Acknowledging this, the cases in this book thus also root problematic cross-cultural differences in phenomena which are not normally considered by mainstream CCM.

Conclusion: Critical CCM in Practice

Teaching and practicing an intersectional approach to culture requires 'the full picture'; therefore, it must move beyond simplified models or a merely conceptual critique. At the same time, the analysis cannot be overly complicated to be useful in teaching and practice. The chapters in this book combine these requirements: each case not only refines the analysis, but also introduces potential tools for navigating it. Each case also rests on the insight that CCM is more about a power-sensitive, diversity-conscious, historically aware and reflexive 'puzzling' with culture in context than about having ready-made answers and solutions (as suggested by Mahadevan, 2017). To that extent, the chapters in this volume bring the emerging and increasingly relevant field of Critical CCM (Mahadevan, 2017; Romani et al., 2018; Romani et al., forthcoming) to the next level.

References

Barth F (1998 [1969]) *Ethnic Groups and Boundaries: The Social Organization of Culture Difference*. Long Grove: Waveland Press.

Collins PH (2000) *Black Feminist Thought: Knowledge, Consciousness and Empowerment* (2nd ed). Boston: Unwin Hyman.

Crenshaw K (1989) Demarginalizing the intersection of race and sex: A black feminist critique of antidiscrimination doctrine, feminist theory and antiracist politics. *University of Chicago Legal Forum* 1(8): 139–167. http://chicagounbound.uchicago.edu/uclf/vol1989/iss1/8 (accessed 01 June 2019).

Eriksen TH (2010 [1993]) *Ethnicity and Nationalism*. London: Pluto Press.

Hall S (1990) Cultural identity and diaspora. In: Rutherford J (ed) *Identity, Community, Culture, Difference*. London: Lawrence and Wishart. pp. 222–237.

Klarsfeld A, Boysen LAE, Ng E, Roper I and Tatli A (2014) Introduction: Equality and diversity in 14 countries: Analysis and summary. In: Klarsfeld A (ed) *International Handbook on Diversity Management at Work*. Cheltenham: Edward Elgar Publishing, pp. 1–12.

Lentin A (2008) Europe and the silence about race. *European Journal of Social Theory* 11(4): 487–503.

Mahadevan J (2017) *A Very Short, Fairly Interesting and Reasonably Cheap Book about Cross-Cultural Management*. London: SAGE.

Peltonen T (forthcoming 2020) The role of religions in cross-cultural management: Three perspectives. In: Szkudlarek B, Romani L, Osland J and Caprar D (eds) *The Sage Handbook of Contemporary Cross-Cultural Management*. London: SAGE.

Prasad P, Pringle JK and Konrad AM (2006) Examining the contours of workplace diversity. In: Konrad AM, Prasad P and Pringle JK (eds) *Handbook of Workplace Diversity*. London: SAGE, pp. 1–22.

Primecz H, Mahadevan J and Romani L (2016) Guest editorial: Why is cross-cultural management blind to power relations? Investigating ethnicity, language, gender and religion in power-laden contexts. *International Journal of Cross-Cultural Management* 16(2): 127–136.

Romani L, Mahadevan J and Primecz H (2018) Critical cross-cultural management: Outline and emergent contributions. *International Studies of Management & Organization* 48(4): 403–418.

Romani L, Mahadevan J and Primecz H (forthcoming 2020) Methods of critical cross-cultural management. In: Szkudlarek B, Romani L, Osland J and Caprar D (eds) *The Sage Handbook of Contemporary Cross-Cultural Management*. London: SAGE.

Tylor EB (1871) *Primitive Culture: Researches Into the Development of Mythology*. London: John Murray.

1

THE PARADOXICAL CONSEQUENCES OF 'THE PERFECT ACCENT'!

A Critical Approach to Cross-Cultural Interactions

Jane Kassis-Henderson and Linda Cohen

Introduction

The simplistic, essentialist model of language and culture prevalent in main-stream cross-cultural management (CCM) has sidelined the complexity of interactions in today's world. This case shows how coming to terms with the multiple markers of identity, together with a more subtle understanding of language and culture, can transform communication and power strategies in interpersonal relations and lead to paradoxical findings. This is the story of how an American lawyer in France breaks from the traditional rules of communication in multilingual intercultural settings by playing with her accent to suit her ends.

Methodology

A critical interpretive approach is applied to this case, highlighting the value of intersectionality and reflexivity to bring to the fore the complex interplay of language and identity and their resulting power effects (Mahadevan, 2017; Primecz et al., 2009; Primecz et al., 2016; Zanoni et al., 2010). In order to deconstruct cross-cultural interactions it is important to move beyond the static categories inherent in the cultural values dimensions literature. Interactions are necessarily dynamic due to the multiple facets of identity which become more or less salient as they are played out in ever-changing contexts. Depending on the desired outcome, an individual draws on different aspects of their identity, behind which lie a multiplicity of *voices*. These voices compose the varied language repertoires, or resources, derived from the experiences of each individual. We therefore adopt the negotiated, situated approach to cross-cultural communication as developed by social identity theorists and sociolinguists who focus on the way in which different aspects of personal background condition expectations and reactions within the context of specific encounters (Blommaert, 2010; Gumperz, 2003; Martin-Jones et al., 2012).

When interacting with others, individuals are constantly interpreting what they see and hear in order to make sense of what is happening. At the same time, they deploy their linguistic resources and send signals as to who they are which influence the perception the other has of them and the relationship between them. The negotiated, situated approach to the analysis of interactions allows us to demonstrate how changing voice according to context can have a positive impact on empowerment in a communication strategy (Steyaert and Janssens, 2015; Kramsch, 2012; Ozkazanç-Pan, 2015).

Case Presentation

In this section, we present a case narrative which illustrates the importance of being aware of the multiple identity markers embedded in each individual. Our analysis highlights the value of adopting an intersectional approach to make sense of the paradoxical situations which often arise in cross-cultural encounters because of accents and the way people speak.

Case Narrative

An American lawyer specializing in international mergers and acquisitions took a new position in the Paris headquarters of a French multinational firm. According to the Human Resources director, the fact that this lawyer not only had the requisite professional credentials and experience, but had studied French and was a true 'Francophile', was decisive in the recruitment process.

The authors interviewed this lawyer in the context of a study of multicultural/ multilingual teams. The lawyer had been in this job for 24 months. The narrative that follows spontaneously emerged while discussing the experience of integration in France.

> I arrived in Paris 2 years ago, very much looking forward to taking on this new position in a city I have always loved from my frequent but short visits. I speak French, have always tried to keep up with French culture and news coming from France, but this is the first time I've lived outside of the U.S. One of the first things that surprised me in dealing with the French on a daily basis, in day-to-day life, was that the first thing they would say is: 'Oh! You're American'! They immediately identified me— because of my accent—as being 'American'. I was at first taken aback as it was the first time I could say—to others, as well as to myself!— 'Yes, I'm American'! Because in the U.S., I'm 'African American'—and

my belonging to the black community has always *identified* me first. People have always labelled me as such and I have always felt rooted in my community. 'American' for me was 'mainstream' America, 'white' America—I, on the other hand, have always felt, and been labelled, 'African American'. So imagine my surprise—and, I must admit, in a certain way which surprises even me, a new-found pride—at being seen, identified, by my French peers and neighbors as 'American'! In the U.S. I had to fight to become a lawyer, to build a professional reputation feeling an 'outsider' in mainstream America. And here I was in Paris: the American lawyer—not the 'African American' woman, the black woman lawyer who 'made it'—with the undertones of the negative stigma of affirmative action never far away. I must admit I enjoyed this 'new' skin, this new identity!

Then something changed. My French became more proficient, more natural, I felt I was finally losing my American accent that French people quickly recognized. Personally, I was looking forward to better exchanges, communication with the French. But instead I realized I was getting certain looks, there was a certain hesitation in interactions, and certain kinds of questions started coming up more frequently. It wasn't 'oh, you're American!' but 'where are you from, the *Antilles*—the French West Indies?'—And little by little I started connecting the dots—the strange reaction I was getting—or what I felt was a strange reaction—was due to my losing the 'American' status as I was losing the American accent and with it the privilege of being the 'American in Paris.' Instead I realized I was being seen—and treated—as 'black'—I was living the French stigma attached to the people from the French West Indies when in the *Métropole*—or in Paris. So I started a survival experiment—I exaggerated my 'U.S.' accent and, indeed, I was again treated with the 'respect' I felt when I first arrived in Paris! I recovered my privileged status! I once again became the 'American in Paris'!

Key Insights and Interpretations: Adopting an Intersectional Approach—The Paradoxical Consequences of Superior Language Skills

Mainstream research argues that individuals with 'superior' language skills, measured by the yardstick of native speaker fluency, are imbued with status and power by simple virtue of their language skills (regardless of other competencies—or lack thereof). This notion is based on two assumptions: first, there is a 'one-size-fits-all' evaluation of linguistic proficiency; and second, attaining this 'objective' level of proficiency will necessarily result in communicative efficacy. Our case debunks this equation and questions the relevance of a singular model of linguistic proficiency as defined by an ideal (or idealized) native speaker. By introducing the importance of taking into account the diverse identity markers of each individual when it comes to communication, we demonstrate how a proficient speaker, interacting within a given context, can in fact lose power. This important lesson on language and empowerment can only be understood by using an intersectional approach (Boogaard and Roggeband, 2010; Crenshaw, 1991; Frame, 2016; Zander et al., 2010) and adopting a critical reflexive stance to appropriately interpret aspects of identity that become more or less salient according to context (Ozkazanç-Pan, 2015; Yagi and Kleinberg, 2011). In this case, our protagonist has to deal with her multiple identity markers which, as the narrative shows, determine how her discourse and message is received by others, and therefore impact the quality of communication itself. Thanks to her cross-cultural sensitivity and reflexive stance, she has the counterintuitive realization that gaining superior language skills impacts her negatively in terms of status in her new environment of Paris, France. Her ability to contextualize interactions and her capacity to adopt a 'self-reflexive move' between self and larger contexts proves she has integrated what has been theorized as the 'dialectical approach' (Martin and Nakayama, 2015). This ability has been identified as an important intercultural competence.

The dialectical approach to intercultural interactions highlights the finding that competence does not reside solely in the individual, but emerges while negotiating interaction with the other(s). As this case shows, a standardized, universal measure of effective communication does not exist. Rather, it results from the interrelationship that is constructed in context and is therefore a fluid, dynamic and ongoing process that reflects both individual sociolinguistic competence and an awareness of the societal constraints and geopolitical context within which the interaction takes place. An individual must constantly adjust their mode of communication depending on the dialectical tensions that are at play in a given situation—individual/societal; privileged/disadvantaged; global/local; past/present—to achieve effective cross-cultural communication.

The present case reveals the multiple polarities that exist both within the individual—with which intersectionality allows us to come to terms—as well as between the individual and the context in which they evolve. Here, a black, female multilingual lawyer from the United States confronts, among other things, the heritage of French colonialism and the legacy of French–U.S. cultural and economic relations as they interweave in her everyday encounters. Thanks to her ability to take distance, both reflexively and in establishing rapport with others, she finds a way to deal with this constant dialectical interplay in order to successfully negotiate communication. Indeed, an individual can be both advantaged and disadvantaged according to the different social categories to which they belong and the changing contexts in which they interact. At any one time, and depending on context, an individual can be marginalized or empowered by virtue of the 'cross-cutting' aspects of identity (Boogaard and Roggeband, 2010). As seen in the narrative, she has internalized the fact that status hierarchies are 'cross-cutting.' She therefore silences her fluency by self-censoring her more French-sounding accent to recover her *American* voice, which carries more positive identifying markers in postcolonial France.

By consciously speaking with an American accent, she removes the identifying marker associating her to the French *Antillais* community, which still must contend with postcolonial bias, and recuperates the higher-status marker as 'American.' This understanding of the potential inequities that are at play in intercultural interactions enables her to consciously appropriate communication strategies, thereby empowering her to better negotiate interpersonal encounters.

Power and CCM: Power Relations and the Value of Reflexivity in Intercultural Contexts

When the protagonist first arrived in Paris, her accent immediately identified her to the *French* ear—from a cultural point of view particularly sensitive to accents—as 'American'. Because of her 'strong' accent, the colour of her skin suddenly lost importance; a fundamental aspect of her identity was relegated to the background. In the United States, she never left her 'black skin'. She was always African American, a group marked with a strong identity, as opposed to (both literally and figuratively) mainstream—meaning 'white'—Americans.

When people in France referred to her as *American*—dropping the '*African*'—the multiple facets of her identity were reshuffled. Although in mainstream French culture, the image of the 'American' is far from being unequivocally positive, people from the United States nevertheless are often *positively* associated with power and prestige. As both political allies and economic rivals, the United States and France have long had a 'love–hate' relationship which has played out on different levels over the years.

One aspect of this ambivalent relationship resides in the language issue. The French pride themselves on having 'enlightened' the world over the centuries and are highly protective of their cultural heritage. One of the many ways in which this is manifested is their sensitivity to the place of the French language in the world today, in face of the increasing importance of American English. In France, the language is cherished as a national treasure, embodying the high 'ideals' of the French culture, a message which is conveyed as subtext to learners of French as a foreign language.

Another important aspect to remember in order to appropriately contextualize this case is the fact that in its national narrative, France has been a haven for the oppressed and, as such, has welcomed individuals who had been marginalized by mainstream America. Viewed as a beacon of tolerance, Paris became a creative hub for the many artists, writers, musicians, and others who were ostracized in the United States at different periods in recent history—most notably for being communist or simply because of the colour of their skin. Paris 'adopted' these intellectuals and artists, now able to pursue their careers in a more favorable environment, which gave rise to the favorable image of 'the American in Paris.'

In her narrative, she admitted that being considered 'the American in Paris', with all the connotations that may bring to mind, provoked a feeling of unexpected pride. It is this self-awareness that would help her readjust to eventually successfully navigate through this complex intercultural situation.

As a black woman who was raised and educated in the United States, she was used to dealing with identity politics and confronting difference, especially while pursuing her studies and career. Her resulting self-awareness empowered her to consciously play with *voice*, as she adapted her behavior and way of speaking depending on with whom and where she was speaking (Kramsch, 2012). Here we see that mastering the 'language/cultural specific' elements—in this case the French language and 'classical' French culture—is not enough to (re)-act appropriately in context. This type of reflexive behavior has been identified as an important 'language/culture general skill' (Mughan, 2015), a skill most often found in bi- or multicultural individuals—those exposed to two (or more) national cultures from birth (Hong and Doz, 2013). In this particular case we see how an awareness of the multiple facets of identity, or intersectionality, is an alternative way for an individual to acquire this valuable competence. Intersectionality, therefore, when used strategically, becomes equally empowering.

Ironically, for a white person, speaking 'perfect' French would have elevated status in France. However, as a black person, her perfect French meant that her identity markers were once again reshuffled. 'Perfecting' her French accent meant she was now assimilated to the French black West Indian *Antillais* community. She was experiencing the cultural stigmatization pervasive in mainstream French cultural labelling associated to former French colonies and therefore felt a loss of respect. Rather than be subjected to this feeling, she used the knowledge gained through this self-reflexive stance. She consciously played with *voice* to bring her *American* identity to the fore, alongside her high-status professional identity as a corporate lawyer, and changed the power dynamics to her favour.

Reflexive Considerations

As we are both women, from the United Kingdom and the United States—and 'white'—as well as fluent French speakers living in France, we have observed that the 'better' we speak—that is, without a discernible accent—the better we are received by the host country (French speakers). The stronger our UK/US accents, the more 'derogatory' comments we receive—the more we are placed as 'outsiders' by the French. We were struck by the fact that our personal experiences were contrary to the experience of our protagonist.

In addition, as research professors in language and cultural diversity, we have observed that the role played by accent differs markedly from country to country. Although we take a critical approach to the essentialist model which explains cultural difference through national stereotypes (Cohen and Kassis-Henderson, 2017), there is indeed a French specificity when it comes to language usage. Our personal experience of observing attitudes to language usage in different national contexts has contributed to our understanding of the particular status the French language enjoys in France. A case in point is that the French language even has its own protective body: the Académie Française, created in 1635. Since this time, the French language has been regulated and, indeed, protected by this institution whose function is to set the standards for proper use of the language. Even in a business context, mastering a sophisticated and elegant style of language is a requirement for recruitment (Holden, 1992). Our international students—non-native speakers of both French and English, who rate their fluency better in French than in English—are surprised when they fail to meet recruitment standards in French companies and face no such hurdles in English-speaking organizations. Consciously or not, these high standards are internalized by French people, from all walks of life, and come to the fore in their interactions with 'foreigners'. We are often bemused how quickly, at even the slightest encounter, people comment on accent and take on the role of French teacher, correcting grammar or turn of phrase.

This case interested us because it brought to the fore the intersectional aspect of interaction: the experience of this American lawyer was the 'opposite' of ours due to the colour of her skin, highlighting the multiple levels of difference at play and the importance of an awareness of intersectionality.

Recommendations to Students, Researchers and Practitioners

Our case points to the limits of the simplified and essentialist nation-based models of identity and language which characterize mainstream cross-cultural management education. Gaining a fuller awareness of the complexity of identity and of language usage should be an explicit learning objective (Kassis-Henderson et al., 2018; Holmes, 2015). Understanding that *all* communication is 'intercultural' when viewed through the lens of intersectionality will have a positive impact on social interactions. As this case shows, a static essentializing approach is not an adequate point of entry to understanding language and culture. In order to better adapt professional competencies, language and culture must be viewed through a more complex lens and teaching must go beyond the standardized, nation-based, 'language/culture specific' model—based solely on the 'accuracy' and 'fluency' of the idealized native speaker—too often preached in mainstream cross-cultural curricula and discourse (Cohen and Kassis-Henderson, 2012, 2017), be it at university or during corporate training activities. To implement an intersectional approach to culture, training must allow participants to bring to the surface the multiple facets of their identity—if only by the act of naming them—which are at the source of their diverse cultural and linguistic repertoires or *voices*.

In a cross-cultural communication seminar, for example, one way to achieve this is, first, to invite participants to spontaneously introduce themselves to the group. Once the initial surface identity markers are exposed, they are incited to list the multiple underlying facets of their identity, indeed, the ones they are not used to naming and that usually are not deemed relevant. Through this simple exercise, participants will see the importance—for themselves and others—of recognizing a more complex 'cultural' identity, which will then lead to making their different 'voices' explicit. This in itself becomes part of the resourceful-ness which lies at the core of intercultural competencies. Understanding from where one speaks and how one positions the other will help reorganize the power games at play in intercultural interactions. Indeed, this type of exercise helps demonstrate that depending on how an individual is perceived, they may benefit from enhanced status or suffer from stigmatization.

Language can be used to transform power relations in unexpected ways, as language comes from and forms personal identity. Individuals will be empow-ered if self-awareness and reflexivity based on an intersectional approach become the core of their personal communication strategies. This case shows the importance of agency in order to assume control in interactions by con-stantly re-evaluating the way roles are attributed (Szkudlarek, 2009).

Following the path of critical sociolinguists (Blommaert, 2010; Kramsch, 2012; Makoni and Pennycook, 2012), future research in cross-cultural manage-ment would benefit from a more critical analysis as to how language, as viewed through this lens, impacts power relations as they are played out in communica-tion strategies. Furthermore, incorporating this dimension into cross-cultural management seminars is of utmost importance if individuals are to acquire the full range of competencies required in today's complex workplaces (Jannsens and Steyaert, 2014).

We therefore recommend a new approach, taking into account both the complexity of language use and the complexity of identity—since languages, like identities, can no longer be conceptualized as fixed, clear-cut, ready-made categories. The emphasis can then be placed on a negotiated, situated approach, where multiple linguistic resources are used in complex ways to express voice. In short, through reflexivity and self-awareness, individuals need to simultane-ously adopt an intersectional approach to their language use and their identities.

In order to incite reflection on the concepts raised in this case, we recom-mend the following questions:

- What do you understand by 'cross-cultural' communication?
- In your experience, do you act differently when using a foreign language?
- In what contexts have you been aware of using different 'voices' and how does this reflect the different facets of your identity?

- How do you react to a person using your language differently from the way you do?
- How can an awareness of the multiple aspects of one's own and others' identity influence intercultural interactions?

References

Blommaert J (2010) *The Sociolinguistics of Globalization.* Cambridge: Cambridge University Press.

Boogaard B and Roggeband C (2010) Paradoxes of intersectionality: Theorizing inequality in the Dutch Police force through structure and agency. *Organization* 17(1): 53–75.

Cohen L and Kassis-Henderson J (2012) Language use in establishing rapport and building relations: Implications for international teams and management education. *Revue Management et Avenir* 55: 185–207.

Cohen L and Kassis-Henderson J (2017) Revisiting culture and language in global management teams: Toward a multilingual turn. *International Journal of Cross-Cultural Management* 17(1): 7–22.

Crenshaw K (1991) Mapping the margins: Intersectionality, identity politics, and violence against women of color. *Stanford Law Review* 43(6): 1241–1299.

Frame A (2016) Intersectional identities in interpersonal communication. In: Ciepiela K (ed) *Studying Identity in Communicative Contexts.* Warsaw: Peter Lang, pp. 21–38.

Gumperz J (2003) Interactional sociolinguistics: A personal perspective. In: Schiffrin D, Tannen D and Hamilton HE (eds) *The Handbook of Discourse Analysis.* Paperbacked. Oxford, UK: Blackwell Publishing, pp. 215–228.

Holden, N (1992) Management, language and euro-communication, 1992 and beyond. In: Berry M (ed) *Cross Cultural Communication in Europe.* Turku, Finland: Finnish Institute for European Studies, pp. 40–57.

Holmes P (2015) Intercultural encounters as socially constructed experiences: Which concepts? Which pedagogies? In: Holden N, Michailova S and Tietze S (eds) *The Routledge Companion to Cross-Cultural Management.* London and New York: Routledge, pp. 237–247.

Hong H-J and Doz Y (2013) L'Oréal masters multiculturalism. *Harvard Business Review* 91(6): 114–118.

Jannsens M and Steyaert C (2014) Re-considering language from a cosmopolitan understanding: Toward a multilingual franca approach in international business studies. *Journal of International Business Studies* 45(5): 623–639.

Kassis-Henderson J, Cohen L and McCulloch R (2018) Boundary crossing and reflexivity: Navigating the complexity of cultural and linguistic identity. *Business and Professional Communication Quarterly* 81(3): 304–327.

Kramsch C (2012) Authenticity and legitimacy in multilingual SLA. *Critical Multilingualism, an Interdisciplinary Journal* 1(1): 107–128.

Mahadevan J (2017) *A Very Short, Fairly Interesting and Reasonably Cheap Book about Cross-Cultural Management.* London: Sage.

Makoni S and Pennycook A (2012) Disinventing multilingualism: From monological multilingualism to multilingual franca. In: Martin-Jones M, Blackledge A and Creese A (eds) *The Routledge Handbook of Multilingualism.* Abingdon: Routledge, pp. 439–453.

Martin JN and Nakayama TK (2015) Reconsidering intercultural (communication) competence in the workplace: A dialectical approach. *Language and Intercultural Communication* 15(1): 13–28.

Martin-Jones M, Blackledge A and Creese A (2012) Introduction: A sociolinguistics of multilingualism for our times. In: Martin-Jones M, Blackledge A and Creese A (eds) *The Routledge Handbook of Multilingualism*. Abingdon: Routledge, pp. 1–26.

Mughan T (2015) Language and languages: Moving from the periphery to the core. In: Holden N, Michailova S and Tietze S (eds) *The Routledge Companion to Cross-Cultural Management*. London and New York: Routledge, pp. 79–84.

Ozkazanç-Pan B (2015) Post colonial perspectives on cross-cultural management knowledge. In: Holden N, Michailova S and Tietze S (eds) *The Routledge Companion to Cross-Cultural Management*. London and New York: Routledge, pp. 371–379.

Primecz H, Mahadevan J and Romani L (2016) Why is cross-cultural management scholarship blind to power relations? Investigating ethnicity, language, gender and religion in power-laden contexts. *International Journal of Cross-Cultural Management* 16(2): 127–136.

Primecz H, Romani L and Sackmann SA (2009) Cross-cultural management research, contributions from various paradigms. *International Journal of Cross-Cultural Management* 9(3): 267–274.

Steyaert C and Janssens M (2015) Translation in cross-cultural management: A matter of voice. In: Holden N, Michailova S and Tietze S (eds) *The Routledge Companion to Cross-Cultural Management*. London and New York: Routledge, pp. 131–141.

Szkudlarek B (2009) Through western eyes: Insights into the corporate training field. *Organization Studies* 30(9): 975–986.

Yagi N and Kleinberg J (2011) Boundary work: An interpretive ethnographic perspective on negotiating and leveraging cross-cultural identity. *Journal of International Business Studies* 42(5): 629–653.

Zander U, Zander L, Gaffney S and Olsson J (2010) Intersectionality as a new perspective in international business research. *Scandinavian Journal of Management* 26(4): 457–466.

Zanoni P, Janssens M, Benschop Y, et al. (2010) Unpacking diversity, grasping inequality: Rethinking difference through critical perspectives. *Organization* 17(1): 9–29.

2

RACE AND PRIVILEGE IN CCM

A Cross-Cultural Life Story

Simon Cedrick Nunka Dikuba and Jasmin Mahadevan

Introduction

Recently, race has come to the attention of critical cross-cultural management (CCM) scholars (Jackson, 2017). At first glance it might seem paradoxical that race should be 'cultural' and not, as it is often assumed, 'biological'. Yet, we can see that meaning is attached to race, and that this meaning, as well as perceived markers for inclusion and exclusion, differ across groups of people. For instance, if we examine exclusionary racial comments made towards Barack Obama, we find that he has simultaneously been critiqued as 'not Black enough' (by 'Black' voters) and as 'too Black' (by 'White' voters) when first running for president (Hatch, 2011: 82).

We can also see that race is approached differently in different cultural contexts. For example, many individuals worldwide are of mixed heritage. In North America, race is a very explicit diversity category (Prasad et al., 2006) and individuals of mixed heritage often self-identify as 'biracial'. In Europe, however, race is largely a silent category (Lentin, 2008), and individuals of mixed heritage would therefore rather self-identify as 'bi-cultural'. From this example, we can see how *meaning* is ascribed to race, and how this meaning is specific to a certain cultural context and can also change over time (for example, race was *not* a silenced category in Europe before World War II, see Lentin, 2008).

Not only is race 'cultural', it is also associated with certain hierarchies, regardless of whether race is explicit or silent. For instance, today's world order has developed in certain ways, with Europe—and, later, North America—as its centre. If we interpret this along the lines of racial categorizations, a 'White' population has come to expand its political, economic, sociocultural and military power, resulting in systems wherein 'Whiteness' constituted the most favourable category, e.g. in the colonial societies of the 19th and early 20th century (Cairns and Śliwa, 2008). Historically, virtually all systems of racial segregation constructed 'White' and 'Black' as opposing poles, sometimes with the possibility of in-between categories such as 'coloured' or 'mestizo' (mixed). Often, individuals of mixed heritage needed to prove their 'Whiteness' based on lineage (and in some systems, even 'one drop' of 'non-White blood' disqualified them for being allowed into the 'White' category). Conversely, the category 'Black' was easily assigned to those of mixed ancestry, often solely based on appearance. These ideas seem to linger on today. For instance, in terms of ancestry, Barack Obama is actually half 'White' and half 'Black', but still often referred to as the 'first African American president of the U.S.A.' (see Hatch, 2011: 56, 82).

In cultural contexts wherein race is silent, such as in Europe (Lentin, 2008), the situation is more complicated because perceived differences, and the hierarchies and privileges associated with them, will be explained by means of alternative categories, and people might not believe that this is actually about race. Nonetheless, the hierarchies and privileges associated with 'Whiteness' and 'non-Whiteness' continue to inform managerial decisions and to advantage those who fit the culturally learned makers of 'Whiteness' (Holgersson et al., 2016). For example, in some countries, such as Austria or Germany, the term 'race' is avoided altogether and replaced by 'migration background' (Holgersson et al., 2016; Mahadevan and Kilian-Yasin, 2016). 'Migration background' is a seemingly neutral term; it describes a person who has migrated to Germany or has at least one parent who has migrated to Germany after 1955 (BAMF, 2019). However, in reality, 'migration background' can only be inferred from visible differences, e.g., skin colour, culture or a non-ethnic German name (Mahadevan and Kilian-Yasin, 2016). This suggests that the situation is about race nonetheless (Lentin, 2008), not as a biological fix point but as a constant cultural practice by which 'Whiteness' and 'non-Whiteness' are 'done' (Holgersson et al., 2006). To make clear that we speak of such cultural constructions in this text, we use 'Black' and 'White' in capital letters and in quotation marks throughout.

Methodology

This chapter exemplifies how race and privilege intersect in the life of Ngebi (pseudonym), a female student, who was born to Anglophone Cameroonian parents in Germany, grew up in Cameroon and Germany, and has held German citizenship since birth. The first author conducted three ethnographic interviews (Spradley, 1979) with her in English language. The first author was interested in Ngebi's life story because of his own life experiences as a male student who migrated to Germany from Anglophone Southwest Cameroon at the age of 20. The interviews, lasting about two hours each, took place in spring 2017. All interviews were documented via memory protocol: the interviewer took condensed notes and later expanded them from memory. Afterwards, interpretations were exchanged with the interviewee, points that needed clarification were raised, and further input was given on relevant topics. The second author provided an outside perspective to this analysis which was informed by critical CCM and diversity studies.

Case Presentation

Ngebi's mother, who was raised in a big city in Cameroon, comes from an academic family. She had moved to Germany when she was 19. There, she learned German quickly, and lived and worked there as a journalist until Ngebi was born seven years later in the early 1990s. A few months afterwards, they moved to another big city, to a complete "white neighborhood", as Ngebi puts it. Ngebi's sister was born three years later. Even though her mother, still working as a journalist, raised them single-handedly, Ngebi was always surrounded by Cameroonian friends and family. For example, her mother supported students from Cameroon with housing and helped them to settle in Germany.

Ngebi's father, who is Cameroonian, lives and works in Cameroon, and always has. Her parents had a long-distance relationship for quite a while. Although her father came to Germany a couple of times to visit them, he preferred to stay in Cameroon, and Ngebi's mother frequently flew to Cameroon.

At age three, Ngebi started kindergarten, then the common entry age in Germany. Even without the interviewer asking questions into this direction, Ngebi immediately started talking about what she was confronted with as a "black kid". She recalled that there were "just two black kids" in that kindergarten: one was herself, described in her own words as a "full black kid", and another boy was a "mixed black kid". She recalls:

> Growing up in Germany [in the 1990s and 2000s] as an immigrant or a black child, you don't really go into the world knowing you are black or, in other words, knowing you are different from what is perceived as normal. Then you are confronted with scenarios like those kids who don't want to play with you because you look different, those who like you because you are different, and those who spend most of their time just bullying you. I was confronted with all of that, and that was when I got to realize that: Ohhh! There is a difference between me and the others. However, for some reason I never really asked my mother *why* I was different. I just decided to accept the fact that I am different because I look different. I got mocked on countless occasions because of my skin color and my name. . . . But, I mean, this was kindergarten. One minute you are made fun of, the next minute you are playing together.

Two years later Ngebi started schooling. However, she spent just two days in first grade; her mother had to go back to Cameroon, where Ngebi and her sister then lived for two years in a town in the English-speaking southwest region of Cameroon. Ngebi was just six years old when they moved to Cameroon; she did, however, refer to these two years as the best time of her life as a kid. "It was the best time because it was different", she said:

> All names were 'difficult', everyone looks like you, it was effortless. Everyone wanted to be my friend. Maybe it was because I was from Europe, but as a kid you don't really care about that, but just the fact that I suddenly found myself being accepted by everyone was really a great experience.

In Cameroon, Ngebi lived with her father for the first few months, after which he moved to South Korea for a master's degree program. A few months later her mother moved to Germany for a while, but frequently visited Cameroon, as always. For the rest of their stay in Cameroon, Ngebi and her sister then lived with their mother's sister and a nanny. Despite them being "the European kids", Ngebi felt that "there wasn't too much of a change" since their mother had brought them up "quite African", in an exclusively English-speaking home. Ngebi says:

> Maybe there were differences, but as kids you adapt quite easily and its possible you don't even realize there was a difference in the first place. . . . Generally, I was too excited about the fact that I had moved to somewhere where everybody looked like me, hence I didn't really pay attention to what was different.

Ngebi completed first and second grade in Cameroon. After the turn of the millennium, they moved back to Germany where Ngebi was enrolled in third grade, after some uncertainties regarding which grade to place her in. She referred to this period as one of the most difficult phases in her life, as she had completely forgotten how to speak German. Whereas her sister could start learning how to read and write German from first grade onwards, Ngebi felt like she was "stuck in the middle". She said: "What was funny was that, in Cameroon, we were the German kids, and suddenly I really felt like an immigrant because I just couldn't communicate with the others." After several teachers had commented negatively about 'Ngebi's slow development', her mother got her enrolled in extra classes for every subject, at high expense. During her final (fourth) year of primary school, Ngebi received the obligatory (binding) recommendation on which secondary school suited her.

The recommendation which Ngebi got was either *'Gesamtschule'* or *'Hauptschule'* which are the 'lower' types in the German system, normally preparing for vocational training or practical jobs. However, *Gesamtschule* is considered still better than *Hauptschule* because it does not explicitly exclude the possibility of an academic career. The highest type of school is *Gymnasium* which leads directly to the university entry exam. Reflecting on this, Ngebi said: "I have the best mother in the whole world". Her mother, confident of her academic family background, her own high level of education and her professional status as a journalist, did not just accept the secondary school recommendations. She took the time to ask people and to understand the German secondary school system. After doing her research, she concluded that *Hauptschule* is not what she wanted for her daughter. Ngebi was enrolled in a *Gesamtschule* which was about an hour away from their residence. There was, however, a private Gymnasium a stone's throw away from their home. Ngebi's mother went to this school and spoke to teachers, advocating Ngebi's abilities. Ultimately, her mother succeeded in convincing the school, and Ngebi was enrolled in the *Gymnasium* after a year. She had to retake fifth grade, but she had passed a crucial educational bottleneck. Ngebi reflects:

> When I got there, the start was really rough because I wasn't used to the speed at which they were learning, and I was also struggling with making friends. At that time, my German had really become better, although I had problems with writing. Therefore, I got a lot of extra classes, and with time everything got better, and I found out what my strengths were.

During these years (between 2005 and 2014), she experienced a variety of attitudes towards her: some teachers pitied her for being from Cameroon, others challenged her abilities to make it in the German system. She found friends, but sometimes still found herself being referred to as "nigger" (*Neger*), a practice she did not contest. In retrospect, she offers an interpretation:

> I feel like the fear of losing a friend back then, and not having friends was huge. I feel like at that stage you are not just confronted with being black in a predominantly white milieu but also confronted with the urge of trying to belong to a group especially as a teenager. So, all these factors determined my reactions.

Whenever she left the campus of her privileged *Gymnasium* during breaks and entered the common campus which her school shared with the other two (lower) types of secondary schools she had predominantly negative experiences.

> I realized how mean the real world could be when I left my campus for the common campus. We—my sister and I; we were together most of the times—will get all sorts of racist insults, people throwing things at us and so on. It was crazy. So, I just avoided that area generally.

During one particular day, she was walking home from school, and her sister was walking about ten meters ahead of her. They both had 'Dakine' backpacks (a fashionable American clothing label). Suddenly, a young boy ran up to her sister and asked her if "she thought herself to be better than others because she has a Dakine backpack".

Ngebi recalls herself and her sister being constantly bullied in their neighbourhood, for example by 'Arab' immigrant children. She says: "At some point, I just thought black people are at the bottom of the immigrant pyramid because we were constantly bullied by these white immigrants." When asked at what point in her life she thought that this became better, Ngebi responded by saying:

> I don't think it became better but with . . . age the perception or understanding of racism changes, and one gets to acknowledge things differently. When I was younger, I only recognized racism if one was really screaming and explicitly using racial slurs on me. Right now, I just need to see your countenance towards me, for instance, and I know. I didn't get into public offices as a kid, but right now I go into offices, and the reception is horrible sometimes. So, I think, there is racism on different levels, and I cannot really say if one is better than the other. The perception of the highest form of racism changes over time. As a kid, the highest form was explicit racist slurs. At this point in my life [as a student of medicine], it is different. So, . . . [you] learn to decipher if this is racism or not.

Even though some incidents seem certain to her, she allows herself room for doubt. For example, Ngebi talked of instances in which she was seated in a train and there was a free seat beside her but someone decided to pass or remain standing rather than sit next to her. She recalled a day in which the only free seat in the coach of the tram where she was seated was beside her, but two people rather preferred to remain standing. She thought that "they just didn't want to seat beside me because I am black". However, she also wanted to tell herself that there could be other reasons why they decided to remain standing. "Maybe backache, you know."

In 2014, Ngebi completed her university entry exam. She wanted to enroll in medicine but could not get in immediately, due to insufficient final grades. She therefore enrolled in a Business Administration program at a large international university in Germany, but still investigated ways to get into medicine. At university, she met students from all over the world, also Germans who had spent a year or more abroad after finishing their university entry exam. Hence, she didn't really feel discriminated there. Of course there were difficulties, mainly related to having moved to another level of the academic ladder, which required more time and effort.

However, in another sphere of life, namely, while working in a jean shop, Ngebi started experiencing discrimination again. She says:

> There were customers who just find you friendly and walk up to you, buy their jeans and go, but there were also those who just didn't want to talk to you or snub you when you walk up to them. I recall this day in which this man completely snubbed me when I walked up to him, to ask him if he needed any form of assistance but instances later my German colleague walked up to him and he was like 'yes, sure'. For me, this was racism, but without any racist slurs like what I experienced as a kid. This was on another level.

After studying Business Administration in Germany for a year, in 2015, Ngebi was admitted to a medical school in Cluj, Romania, where she studied for three semesters. Medical school in Germany requires certain final grades, and those who cannot get in often start studying medicine in another country in the hope to get into a German school at a higher semester, when places are available again because a certain number of students will have dropped out. Study fees in Romania are high from a German perspective (university education is free in Germany): about €4,000 per semester. But Ngebi's mother paid for it, and Ngebi was also eligible for a study loan by the German state which needs to be paid back (fully or partially) after graduation.

In Romania, Ngebi still stuck out, but differently. She, "like other Black students" both male and female, had "so much attention" in Romania: "Whistles everywhere I went to, people stopping to take pictures and so on." Ngebi perceived such incidents as being "a positive experience". This suggests that, to her, such othering and being made the object of attention was still preferable to how she was perceived and treated in Germany. This might have been due to her high social status in Romania, of which she was certain: As Ngebi explained, "Romanians assume all non-Romanian students to be wealthy", because of their ability to pay the study fees. So, it seems that Ngebi was assured that, regardless of how she was treated during particular incidents, she was still perceived as a member of a privileged group in general. To deal with these incidents, she might have even subconsciously chosen not to consider her being 'Black' but to interpret the situation solely in term s of her being a 'non-Romanian student'.

After studying in Romania for three semesters, in 2017, Ngebi got an admission to continue studying medicine at a university in former East Germany, which she perceived as a "closed environment". Still, medicine is what Ngebi calls her "dream profession". One of her uncles (Cameroonian) is an oncologist. He works in a day clinic in a comparably poor city in West Germany, and Ngebi interned at this clinic for a few weeks.

She recalls instances in which a patient went to her uncle's office and asked him to bring the doctor. She saw "the shock on their faces" when her uncle said that it was him who is the doctor, and she also experienced instances in which patients said they did not want to be treated by her uncle. According to Ngebi, these were "German and immigrant patients, but all of them were non-black". Ngebi says: "But then I took that as a motivation, too, to strive to climb the academic ladder and try to change the status quo. We cannot ignore the fact that colonialism has made the West have certain pictures of Africans generally."

Ngebi also explains that she consciously positions herself, for instance, regarding her sociolect (class-related 'dialect') when speaking German, which she adjusts depending on context and whom she speaks to. She also reckons that not everyone might be able to do so, but she can, after all (as is typical of middle and higher social classes). She is fluent in English, which she considers an advantage as well. So, where does Ngebi belong? "I am Cameroonian", she says:

> Maybe a Cameroonian with some German character traits but I am Cameroonian. One reason for saying so is due to my upbringing which was mainly with Cameroonian values. I may have German nationality, but my roots are more important for me, and these are Cameroonian. If someone asks me where I am from, I would say I am Cameroonian. I know if I say German, eventually I will get asked where I am *really* from because I don't look German. I am Cameroonian, and that is who I identify as.

Power and CCM

This case shows how race is a cultural category, and how it intersects with social status and the privileges associated with 'Whiteness'. In a context such as Germany wherein race is silenced it might be difficult to interpret Ngebi's story in terms of race, even for Ngebi herself. For instance, initially, she is not aware of the 'non-Whiteness' associated with 'migration background' that separates 'Arab immigrants' from ethnic Germans: both groups are 'White' in her eyes. Ngebi also is a German citizen by birth: why does she not identify as German? If we understand 'migration background' not as a technicality but as a way in which 'Whiteness' and 'non-Whiteness' are constructed, then this implies that those descendants of immigrants who are visibly 'different' in terms of race can never become 'German'. In Germany, this would normally be ascribed to remaining 'cultural differences' between what is called 'the receiving society' and immigrants (Mahadevan and Kilian-Yasin, 2016). However, these presumed 'cultural differences' matter the most if there are additional markers 'non-Whiteness', as in Ngebi's case: she is asked from where she is *really* from and, thus, not identified as German. And she is asked this question because she *looks different*. So, even if this is not labelled racism, the underlying patterns are the same. For CCM, this means that we need to investigate situations for their racial biases even if all believe that the situation is not about race, and to find out *how exactly* ideas of 'Whiteness' and 'non-Whiteness' are produced.

In Cameroon, Ngebi looks like everyone else, but now that she represents 'White' Europe, she becomes "the European kid': She is symbolically 'White'. Because of this high status, she is not challenged (as she is in Germany) and therefore does not dig further into what makes her 'different' in Cameroon: Race 'vanishes' for her. This reminds us that privilege—also in CCM—is invisible to those who have it, whilst being assigned the inferior position is more strongly experienced. This suggests that we need to check presumed CCM normalities—including our own—for implicit racial privileges.

In Romania, race and status intersect in yet another way: Romania has a lower GDP than Western Europe, and is also potentially disadvantaged by a certain history that made Western capitalism the dominant global system (Cairns and Śliwa, 2008). There, Ngebi suddenly became the 'wealthy Black student'. Still, Ngebi speaks of her experiences not as those of "a German student taking a detour to be able to study medicine in Germany." Rather, she categorizes herself as part of a group of 'Black' students, and we may assume that this was a diverse group of students from different countries. Yet, as Ngebi experiences it, they are perceived as a homogeneous group only because of how they look, and, in her interpretation, race dominates over alternative categorizations. We can thus see how race simplifies cultural categories and might even cancel out alternative interpretations. Nonetheless, the situation is experienced as positive by Ngebi, because of the high social status which it involves.

Social status, privilege and race intersect throughout Ngebi's story, but in various context-specific ways. Nonetheless, race as linked to status remains prominent: there is, for instance, the idea that a 'Black' doctor is unfathomable, and even other 'non-White' immigrants seem to entertain this thought. In Romania, the idea of a high-status 'Black' student seems much more out of the ordinary than the concept of someone being a privileged or wealthy 'White Western European' student. This reminds us that there are status expectations linked to the hierarchies of race. For instance, in today's international business, the qualifications of a 'non-White' expatriate from the 'non-West' are more likely to be undervalued than those of a 'White' and 'Western' expatriate (e.g. Al Ariss et al., 2014).

At the same time, there is also the potential to change status expectations attached to race: we can see how entering the German Gymnasium reduces racism for Ngebi, and we can assume that similar effects will change the situation as soon as Ngebi has achieved the status of 'medical doctor': The higher her 'proven' social status in terms of education, the more her perceived 'Whiteness' increases.

Ngebi has not asked to experience race: race came to her, and we may assume that this would not have happened had she not been categorized as 'non-White' in all cultural contexts except Cameroon. Yet, now that she has experienced race in so many facets, Ngebi's strength is to position herself in numerous ways. We can see this, for instance, in the ways in which she speaks German with different sociolects to achieve certain goals. Her English language skills are an asset in a modern and cosmopolitan international business world (Cairns and Śliwa, 2008) which many Germans do not possess. In Cameroon, Ngebi profits from her 'European' status. Thus, education and class partly counterweigh the hierarchies of race.

Reflexive Considerations

Both the first author and Ngebi are related in many ways: in terms of race, both are categorized as 'Black' by others and self-identify as 'Black African'. The first author can recall similar incidents of racial discrimination in Germany; he has developed similar strategies of how to counteract them. Being well-educated and coming from an academic family is an asset to him as well, and he has also experienced privilege because of the 'European' status which is ascribed to him when in Cameroon. However, he only immigrated to Germany at the age of 20, whereas Ngebi was already born in the country; he realized that this, again, is a different story. For example, he speaks German with an accent, whereas Ngebi does not.

The second author is of mixed heritage and her 'Whiteness' is fluid in the eyes of others. She also has been a German citizen since birth, identifies as German and has received most of her education in the country. Because of this 'German' socialization, she has learned that the very word *Rasse* (race), let alone analyzing the social world in terms of race, is taboo: It bears the stigma of National Socialism, a past that may never reemerge. Yet, as a critical CCM scholar, she has also come to realize that censoring a problematic category does not make its power effects vanish: Rather, a taboo seems to only increase the inability to name and deal with the problem, namely the realization that race—as a cultural category, not as a biological fix point—continues to inform our thoughts and actions.

Recommendations to Students, Researchers and Practitioners

As this case suggests, a critical CCM needs to question perceptions of a person's social status, competency or qualification for underlying constructions of 'Whiteness' or 'non-Whiteness'. This requires becoming aware of the categories by which we have learned to 'do' and 'see' categories such as 'White' and 'non-White'. We should also investigate our individual and organizational practices for how 'Whiteness' is 'done' in the sense of a culture-specific process that produces the hierarchies of race and affirms the privilege of those that are constructed as 'White'. This is of particular importance in cultural contexts wherein race is silenced, and related categorizations are not thought of as involving race.

References

Al Ariss A, Cascio WF and Paauwe J (2014) Talent management: Current theories and future research directions. *Journal of World Business* 49(2): 173–179.

BAMF (2019) Glossar: Migrationshintergrund (Definition) [Glossary: Migration Background (Definition). Available at: www.bamf.de/DE/Service/Left/Glossary/_function/glossar.html?lv3=3198544 (accessed 1 February 2019).

Cairns G and Śliwa M (2008) *A Very Short, Reasonably Cheap and Fairly Interesting Book about International Business.* London: SAGE.

Hatch M-J (2011) *Organizations: A Very Short Introduction.* Oxford: Oxford University Press.

Holgersson C, Tienari J, Merilainen S and Bendl R (2016) Executive search as ethnosociality: A cross-cultural comparison. *International Journal of Cross-Cultural Management* 16(2): 153–169.

Jackson T (2017) Should cross-cultural management scholars study race? *International Journal of Cross Cultural Management* 17(3): 277–280.

Lentin A (2008) Europe and the silence about race. *European Journal of Social Theory* 11(4): 487–503.

Mahadevan J and Kilian-Yasin K (2016) Dominant discourse, orientalism and the need for reflexive HRM: Skilled Muslim migrants in the German context. *International Journal of Human Resource Management*: 1–23. DOI: 10.1080/09585192.2016.1166786.

Prasad P, Pringle JK and Konrad AM (2006) Examining the contours of workplace diversity. In: Konrad AM, Prasad P and Pringle JK (eds) *Handbook of Workplace Diversity.* London: SAGE, pp. 1–22.

Spradley JP (1979) *The Ethnographic Interview.* Belmont: Wadsworth.

3

FROM IMPOSSIBILITY TO VISIBILITY

An Intersectional Approach to LGBT Muslims and Its Benefits for CCM

Momin Rahman and Sébastien Chehaitly

Introduction

This case study is drawn from a research project on experiences of Lesbian, Gay, Bisexual and Transgender (LGBT)[1] Muslims in Canada. We use these life stories to demonstrate the benefits of an intersectional approach to culture and identities. In terms of cross-cultural management (CCM), this case highlights that we should accept neither assumptions of a unified national or ethnic culture nor assumptions that there are uniform attitudes amongst the people that are equated with such cultures or groups. Specifically, there is a widespread assumption in Western cultures that LGBT rights are only possible in the West and a related assumption that Muslim cultures and people are inherently homophobic. This assumption illustrates a fundamental organizational aspect of culture in which dominant or *normal* identities are formed in opposition to a perceived minority or *other*. In this context, the recent emergence of LGBT rights in the west (Hildebrandt, 2014; Weeks, 2007) and subsequent attempts to internationalize LGBT rights have provoked resistance from Muslim states and cultural/religious community groups in both majority and minority populations. So LGBT rights have become identified with a Western culture of human rights and progressive values, and this is used to define Muslim cultures as traditional and backwards. This dichotomy creates a sense of mutual exclusivity between LGBT and Muslim. To challenge these assumptions, we use intersectionality theory to focus on the identities caught between these assumptions—those of LGBT Muslims. In doing so, we show why intersectional theory and related methods challenge dominant forms of thinking and allow new forms of knowledge to be produced. Crucially, these new forms of knowledge create a more accurate basis for the understanding of culture in societies and organizations and, in particular, alert us to key issues in LGBT equality, specifically, racism and Islamophobia in LGBT communities, assumptions of a transcultural model of the 'coming out' process and assumptions of monolithic homophobia with Muslim communities. Intersectionality therefore complicates the assumptions of distinct aspects of national cultures that we often see in CCM. Homophobia, racism and Islamophobia all are such examples of cultural hierarchies that are not limited to one national culture. We base our brief recommendations on these issues, emphasizing that it is the intersectional methodological approach that has permitted the creation of more accurate evidence on which to base these recommendations.

Methodology: An Intersectional Approach to LGBT Muslims in CCM

The dominant political understanding of the relationship between LGBT rights and Muslims is one of inevitable opposition. This has resulted from various facts, including that most Muslim majority states regulate homosexuality severely, and surveys of both those countries and Muslim minority immigrant populations suggest higher levels of homophobia than Western populations (Carroll and Mendos, 2017; Pew Research Center, 2013; Rahman, 2014). For example, Muslim majority states were largely unified in their opposition to the successful appointment of an international expert to report on LGBT rights at the United Nations Human Rights Council in 2016. Moreover, research shows that LGBT citizenship rights have progressed more widely and more quickly in Western countries (Western Europe, North America, Australia and New Zealand) than in other regions (Hildebrandt, 2014). Given these facts, it is no surprise that there is a widespread cultural understanding that 'Western cultures' are LGBT friendly and 'Muslim cultures' are homophobic.

One of the consequences of this oppositional understanding is that the idea of LGBT Muslims becomes a difficult one to imagine. Opposition to LGBT rights from Muslim governments and communities involves increasingly rigid interpretations of Islam and monolithic characterizations of contemporary Muslim cultures, and thus renders invisible contemporary forms of sexual and gender diversity in Muslim cultures. Moreover, the current political homophobia also renders invisible the historical evidence and acceptance of gender and sexual diversity in a wide range of Muslim cultures from North Africa to Southeast Asia (De Sondy, 2015; Hamzic, 2016). There is, however, a small body of research that demonstrates that LGBT Muslim identities have existed historically and continue to do so in contemporary times, both in minority immigrant populations and in Muslim majority countries (Rahman, 2018). Based on this research, our first step was therefore to focus on LGBT Muslims as an identity that challenged the assumptions of inherent or inevitable opposition between Western and Muslim cultures. Moreover, the increasing body of research on LGBT Muslims demonstrates that LGBT Muslims are caught in between mainstream Western LGBT politics and communities and heteronormative (heterosexually organized) Muslim identity and politics (Dhoest, 2016; Gandhi, 2012; Jaspal, 2012; Jaspal and Cinnirella, 2012; Kugle, 2010, 2014; Rahman and Valliani, 2016; Yip, 2004, 2007, 2008). This suggested to us that an intersectional theoretical and methodological framework would be relevant in studying LGBT Muslims, since intersectionality asks us to consider those within oppressed identity categories (such as LGBT) that also suffer from other hierarchies of oppression (such as racism). Hence, oppressions *intersect*, and those at the point of intersection have a distinct experience of each hierarchy. In this case, LGBT Muslims are the intersectional identity that suffers both racism/Islamophobia and homophobia.

LGBT Muslims experience their lives as a combination of ethnoreligious, gendered, sexual and racialized identities in specific national and transnational contexts. They are, therefore, an *intersectional* social identity because they exist at the intersections of these various identity markers. More precisely, taking an intersectional approach means that we are also considering LGBT Muslims as distinct identities *within* larger categories of identity—in this case, the broader category of Muslim *and* the broader category of LGBT. This is linked to a critical multiples cultures perspective in CCM (Mahadevan, 2017) that helps us consider alternative, multilayered and more complex cultural identities than mere national cultures.

By centering our research on the experiences of LGBT Muslims, we reorient the oppositional understandings of Muslim *versus* LGBT and instead start with an analytical framework that assumes that LGBT Muslims are equally valid and intersecting expressions of *both* Muslim and LGBT, rather than simply being a minority 'version' within each those categories. Furthermore, researching and disseminating the experiences of those who inhabit this site of intersection enables their points of view to be illuminated in order to contest established dominant knowledge of both Muslim cultures and LGBT cultures. This leads us to specific intersectional methods of learning about identities.

Providing new knowledge on intersectional identities means that we must allow the specificity of these intersectional identities to come through. This requires research methods that allow individuals to talk about their life stories in their own terms, without the imposition of pre-existing themes of analysis or—put more simply—without assumptions drawn from current cultural conditions. This means that intersectional studies often draw on the feminist tradition of *standpoint* methods. This is a methodological tradition that attempts to research the experiences of marginalized or oppressed groups by understanding their 'standpoint' on objective reality (Harding, 1986; Smith, 2006). It therefore contests the notion that there is an objective reality that all people experience in the same way, arguing that those who are oppressed experience the everyday world differently than those who are privileged. Intersectionality falls firmly within this tradition and so takes all knowledge as relative, arguing that a group's location in social hierarchies of difference reflect divisions of power and thus affect their ability to make their knowledge (of their particular experience) both heard and taken as legitimate. Standpoint methodologies include a range of specific methods (such as unstructured interviews) but are qualitative and aim as much as they can to allow individuals to produce knowledge in their own terms and frameworks, rather than attempting to fit knowledge into preconceived or dominant categories of analysis (Collins, 2000; Harding, 1986; Smith, 2006). In this specific case, this means thinking about the fact that LGBT Muslims may suffer from Islamophobia or racism as other Muslims do, but that they may also experience this from within LGBT communities. Furthermore, they also suffer from homophobia, both from the wider society and from within Muslim communities. Thus, their experiences of oppressions connect to, but are distinct from, the dominant groups that they inhabit.

Case Presentation

Our case study draws on unstructured qualitative interviews with eight participants from October 2016 to August 2017, and who were all from Muslim families. Five of them are immigrants of first generation that have been living in Montreal from three to 20 years, and three are second-generation immigrants. Overall, our results demonstrate that negotiating a queer Muslim identity is a difficult, intersectional process because of limited engagement from LGBT groups with issues of racism and Islamophobia, and an even more limited acceptance of the legitimacy of LGBT Muslim identity by mainstream Muslim groups, either politically or theologically. Moreover, the research also suggests that our interviewees use both Western and Muslim identity resources when they negotiate their identities. In this process, they also adapt these categories and create a 'third space' for themselves. This way, our case shows that, despite common understanding, LGBT is much more than purely Western, and that there is no singular LGBT identity or identity negotiation process.

Key Demographics and Definitions

Amongst our eight participants, seven believe in Islam, and one is not specifically adherent but identifies culturally with Islam. Amongst those who are believers, one practices the religion. All our participants have engaged or completed university studies. Six participants are in their late 20s, and two are aged from 35 to 50 years old. They are all first-generation immigrants, except one who is second-generation. Relatively to gender identity, five of our participants are cis (meaning they identify with the gender they were assigned at birth) and three are trans (they do not identify with the gender they were assigned at birth). One is a trans woman, one is nonbinary (their gender identity is not defined by the binary of being either a man or a woman), one is genderfluid (their gender identity shifts on the gender spectrum depending on situations and contexts they are in), two are cis women and three are cis men. Our participants are of diverse sexual orientations: two are pansexual (they are attracted to people of the whole gender spectrum), four are homosexual, one is asexual, and one did not define their sexual orientation. Our research ethics approval requires us to protect the confidentiality of our participants, so we do not disclose the country of origin and the ethnic backgrounds of our participants.

The Importance of Being Muslim

All of our participants maintain strong links to Islam and cherish that part of their heritage. In spite of their internal conflicts with Islam, they all came back to reconcile with it or never left it. Yet, for many of our participants, their relationship to their religion has been uneasy.

Some, like Nazanine, have turned their back on Islam for a time. She chose to leave the religion when she became aware that she was gay: "I was very religious before I knew I was gay. . . . But when I found out I was gay, I couldn't find a good excuse to keep Islam. That's why I got out of Islam, and I changed my religion", converted to Christianity, a religion that she "found to be more open on homosexuality". Although she realized later on that this wasn't exactly the case, she still chose to keep Christianity in her life, and to welcome back Islam: "I am still Christian, and still Muslim. I can't quit Islam. I think we should look at Christianity with Islam [and vice versa]." She also affirms that "in general, I am atheist. Sometimes, I become religious, sometimes, I become atheist, that's why I can't say I'm this or that." Her ambiguity is explained by her critical views on religion and her urge to understand the "meaning of life":

> I look at religion like this, like a light. Arts, science and philosophy cannot give a good answer, but religion can't give an answer, but can give a light [to the signification of life], light up things that are dark." Without this light, she says, "I would commit suicide easily. Why should I keep living on like this? Why? Life is not easy. Especially for us [queer and trans people]."

Accordingly, if Islam came to her by default, it became a part of her spirituality, something that she relies on to guide her life. This concurs with what Salim shared with us. He witnessed some of his Muslim homosexual friends rejecting Islam to choose their sexuality, but he believes "this didn't work well on them". People who left Islam, he observed, had a crisis of conscience and experienced spiritual emptiness. On the opposite side, for his friends who have chosen religion (and practised it according to its mainstream interpretation), evacuating their sexuality "did not turn well on them" and "did not respect who they were". Yassine also shared with us a story of a Muslim friend who was questioning his sexuality, who started writing to imams in search for answers. Yassine disapproved of this, declaring: ". . . it's not a way to be in peace with yourself". The reply of the imam, as he recalls in his own terms, was: "God gave you this burden, it is your jihad, you'll have to fight against this, work on this, find a woman and . . ." which he completed by saying ". . . and like shut up!"

Like Wafaa, who stated that she practices "an Islam à-la-carte", he believes one does not need imams to practice Islam because his relationship with God does not concern them. Mourad and Mohammed (both male) summarize well the importance of religion for our participants; Mourad explains that Islam "is part of my fabric", and Mohammed says: "I still relate to Islam and Muslims, it's still a part of my identity and who I am going to be. What I believe, how I look at the world, it's all a part of me". Indeed, Islam became part of their identity and who they are as much as—or, in some cases, more than—their sexual orientation or gender identity. Cutting them forcibly from one aspect of their identity provoked unwanted suffering.

Difficulties With the Western Model of 'Coming Out'

Coming out has historically been seen, by gay and lesbian activists of the 20th century in the West, as one the ultimate act of visibility that one can do to improve the life of LGBT people because it allows for political organization to achieve greater freedom from oppression. Indeed, it is not possible to imagine the advances in LGBT rights without the public organization of LGBT activist groups based on people who are willing to identify as LGBT. However, there are also assumptions and judgments about the 'coming out' process, particularly, that someone who does not come out can never be who they *really* are, or even worse, can be perceived as a coward or a liar. Yet, our participants mostly believe that the mainstream discourse about coming out does not and should not apply to them. When we asked Rafik if the concept of coming out resonated in them, they answered:

> Not so much. But I respect all it has of an importance, that for a lot of people, talking about it has a very, very, very, very great value. . . . There are a lot of reasons not to do your coming out. . . . I had this talk with a White person . . . "Yeah, but one should be proud of their sexual orientation! If people don't say what they are . . ." . . . but it's not that simple! There are people who get murdered, you can lose a job, you can get insulted in the street . . ., you can get rejected from your community. It's no small matter! Or from your family . . . And those are the people who are the closest from us . . . It's terrible! No, there are a lot, a lot of reasons not do it, not to put yourself in danger.

Rafik recognises the value of coming out for some, but insists we should take into consideration the lived context of each individual. Yassine mentioned that he got a lot of pressure from his gay white friends to come out to his parents, but he did not understand why this was expected of him, since sexuality is not discussed in his family. Salim warned against the danger of pushing people to come out, since we cannot predict the outcomes of it, nor if it can be done safely for anybody in any context.

The reality of coming out is different for trans people, as Nazanine explained, as their coming out can be done automatically when they transition. On the matter, many participants have observed that trans rights and acceptability are not sufficiently developed in Canada, and it can be dangerous to live as a trans person there.

Coming out is not something to be avoided at all costs, either. In most cases, our participants were comfortable coming out to siblings and friends. The situation is not the same with parents, but it varies from family to family and on the lived circumstances of the individual. Widad did not plan to come out to her mother, but she was depressed, and her mother worried. Athough Widad's mother did not initially react with happiness, she eventually became supportive of her daughter. Mohammed does not consider coming out to his parents, but he speaks positively about homosexuality with them and they discuss it relatively well. Yassine and Wafaa envisioned telling their parents about their hypothetical same-gender partners if they ended up in long-term relationships.

Therefore, depending on the situation of the person, coming out can be seen as desirable or unwanted and the key issue is to listen to the views of the individual concerned. Most importantly, in a cross-cultural context, we cannot assume that the pathways to equality are the same for all LGBT people; cultural differences shape those pathways differently and should be considered when we are working for social justice.

Caught 'In Between' Cultures

Globally, our participants have mixed feelings about the different cultures they live in, whether Canadian, LGBT, Muslim or ethnic. About their lives in Canada, they all appreciate the human rights they benefit from, especially LGBT rights. As Salim puts it, "the most important thing is I live here without fear". Most of them live more openly their sexual orientation or their gender identity in Montreal than in their countries of origin, and some feel their countries of origin are more patriarchal than the West. This leads a part of our sample to ask the Canadian government to campaign more actively in favor of the advancement of LGBT rights internationally. Nazanine explains this by saying:

> I don't think we can change a lot of things in Muslim and conservative
> societies. But I think we can change things here, and societies elsewhere

would get influenced. I know the lifestyles always come from Western countries. I think we should be doing activism because of that.

Yassine disagrees with this position, and is critical of LGBT activism led by Western organisations:

Their activism . . . if I had to be following what they were doing, I would become homophobic! Those White gay men who know nothing about LGBTs around the world, their struggles, and our realities . . . they talk as they know their stuff. By doing what they're doing, they're throwing us under the bus. They seem to want to achieve a white gay supremacy, which I don't find interesting. I don't care about what they have to say, what matters to me is that we get a voice and we develop it.

Folks like Yassine, are critical of Western states and nongovernmental organisations (NGOs) that conduct human rights campaigns in their countries of origin while ignoring their sociohistorical context. This includes the impacts of European colonialism on contemporary Muslim-majority societies, and on the configuration of non-heterosexual sexualities and nonconforming gender identities. Homosexual behaviors were part of Muslim cultures before European colonisation, and where Muslim-majority societies were criticized by European countries for being too liberal sexually during that period, they are now seen as too conservative and restrictive (Said, 1979). This leads some to be critical of *homonationalism*, which means one nation considers itself superior to others because it supposes it has "abolished sexual oppression"—while LGBT people from that very country continue to suffer from oppression and discrimination (Puar, 2007).

This kind of critical position can be explained by the frustration experienced by LGBT Muslims from seeing part of their heritage and culture being discarded and seen as "barbaric" (Bilge, 2010). Salim feels white people can be unappreciative of the richness of gay life abroad, even in contexts where repression is strong. Other participants, like Mourad, are frustrated by the dichotomic representations of Muslim people, who can be seen either as "footballers" or "terrorists". Even though our participants haven't always used this word specifically, they want their intersectional identities to be acknowledged and respected.

Intersectionality in Focus: Family, Religion, Culture and Sexual Identity

The harsh reality of our participants is that they don't get the privilege of living in a world shaped to their image, wherever they go. They have to deal with different systems of oppression depending on where they are, what they do, what they look like. Sometimes, it isn't even clear for them why they can be subjected to discrimination. As Yassine explains, "all your identities will clash according to the spaces where you are". Moreover, he says:

> If we're talking about struggles, if we're talking about getting yelled insults at us in the street or looked strangely at, me, I never know really if it is because I look too faggy or if I look too brown, or if . . . We have multiple reasons to get hated!

Because of this, our participants have to relinquish access to certain types of spaces. One example of this is Rafik, who would like to go to the mosque:

> Now that I see that I am trans and nonbinary, I wonder, do I have a place in that community? I would like to go back to the mosque, but phew! I am not going back with the men! So I was wondering, will it go well if I go with the women? I am not sure too. . . . So I was wondering what can I do regarding this, do I have a place in this community, can I have one?

Rafik's challenge of their assigned gender identity also challenges the social configuration of mosques, where people are separated according to their perceived gender. We can observe, in their desire to go to the mosque, a wish to stay connected to their faith and their culture, but also a will to be able to do so while refusing to comply with gender binarism. Wafaa also has a complex relationship with elements of her cultural background. When we asked her how was her relationship to her home country, she replied with much enthusiasm and spontaneity "very beautiful relation! I love my country!" Yet, she quickly added "it's a bit difficult however to have your liberty, though." When she visits her country of origin, she is critical of how controlling her family abroad can be with her, but this does not prevent her from spending her summers there almost every year. She also adores and values her family enormously, despite having a complex relationship with them. Over the years, she developed more and more strategies to be able to negotiate those complexities.

The same goes on the other way. Although Mourad was the participant who was the most critical of Islam and of his community of origin, he was also the only one who ascribed more importance to his cultural background than to his sexuality; as a matter of fact, he does not consider sexuality to be an element of his identity at all. However, he experienced a strong feeling of belonging with LGBTs when he got to hang out with a group of queer and trans people of his ethnic background:

> The only time where I have felt a little bit this [LGBT] community feeling, it was when we were in a LGBT group with people from the [world area where I come from], because there was a cultural reality, because

we had experiences that were similar. Even if we could have been from different religions or different regions, we have these common points.

Widad, who is involved in LGBT activism, does not accept that the LGBT world stays a space tailored "for white gay men". Salim, who has a lot of white friends, yet expressed frustration on the way his romantic life has been going with them, feeling "they don't know how to act properly with Muslim people, and don't know much about Islam". Our participants have also expressed the wish to see a gay mosque appear in their city since they are aware that such spaces have existed in Toronto for some time, although on a very small scale.

In short, our data show that for all of our participants, they feel best when all parts of their identities are validated and conjugated together. The need for spaces shaped to their image, and where they can feel belonging and safety, was adamant. Our participants have also expressed appreciation of being able to connect with peers who live similar lives, as Yassine explains:

> Well, it's clear it always feels good to find yourself with those who are like you, close to your struggles. I don't know if it's we understand each other better. It doesn't mean you will necessarily be best friends, or that your love relationships, for instance, will be better, because I've had very good love relationships with White people or non-Muslims, but it's always like reassuring maybe to find yourself amongst Muslim people or [people from your cultural background].

As we can see, this does not mean LGBT Muslims wish to exclude white people from their lives; as Yassine explains, he had very fulfilling relationships with them. The subjects do not want to cut ties with heterosexual and cis people, and as we have seen, they wish to maintain links with their ethnic group and their coreligionists who do not share their sexualities or their gender identities. It does certainly mean that intersectionality allows us to challenge the perceived opposition between Islam and LGBTs, and that it should be taken in consideration when we are confronted with dominant discourses trying to maintain this dichotomy.

Summary: Power and CCM

Our case study is focused on making visible the LGBT Muslim experiences of being and belonging and of the complications in achieving that condition. By using an intersectional analytical framework, we have shown that we must resist the dominant assumptions in culture that exist about both Muslims and LGBT identities and politics. In this sense, we need to understand that power hierarchies of oppression around racism, Islamophobia and homophobia all combine to structure the experiences of LGBT Muslims in different but compounding ways. One the one side, the Western model of coming out and the assumptions of Muslim homophobia exert pressures on LGBT Muslims that white LGBT people do not have to deal with; on the other, family and cultural homophobia makes it difficult to feel secure and happy in an LGBT Muslim identity, forcing our participants to negotiate power hierarchies in complex and multidimensional ways.

Reflexive Recommendations to Students, Researchers and Practitioners

Our recommendations to students and practitioners of CCM center on the need for reflexivity. They demand moving beyond dichotomist labels and to imagine how seemingly contradictory ideas about who we and others are, might come together.

Our first point is that we often assume key facts about a culture and we need to be aware that these may hide other important and distinct aspects of this culture. Muslims may seem to have a homophobic culture, but an intersectional approach in fact demonstrates that this is not completely accurate. We can then approach the neglected intersections of CCM, e.g., LGBT Muslim life experiences: they become a 'possibility' of CCM. This is the second point: good CCM practice can identify apparently opposing aspects of different cultures, and focus on identifying what connects them, not what divides them. Next, we can then work on making them 'visible' in order to illuminate both these specific experiences but also to show that there are points of connection between apparently opposing cultures. This should help to change both sets of cultures by achieving a recognition that those caught 'in between' are, in fact, legitimate members of both groups, and so the self-belief about each group should expand or change to acknowledge this diversity.

We can then restrain ourselves from dichotomist and mono-causal explanations, e.g., from automatically assuming that Islam is intrinsically homophobic, because it is not. Islam is not only a religion, it is a cultural phenomenon that takes different shapes depending on where it is in the world, in what time in history it takes place and whom it concerns. For an inclusive CCM, we need to consider these alternative standpoints in Islam and as related to other standpoints outside of it.

We can then also step back and reflect upon what seems 'normal' and ask ourselves how CCM is informed by these implicit and historically learned normalities. For instance, we could acknowledge the history of homophobia in contemporary Western countries. How did homophobia exist in the West before the 21st century? Were there moments where homosexuality was more accepted than others? Were there times when it was less tolerated than in other parts of the world? Has the acceptance of homosexuality evolved in a linear way? Answering those questions allows us to appreciate how culture is dynamic and changes over time and space. A more thorough investigation allows us to see that there has been a very negative history of homophobia and transphobia (the oppression of nonheterosexual gender identities) in Western cultures until very recently. Moreover, homophobia has not disappeared in contemporary times from various Western cultures.

The same need to question assumptions applies to Muslim-majority countries, societies and communities. This kind of reasoning can be applied to interrogating how gender identity and sexual identity were understood and regulated in different times and spaces in the huge variety of Muslim cultures. We know that, in fact, many Muslim national cultures were accepting of gender and sexual diversity, within certain limits for sure, but nonetheless much more open than the positions of contemporary Muslim communities or governments. Accepting this complicated history means we should *not* let ourselves simply accept that one part of the world (namely, the West) is more civilised and progressive than others (like the Muslim-majority countries) because they are supposedly champions of LGBT rights. The reality is much more complex, especially when we know that homophobia and (especially) transphobia are well and alive in many parts of Western countries.

Note

1. While LGBT is the common public term for sexual minorities, this is a simplification that ignores some contemporary identities, such as pansexual (people who are erotically attracted to all gender identities and expressions). It also simplifies transgender, which can include a huge variety from people who want to or have physically changed their gender anatomy to those who identify as another gender or as nongendered (non-binary) and adopt a range of clothing, names and pronouns to signal their gender expression and identity.

References

Bilge S (2010) ". . . alors que nous, Québécois, nos femmes sont égales à nous et nous les aimons ainsi" : La patrouille des frontières au nom de l'égalité de genre dans une "nation" en quête de souveraineté. *Sociologie et sociétés* 42(1): 197–226. https://doi.org/10.7202/043963ar.

Carroll A and Mendos LR (2017) State Sponsored Homophobia: A World Survey of Sexual Orientation Laws, Criminalization, Protection and Recognition. Available at: https://ilga.org/downloads/2017/ILGA_State_Sponsored_Homophobia_2017_WEB.pdf (accessed 26 July 2018).

Collins PH (2000) *Black Feminist Thought: Knowledge, Consciousness and Empowerment* (2nd ed). Boston: Unwin Hyman.

De Sondy A (2015) *The Crisis of Islamic Masculinities.* London: Bloomsbury.

Dhoest A (2016) Media, visibility and sexual identity among gay men with a migration background. *Sexualities* 19(4): 412–443.

Gandhi NM (2012) Siraat-e-Mustaqeem or the straight path. *Journal of Lesbian Studies* 16(4): 468–484.

Hamzic V (2016) *Sexual and Gender Diversity in the Muslim World: History, Law and Vernacular Knowledge.* London: I. B. Tauris.

Harding S (1986) The instability of analytical categories in feminist theory. *Signs* 11(4): 645–664.

Hildebrandt A (2014) Routes to decriminalization: A comparative analysis of the legalization of same-sex sexual acts. *Sexualities* 17(1–2): 230–253.

Jaspal R (2012) Coping with religious and cultural homophobia: Emotion and narratives of identity threat among British Muslim gay men. In: Nynas P and Yip AKT (eds) *Religion, Gender and Sexuality in Everyday Life.* Farnham, Surrey: Ashgate Publishing, pp. 71–90.

Jaspal R and Cinnirella M (2012) Identity processes, threat, and interpersonal relations: Accounts from British Muslim gay men. *Journal of Homosexuality* 59(2): 215–240.

Kugle SS (2010) *Homosexuality in Islam: Critical Reflections on Gay, Lesbian, and Transgender Muslims.* Oxford: Oneworld Press.

Kugle SS (2014) *Living Out Islam: Voices of Gay, Lesbian and Transgender Muslims.* New York: New York University Press.

Mahadevan J (2017) Chapter 1: Workplace diversity, Muslim minorities and reflexive HRM: concepts, challenges and power implications in context. In: Mahadevan J and Mayer CH (eds), *Muslim Minorities, Workplace Diversity and Reflexive HRM.* New York: Routledge, pp. 1–12.

Pew Research Center (2013) *The Global Divide on Homosexuality.* Available at: www.pewglobal.org/2013/06/04/the-global-divide-on-homosexuality/ (accessed 27 July 2013).

Puar JK (2007) *Terrorist Assemblages: Homonationalism in Queer Times.* Durham: Duke University Press.

Rahman M (2014) *Homosexualities, Muslim Cultures and Modernity.* Basingstoke: Palgrave Macmillan.

Rahman M (2018) Contemporary same-sex Muslim sexualities: Identities and issues. In: Woodward M and Lukens-Bull R (eds) *Handbook of Contemporary Islam and Muslim Lives.* Springer, pp. 1–21.

Rahman M and Valliani A (2016) Challenging the opposition of LGBT and Muslim cultures: Initial research on LGBT Muslims in Canada. Special Issue of *Theology and Sexuality, "Approaching Islam Queerly"* 22(1–2): 73–88.

Said EW (1979) *Orientalism.* New York: Vintage Books.

Smith D (2006) *Institutional Ethnography as Practice.* Lanham, MD: Rowman and Littlefield.

Weeks J (2007) *The World We Have Won: The Remaking of Erotic and Intimate Life.* New York: Routledge.

Yip AKT (2004) Embracing Allah and sexuality? South Asian non-heterosexual Muslims in Britain. In: Jacobsen KA and Kumar P (eds) *South Asians in the Diaspora.* Leiden: Brill, pp. 294–310.

Yip AKT (2007) Changing religion, changing faith: Reflections on the transformative strategies of Lesbian, Gay, and Bisexual Christians and Muslims. *Journal of Faith, Spirituality and Social Change* 1(1). Available at: www.fsscconference.org.uk/journal/1-1.htm.

Yip AKT (2008) The quest for intimate/sexual citizenship: Lived experiences of Lesbian and Bisexual Muslim women. *Contemporary Islam* 2(2): 99–117.

4

CORPORATE CHRISTMAS

Sacred or Profane? The Case of a Hungarian Subsidiary of a Western MNC

Anna Laura Hidegh and Henriett Primecz

Introduction

As part of the modernity project, workplaces are presumed to be secular in many Western countries (Hicks, 2002). The European Union Article 13 of the Treaty of Amsterdam, which came into force in 1999, forbids discrimination on the grounds of sex, racial or ethnic origin, religion or belief, disability, age or sexual orientation (Claes, 2019). Free choice of religion is assumed, religious practices are not considered relevant to work situations, they are rather expected to remain in the private sphere of employees' lives (Primecz and Romani, 2019). While this might be compatible with contemporary Christian religious practices, other religions, such as Muslim or Hindu religious practices, are more visible than Christian practices (Mahadevan, 2012) at an individual level. Furthermore, in religions describing themselves as a way of life, the separation of religion and work cannot be assumed and might not even be conceivable (Alexis, 2012). Policies built upon workplace secularity might have a disparate impact upon religious minorities in Western societies (Alexis, 2012).

While secular principles are often explicitly or implicitly expected (Hicks, 2002), references to the Christmas celebration, a highly visible religious practice, are frequently present in organizational life. In this setting, the celebration of Christmas is often taken for granted, as it is perceived as part of a presumed global culture and not merely as one of many religious traditions that are practiced. One might argue that Christmas in capitalistic consumerist societies is a secularized rather than sacralised ritual (Bartunek and Do, 2011; Hancock and Rehn, 2011) and might not challenge the concept of the secular workplace. In order to understand the sacred and the profane layers of corporate Christmas, Evans (2003, in Bartunek and Do, 2011) distinguishes between three ways of approaching the sacred: the religious, the transcendent and the set-apart. Understanding the sacred as religious or transcendent, which presupposes the existence of a supernatural force or ultimate truth (Bartunek and Do, 2011), is a broadly shared meaning. The third reading of the sacred is the set-apart, which indicates that the sacred incorporates a set of *'particular beliefs, rituals and duties'* and becomes a source of social cohesion (Bartunek and Do, 2011: 796). Thus, the sacred is a social product in contrast to the profane, which refers to *'the mundane, ordinary, everyday state of the world'* (Bartunek and Do, 2011: 797).

In the layers of meaning of Christmas, the three interpretations of the sacred are coexisting and enwreathed: Christmas cannot be regarded as an originary *Christian* religious holy day, since the Christian Church aligned the celebration of the birth of Jesus with the winter solstice and, in this way, sanctioned existing pagan traditions (Forbes, 2007). We can also observe two parallel tendencies reflected in the debates around the nature and role of Christmas in contemporary society. The first one is that, due to commercialization and corporatization, Christmas has become increasingly secularized, and the sacred layers of Christmas rituals have become exhausted. The second one is that, in the Christmas season, otherwise mundane activities such as shopping or celebrating with the company are included in Christmas rituals and become 'sacred' under the realm of Christmas. In our ethnographic case study, we identify those contradictory and co-existing processes in the construction of the meaning of corporate Christmas, and we interpret our results through the critical lens of cross-cultural management (CCM). We argue that it is mainly cultural blindness that makes corporate Christmas' religious elements invisible and accommodates the celebration of corporate Christmas to the concept of secular workplace.

Methodology

Research was conducted at the Hungarian subsidiary of a Western multinational company. Research was informed by critical ethnography (Thomas, 1993), since the focus was on the control mechanisms and the repressive and constraining aspect of corporate culture (Duberley and Johnson, 2009). Empirical material was collected by the first author by participatory observation of the Christmas party and via semistructured qualitative interviews with 11 employees during corporate Christmas time. Six interviews took place before the Christmas party and five interviews afterwards. Two organizational members were interviewed twice, both before and after the Christmas party. During the interviews, open questions were raised about topics such as organizational context and culture, previous Christmas parties, the Christmas season itself at the company, the current Christmas party and its relation to family Christmas Eve, which is celebrated on December 24 in Hungary. The previously defined topics were completed with topics introduced by interviewees to the conversation. The second author was involved in the process of data analysis.

Case Presentation

Christmas at the Transport Services Co.

Fieldwork took place in a Hungarian subsidiary of a Western multinational company (Transport Services Co.), which functions as the regional headquarters for Central Europe. In the Hungarian subsidiary, 65 people were employed at two different sites, most of them with qualifications in business administration at the headquarters in central Budapest, and only a few employees in the areas of sales and logistics in a suburb of the city. There were three non-Hungarian employees, including the CEO; thus, the majority of the employees were Hungarian.

At this multinational company, Christmas was perceived as a normal social event to close the year. However, the historical context of celebrating Christmas at a workplace in Hungary is slightly different due to its socialist past. Despite the official and dominant atheist discourse during the socialist period (1948–1989), the celebration of Christmas did not disappear, but was reframed as 'Pine Tree Feast'. The religious content of Christmas traditions was eliminated from official discourse, but the distinct function of the feast was kept. In socialist companies, the emphasis was put on celebrating "Father Winter" (the name of Santa Claus suited to communist ideology), who brought presents for employees' children on December 6th. Corporate Christmas parties grew popular after 1989 and became common corporate practice due to Western multinational companies.

Corporate Christmas at Transport Services Co. has been organized every year in December. Employees from both company sites in Budapest were invited. The event has always taken place in an elegant restaurant off site. Participation is encouraged by top management, yet participation rates are usually higher among the employees of the central office, and lower among the employees working in the suburbs. Employees' partners and children are not usually invited to the corporate Christmas party. The Christmas party on which we focus was organized by a team of employees nominated for the task by the CEO, but the final decisions about the budget, the concept and the program were made by the CEO.

The script of the Christmas party was as follows: Employees arrived around 17:00 hours at the restaurant, and received a small welcome package containing corporate presents (a USB drive and a calendar). Socializing was still ongoing, there was a buzz of speech in the room, when the CEO's voice—amplified by the microphone—cut through it, and people turned around. He spoke in English and expressed how nice it was to be there together. Then, the speech covered changes in the personnel and financial achievements. The contribution of each organizational unit to corporate profits was highlighted, and followed by applause. Finally, the CEO wished "bon appétit", people searched for a seat around the tables, and dinner began. There was no allocated seating, although the CEO chose his fellows for the table unobtrusively. Dishes were of high quality. The main dishes were not traditional Christmas dishes; however, the dessert was poppy-seed roll, which is a traditional Christmas dish in Hungary. During the dinner, wine was served, but otherwise the consumption of alcohol was not allowed at the party. The theme of the party was a casino: participants were invited to play blackjack and roulette at gaming tables borrowed for the event from a casino. The winner of the game also received a prize from the CEO. Then one of the marketing staff announced "the charity", that is, the employees of the company were invited to donate goods to an orphanage. The donated goods were collected the following week in the company's offices and their transport to the orphanage was organized by the marketing department. The next program was the lottery with the opportunity to win expensive prizes. After that, informal small talks among participants continued, and people started leaving the restaurant shortly afterwards.

In the following, we present the shared symbolic meanings of the script elements of the corporate Christmas party, relying upon the coexisting narratives of sacralization and secularization.

Narratives of Sacralization

Gathering the Corporate Family

All interviewees regarded corporate Christmas as a good occasion to be together and spend time together informally. The togetherness at Christmas provided the employees with the opportunity of breaking the routine of everyday work and to be more than merely an 'instrumental human resource'. All interviewees pointed out that it was important to care about relationships with colleagues, and to acknowledge that they spend large parts of their days with each other (more than with their family members or friends). In the perceptions of the interviewees, the Christmas party was a good occasion for galvanizing life into instrumental workplace relationships.

> To get out from this prosaic environment full of work, and then to be together with these people, in a more familiar, friendlier atmosphere. And then it changes the everyday as well. . . . Thus, it helps in making the everyday more comfortable.
>
> *(Tamás)*

Breaking everyday routines in order to create space for reflection was supported by the fact that the Christmas party was held off site in an elegant restaurant.

Participants wore elegant clothes; statements suggested that this is important in Transport Services Co., in particular, because those working with clients wear uniforms during workdays. Dressing up at Christmas helps the employees symbolically break out from everyday work.

> It's much better [to go outside] than to stay here [in the office]. . . . If you are here eight to nine hours a day, then you don't wish to be here at the Christmas party as well. And somehow everybody prepares to, wow . . . at least the female colleagues, that they dress up to the nines. . . . This is necessary [for them], I guess.
>
> *(Pisti)*

Having dinner together and sharing fellowship at the table is an important element of corporate Christmas: a temporary intimacy among participants may evolve (Rosen, 1988). Interviewees discuss the presence of Christmas traditions and search for parallels. The feasts of Christmas bestow additional value upon the corporate occasion, but there is a certain insecurity in the interviews, whether the similarity is valid or not.

> This is also a Christmas tradition: let's eat good dishes, and it brings people together a little bit. . . . It is such a physiological thing, what everybody loves: sit down, eating delicious meals, and [do so] among people one likes. Everybody chooses a table where his or her colleagues are near at hand.
>
> *(Ani)*

A family metaphor is applied to the company community, which is the most common metaphor for organizational culture (Casey, 1999). Celebrating Christmas together nurtures this metaphor by strengthening group identity.

> And what is common [in family and corporate Christmas]? The common thing is, that behind the party, there is the same corporation that links us to each other.
>
> *(Éva)*

The Christian tradition places the Holy Family (Jesus, Maria and Joseph) at the centre of celebration: the nuclear or the extended families celebrate together in their homes on Christmas Eve. Thus, the common celebration of Christmas designates also the boundaries of the family and reinforces family membership. Celebrating Christmas with the corporate community indicates the application of the family metaphor to organizational culture: it demonstrates the strong social relations among employees and their managers. The message is outlined similarly by Rosen (1988): "your work is your life, and these are your friends".

At the Transport Services Co., play is a recurring element of the Christmas parties. Playing together is an activity that supports the building of informal relationships, similar to children playing under the Christmas tree in a family Christmas. Therefore, it supports the family metaphor and advocates a smooth atmosphere. The assessments of the games at the corporate Christmas were ambivalent: some interviewees underlined that playing together is a good instrument to help people to get in contact with each other by moving beyond initial feelings of discomfort.

> In my mind, such games or a sort of common activity on a Christmas party are very important in that they connect people, and that they become a little bit relaxed, to dissolve this cramped, embarrassed attitude a little bit.
>
> *(Ági)*

Others pointed out—referring to previous Christmas parties—that games also involve a kind of performance orientation, which they refused, and also that games put employees into the roles of children, which they perceived to be somewhat humiliating. By shedding light on the dark side of the family metaphor, such perceptions both challenge and reinforce the family metaphor: corporate children (employees) complain about their overburdened everyday life. At Christmas time, they want to be relaxed and pampered. Thus, the child role is not refused as a whole, but only in its 'being controlled' part.

> Those quizzes, and to work in teams, and a drawing competition, and so on. . . . We are not five years old anymore.
>
> *(Márti)*

Gift Giving

Giving was also a central element of corporate Christmas in several ways. First, employees received welcome gifts upon arriving at the party. These identical presents symbolically acknowledged the belonging to the company. Employees could also win presents in the casino and, besides this, there was a lottery where the most expensive presents were drawn by lot. Many interviewees pointed out that this part was the high point of the event. Although the CEO did play blackjack, in the last moment, he lost all of his chitons. Interviewees interpreted it as an intentional act. Also, he did not take part in the lottery. Last, but not least, as mentioned earlier, a company charity activity is also organized every year in which employees can donate voluntarily to orphans.

In Hungary, the story of Christmas presents for children is that presents are brought by little Jesus (not by Father Christmas or Santa Claus as in other traditions). Of course, as children get older, they realize that presents are given by their parents. In the company, presents are paid for from corporate budget, but symbolically, they are given to the employees by the CEO. Thus, the role of the parent is fulfilled by the CEO. Donation is also higher in the Christmas period. Many interviewees interpreted the rite of giving in relation to Christmas traditions, and the obligation to receive a present and to donate was framed by the obligations embedded in Christmas traditions.

> I think, little Jesus was really generous [laughs].
>
> *(Ági)*

Mauss (1923[2002], in: Lemmergaard and Muhr, 2011) points out that gift giving symbolizes the giver's superiority, and that if someone accepts the gift without reciprocation of equal or higher value, it means that they acknowledge their inferiority in that given relationship. Since the gift in the Transport Services Co. was one-sided, as the employees did not give presents to the CEO, it reflects an asymmetrical power relationship (Lemmergaard and Muhr, 2011). Accepting a Christmas gift from the company and from its official representative is also accepting the parent–child relationship, and it reinforces the family metaphor and the hierarchical structure of the organization.

> It is an occasion for the company to say: "thank you for your work", and to organize a thing like this [Christmas party]. From the employer's part, I think it is part of it that we realize, maybe, at that time that human beings are working here and not robots.
>
> *(Tamás)*

The Christmas party itself is interpreted as a gift. Through this reading of corporate Christmas employees accept their everyday routines as well: that they have to work to the best of their ability, and that they deserve compensation for it. Although recognition could be reflected in salary, they need another ritual act, in order to be acknowledged as complex human beings, not just as employees or at least the symbolic acknowledgement of their performance.

Reflection

Christmas time is also a time for reflection, as it indicates the end of the year as a cultic unit (Bálint, 1973). In corporate Christmas, reflection is institutionalized in the CEO's speech, which is an indispensable element of Christmas parties. The speech is a retrospection on the past year from the point of view of the company, touching upon business performance and important changes in organizational structure or in the staff. In the Transport Services Co., the speech of the CEO also provided a good occasion for reflecting upon the relationship between CEO and employees.

So, this Christmas, it is okay, let's sit down, let's calm down a little bit, and let's think about what results have been achieved so far, and then where to go. A short break, I would say. And that's an evening.

(Kati)

In sum, narratives supporting the sacralization of corporate Christmas make sense of the sacred in terms of setting-apart. The function of the rites of having dinner, playing together, and the symbolical meaning of being outside the company and of dressing in elegant clothes was to establish a company identity, to strengthen social relationships and to open up a space for reflexivity that facilitated seeing each other as complex human beings.

Corporate Christmas rituals contained elements from Christian Christmas traditions as well. Interviewees mentioned material symbols such as nativity figures (Joseph, Mary and the baby Jesus in the manger) and the Christmas tree (decorated pine tree, a symbol of Christmas); between the lines, we discovered rites that reflect the symbols of the Holy Family and the Gift of the Saviour (Jesus), although they are not mentioned explicitly. The celebration of the end of the year as a cultic unit has also a transcendent meaning, albeit not necessarily religious.

Narratives of Secularization

It was surprising that references to Christian Christmas were invalidated by the interviewees when the researcher asked a direct question to make comparisons between family Christmas and corporate Christmas.

Team Building Without Intimacy

The sacred nature of corporate Christmas is undermined by management striving to use it as a team-building event. Previous Christmas parties had been instrumentalized by corporate management to create a space wherein employees belonging to different informal groups could intermingle. In order to achieve this goal, in the previous year, seating was allocated and certain training elements were deployed. Employees complained about this as destroying the Christmas atmosphere, since it interferes with the lived experience of informal intimacy evolving among good colleagues.

So, for example, last year's event's biggest mistake was that. So it was such a team building training that it lost its Christmas atmosphere completely.

(Márti)

It's Just a Party, Not Christmas at All

When triggered by the researcher, interviewees acknowledged that there are some similar ritual elements in corporate Christmas and Christian family Christmas, but, they argued, their content, depth and the emotions in relation to it were completely different. They even questioned the right to call this corporate party a "Christmas party", saying that it did not deserve the name. Questioning the right to call it Christmas means also challenging the idea that the corporate Christmas is sacred.

> The two have nothing to do with each other. Christmas, as a festivity, has no significance in that event. Really, I would rather call it an event, or a corporate party, than Christmas.
>
> *(Ági)*

Most of the interviewees differentiated between the working self and the private self, arguing that it was mainly their working self who took part in the corporate Christmas party.

> So I like to set apart this: the private and the work. And what do you leave outside from Kati, when you join the corporate Christmas party? Well, I bring myself which is working here. So, the one who is the employee. Not the private person.
>
> *(Kati)*

The division is reflected also in emphasizing the differences between the corporate party where working selves are celebrating, and the sacred realm of family Christmas where private selves are celebrating. The division is a tool of resistance against the effort of the company to build a common corporate identity: normative control mediated by corporate Christmas can be exercised only on the working self.

> I don't know, the corporate Christmas is still just a dinner, a party, not an intimate feast. Christmas is, after all, a family event. Then, you rather think about the love you feel for the family, then about your employer. Sure, there might be some gratitude for the employer. But this, I've never. . . . Family touches upon a deeper layer than a Christmas dinner like this one.
>
> *(Ani)*

Explicit references to the Christian religion were almost entirely missing from the interviews despite the use of Christian traditions and symbols (for example, nativity figures and gift giving). Religion entered into the conversation when comparisons were made between the family Christmas celebrated on December 24 and corporate Christmas. Statements about not being religious were made, although references to the transcendent were discoverable.

> For me, there is no religion. So, if I go anywhere—my grandma died, and a few years later my grandpa as well—I always light a candle for them. If I am in a cathedral abroad, anywhere, anytime, Christmas, summer. . . .

What is a tradition in my family at Christmas is that I make the Advent wreath, and that's all.

(Melinda)

In sum, narratives supporting the secularization of corporate Christmas underline the missing religious and transcendent content of it. Christian rituals and symbols are subtracted from the realm of religion even in a family Christmas in several cases, although there is a vague relationship with the transcendent. The set-apart function of corporate Christmas is not challenged. The division between the working self and the private self provides a rationale for why not to consider corporate Christmas as a religious or transcendent event; at the same time, it challenges the success of renewing corporate membership and identity.

Power and CCM

Despite the ambiguities presented previously, interviewees shared the opinion that celebrating Christmas with the corporate community is a must. From the three interpretations of the sacred, the *set-apart* is dominant in the accounts of the interviewees of Transport Services Co. The meaning of corporate Christmas is mostly detached from its religious or transcendent content on the surface, but in the arguments about the justification of corporate Christmas, interviewees relied upon Christian (religious) traditions. There is an inner need for being together, receiving gifts and reflecting upon themselves in a broader context—an inner need for experiences enabled by the corporate Christmas party. Thus, the deeply symbolic structure of corporate Christmas is based on Christian traditions and the moral values and obligations embedded in them: putting family in the centre, taking care of beloved ones, practicing active love and forgiveness, being altruistic when giving presents to each other and providing a helping hand for those in need, engaging in retrospection and introspection.

Thus, the presumed secularity of European workplaces fails with the celebration of corporate Christmas. With this failure, the taken-for-granted nature of the celebration of Christmas and the implicit usage and renewal of religious rituals raises questions concerning exclusion of people with non-Christian and alternative worldviews. The most important question is *why* corporate Christmas is not challenged as a religious and potentially exclusive event in an alleged secular corporate life. Why is the sacralised aspect of corporate Christmas less visible 'culturally' than, for example, a Muslim headscarf, which is strongly critiqued as being backward and oppressive (Mohanty, 2003) and also immediately considered to be 'religious'? Could it be that the major difference between the two phenomena is that Christmas is a tradition embedded in the dominant Western culture (Jack and Westwood, 2009; Said, 1978) which is historically shaped by Christianity, while the 'Muslim' headscarf is a phenomenon related to Islam which is a minority belief in the West?

We argue that this cultural blindness toward Christmas is a symptom of the postcolonial power asymmetry inherent in the concept of the secular workplace, since it is more commensurate with not only atheism but also with contemporary Christian religion—rather than with Islam or Hinduism, for example. Critiques of the secular workplace claim that it forces people to fragment their lives into private/personal (potentially religious) life and working life, thus denying the essential aspects of employees' identity when they are working (Hicks, 2002). The pressure for fragmentation might weigh more heavily on those who adhere to religious beliefs which do not separate life and work (Alexis, 2012). For example, Islam is strongly rooted in visible and regular social practice (e.g. Mahadevan and Kilian-Yasin, 2017) and Hinduism is not a 'book religion' but a way of life (e.g. Mahadevan, 2012). This means that the 'Western' idea of the secular workplace is limited in the sense that it is built on the idea of the separation of life and work, as shown by the example of corporate Christmas. The celebration of corporate Christmas maintains the fragmentation by positioning the Christmas party after working time and 'outside' of the office, but, at the same time, it also disrupts it, bringing private and spiritual elements of social life 'inside' to the workplace (Rosen, 1988).

Challenging the viability of the secular workplace through the example of corporate Christmas, we propose the concept of a 'postsecular' workplace in consonance with the notion of post-secular society (Habermas, 2008). A postsecularist approach recognizes the achievements of Western Enlightenment; namely, 'the inclusive religious freedom that is extended to all citizens alike' (Habermas, 2008: 22). At the same time, it advocates a change in consciousness about the role of religion in contemporary societies with growing plurality of cultures and world views (Habermas, 2008). Including all citizens as equals in society requires a more nuanced approach to religion (Martin, 1996 in Geoghegan, 2000); that is, institutionalized secular practices such as the concept of secular workplace should not have a disparate impact (Alexis, 2012) on religious employees whose beliefs and practices intertwine in all spheres of life. Thus, while we acknowledge the historical reason behind the Western idea of the secular workplace, namely to ensure 'free' choice of religion, we also argue that it should be reconsidered, as it is impregnated with power asymmetries. Raising the consciousness of the presence of cultural traditions intertwined with the Christian religion in organizational life such as corporate Christmas, we argue for a more sensitive and inclusive attitude toward non-Christian ways of being religious.

Reflexive Consideration

The authors of this chapter were born and grew up in Hungary, a Christian-majority country in Europe. However, their childhood was marked by socialist times, when the official and dominant discourse was atheist. In those times, people who actively practiced religion were considered backward and unenlightened.

Even though Christmas did not vanish during those decades, the religious content was suppressed in the official narrative. In the 1950s, the second day of Christmas (December 26) was a working day. Families celebrated Christmas, but attending church services was suspicious in the political sense, and few people dared to risk living openly religious lives.

After the political change of 1989–1990, expressions of religiosity grew in postsocialist countries and previous attempts to secularize Christmas traditions were replaced by official religious ideologies. Christian religious institutions became stronger and more prevalent in everyday life in Hungary. This change in the intensity of religiosity during our lifetimes made it possible for us to reflect on the Christmas tradition. The deep reflection would not have been possible for any of us without meeting and discussing religious issues with adherents of alternative worldviews and religions. The research process, both empirical material collection and later the analysis, was reflected in the light of alternative worldviews as well. It was not an easy process, as Christmas as a feast has been and still is taken for granted in our lives as well.

Recommendations to Students, Researchers and Practitioners

In this chapter, we argue for a 'postsecular' workplace supporting the plurality of world views and acknowledging that the complete elimination of any religious content from the workplace might result also in the repression of employees who cannot or do not wish to separate work and life. We stress the importance of ensuring the freedom of belief and worldview in organizational practices, and open up a discourse about how seemingly innocent organizational practices such as a Christmas party might reinforce existing power structures—if the organization remains blind to the intersection of organizational position and religion. Thus, we would like to encourage managers and practitioners in organizations to reflect upon the way they celebrate Christmas at their workplaces. We would also like to advocate for more sensitivity and openness among practitioners and management towards multiple religious traditions and worldviews.

Questions like the following might be raised: Is the present practice of celebrating Christmas exclusionary for certain groups of employees? What is the function of celebrating Christmas together? For example, if the function of the Christmas party is team building, then what practices serve this goal and what practices do not? Are Christian rituals and symbols necessary to achieve the defined goal? How could the end-of-the-year celebration be changed to make it a more inclusive event? How might a corporate Christmas event raise employees' consciousness about the role of tradition and religion in their own and others' working life? Looking at Christmas from a different perspective might support reflection regarding how cultural or structural power is exercised (unconsciously) through the given way of celebrating Christmas at the workplace, and how it can be changed.

References

Alexis GY (2012) Not Christian, but nonetheless qualified: The secular workplace: Whose hardship? *Journal of Religion and Business Ethics* 3(1): 1–24.

Bálint S (1973) *Karácsony, Húsvét, Pünkösd [Christmas, Eastern, Pentecost]*. Budapest: Neumann.

Bartunek JM and Do B (2011) The sacralization of Christmas commerce. *Organization* 18(6): 795–806.

Casey C (1999) "Come, join our family": Discipline and integration in corporate organizational culture. *Human Relations* 52(1): 155–178.

Claes MT (2019) Diversity in Europe: Its development and contours. In: Risberg A and Mensi-Klarbach H (eds) *Diversity in Organizations: Concepts and Practices*. Houndmills: Palgrave Macmillan.

Duberley J and Johnson P (2009) Critical management methodology. In: Alvesson M, Bridgman T and Willmott H (eds) *The Oxford Handbook of Critical Management Studies*. Oxford: Oxford University Press, pp. 345–368.

Evans MT (2003) The sacred: Differentiating, clarifying and extending concepts. *Review of Religious Research* 45(1): 32–47.

Forbes BD (2007) *Christmas: A Candid History*. Berkeley: University of California Press.

Geoghegan V (2000) Religious narrative, post-secularism and Utopia. *Critical Review of International Social and Political Philosophy* 3(2–3): 205–224.

Habermas J (2008) Notes on post-secular society. *New Perspectives Quarterly* (25): 17–29.

Hancock P and Rehn A (2011) Organizing Christmas. *Organization* 18(6): 737–745.

Hicks DA (2002) Spiritual and religious diversity in the workplace: Implications for leadership. *The Leadership Quarterly* 13(4): 379–396.

Jack G and Westwood R (2009) *International and Cross-Cultural Management Studies: A Postcolonial Reading*. London: Palgrave MacMillan.

Lemmergaard J and Muhr SL (2011) Regarding gifts: On Christmas gift exchange and asymmetrical business relations. *Organization* 18(6).

Mahadevan J (2012) Are engineers religious? An interpretative approach to cross-cultural conflict and collective identities. *International Journal of Cross-Cultural Management* 12(1): 133–149.

Mahadevan J and Kilian-Yasin K (2017) Dominant discourse, orientalism and the need for reflexive HRM: Skilled Muslim migrants in the German context. *The International Journal of Human Resource Management* 28(8): 1140–1162. DOI: 10.1080/09585192.2016.1166786.

Martin B (1996) *Politics in the impasse: Explorations in postsecular social theory*. Albany: State University of New York.

Mauss M (1923[2002]) *The gift: The form and reason for exchange in archaic societies*. London: Routledge.

Mohanty CT (2003) "Under western eyes" revisited: Feminist solidarity through anti-capitalist struggles. *Signs: Journal of Women in Culture and Society* 28(2): 499–535.

Primecz H and Romani L (2019) Diversity categories across cultures. In: Risberg A and Mensi-Klarbach H (eds) *Diversity in Organizations: Concepts and Practices*. Houndmills: Palgrave Macmillan.

Rosen M (1988) You asked for it: Christmas at the bosses' expense. *Journal of Management Studies* 25(5): 463–480.

Said E (1978) *Orientalism*. London: Routledge & Kegan Paul Ltd.

Thomas J (1993) *Doing Critical Ethnography*. London: SAGE.

5

WASTA IN JORDANIAN BANKING

An Emic Approach to a Culture-Specific Concept of Social Networking and Its Power Implications

Sa'ad Ali and David Weir

Introduction

Contemporary cross-cultural management (CCM) theory and practice is Westocentric, as they tend to rely on theories, practices, concepts and methods drawn from research conducted in Europe and North America—geographically, mostly located in the Northern Hemisphere (Leung et al., 2005). There is a dearth of *indigenous* research on alternative social concepts from other regions, and culture-specific (emic) concepts such as *guanxi* (relationship management) in China, *blat* (getting things done through personal contacts) in Russia or *caste* in India tend to be described from an outside (etic) perspective (Hutchings and Weir, 2006; Barnett et al., 2013). The call for "the concurrent analyses of multiple, intersecting (and interacting) sources of subordination/oppression" (Denis, 2008: 677) is often derived from contemporary feminist discourse that in itself might be understood as Western-infused and thus implies an etic approach (Denis, 2008). For a more balanced and inclusive CCM theory and practice, we would need to discover specific cultural concepts from the Global East and South, and to view them in their own inside (emic) terms.

To answer this call, this chapter sheds light on *wasta*, a specific social and organizational phenomenon in Jordan which is explored in relation to the Jordanian banking industry. The literal translation of *wasta* is mediation, or intermediary. In daily usage, *wasta* refers to the use of connections in order to get something done. Someone who 'has *wasta*' either has a degree of influence, or has access to those who do (Hutchings and Weir, 2006). A Jordanian might seek out someone with influence, who is then also called 'a *wasta*' in spoken dialect Arabic or '*waseet*' in classic Arabic, in order to find a job, secure a place at a university or navigate the bureaucratic red tape that is so common in Jordan

(Cuninngham and Sarayrah, 1993; Jones, 2016). *Wasta* refers thus both to the action and to those facilitating it. It has been suggested that *wasta* impacts nearly every facet of a Jordanian's life and it is also a common source of discussion and complaints among Jordanians (Ali, 2016). Yet how *wasta* is practiced in this context, and how it is experienced, remains a largely unknown phenomenon.

As a practice, *wasta* is widespread and influential throughout the region (Cunningham and Sarayrah, 1993, Barnett et al., 2013; Weir et al., 2016), and also exists in other Arab countries. As a cultural phenomenon, it is not remote from other practices and ideas of a reciprocal social relations, such as *guanxi* in China or the general idea of a relational give and take in the business world (Smith et al., 2012). The etymology of *wasta* as an action and a person generally is associated with the notion of occupying a middle place in a network. When one looks further into the linguistic roots of the word, one can simply understand it as the ability (or the person) "to get things done through the use of social connections".

In Jordan, *wasta* impacts different social and business issues, from applying for trade licenses and government services to securing governmental bids. In particular, it influences recruitment and selection: job seekers use *wasta* as a medium to secure employment, and organisations use it to secure qualified employees (Ali, 2016). From a Westocentric perspective, *wasta* tends to be perceived as favouritism or nepotism which contrasts the idea of a 'modern' (implicitly, 'Western') workplace. Also within Jordan, there is a widespread debate whether *wasta* should be abolished for the sake of Western-style 'modernization' and in order to ensure equal employment opportunities for all (Al Harbi et al., 2017).

Jordan is often described as a 'tribal' society (Sharp, 2012), and this can be considered the first etic concept which we need to deconstruct in order to view *wasta* in its own terms. Whilst Western literature often treats tribalism as a primitive 'lifestyle' associating it with an underdeveloped culture or society, Rowland (2009) argues that tribalism can be viewed as an intangible emotion that entails a varying degree of loyalty to a tribe, as well as the social sense of belonging to a certain people which predates the advent of Islam and Christianity (Jordan's majority and minority religions). Indeed, Chua (2018) claims that Western society is becoming increasingly tribalised in the sense used by Ibn Khaldun as *asabiyya*, an Arabic word conveying something stronger than mere social solidarity. If we wish to understand why such affiliations are of importance in Jordan, the Bedouin experience of the desert and its harsh environment can help to understand the strength of values of friendship, mutual support and trust which, it is generally argued, must have been foundations of survival in such an environment (Branine and Analoui, 2006; Sharp, 2012). Weir (2018: 11) recently referred to *wasta*, which he argues is a product of tribalism, as one of the "pillars of Arab leadership".

To avoid the developmentalist connotation which 'tribal' and 'tribalism' might have, we therefore understand the term neutrally, as the idea of identifying with and drawing on certain in-group affiliations based on a combination of ancestry, religion, ethnicity and extended family networks to achieve one's social, political and economic needs.

By making this point for the specific cultural phenomenon of *wasta*, we contribute to a more intersectional approach to culture in CCM, because we show how a seemingly merely nepotistic practice actually fulfills multiple roles and is balanced by other requirements. We do so for the banking industry, as a highly internationalized business sector of Jordan, which at the same time is also linked to specific cultural requirements, such as the ideals and regulations of Islamic banking (Al Khayed et al., 2014). The banking sector illustrates the complexity of cultural phenomena as being both different and related, and as both global and local, which is an underlying implication of an intersectional approach to culture.

Methodology

Our main objective was to understand *wasta* in depth and from the inside (emic) point of view: to uncover the meaning given to the term by those involved and to better understand the power implications of the concept. To this end, the first author conducted 17 semi-structured, qualitative interviews with managers from 14 banks operating in Jordan. When interpreting the material, we looked for how the interviewees perceived *wasta*, how they had experienced it and whether they believed it to be positive or negative and for whom.

Case Presentation

In this section, we first present the wider sociopolitical and economic context wherein *wasta* in Jordan is situated. We also highlight the role of the banking sector in Jordan. Next, we present quotations from the interviews that let us approximate *wasta* from an emic perspective.

The Wider Context

Jordan is a hereditary monarchy that has been led by King Abdullah II since 1999. Although the parliament is elected by the people, democracy is limited by the intervention of the state, the secret service, or '*mokhabarat*', and the one-vote system which was used from the 1993 elections until 2015 when reforms were implemented. These reforms were critiqued for reducing the voting process into a tribal and family-based election and limiting the role of parliament members into service providers to their area, family and tribe rather than community representatives (Jones, 2016). Furthermore, the king has extensive powers, since he appoints governments, approves legislation and can dissolve parliament.

Over the past few years, the king has been facing growing demands for political reform, especially in the wake of the popular uprising in Tunisia that led to political turmoil in many Arab countries after 2011. King Abdullah dismissed his government at the time and appointed the first of a series of prime ministers to oversee the introduction of political change, which included reforming the voting system in the 2015 elections, but concerns over the cost of living and income tax reform have led to regular street protests (BBC, 2018).

In-group and out-group differentiation can be found in various areas of Jordanian society and organizational life. The population is usually classified by Jordanians into two distinct groups: East Bank Jordanians and West Bank (Palestinian) Jordanians. The former lived in Jordan before the 1948 and 1967 Arab–Israeli wars, and, historically, can be linked more explicitly to tribalism (Rowland, 2009). The latter are Palestinian-Jordanians who immigrated to Jordan as refugees from Palestine after the wars and whose lives tend to be more urbanized (Ali, 2016). It is important to understand that identity is more complex and that Jordanians do not in their everyday discourse limit themselves to "East Bank Jordanians" or "Palestinian Jordanians". Indeed, religion, city of birth and economic status all play a role in setting these different insider/outsider groups which most previous research on *wasta* neglects (Ali, 2016; Jones, 2016).

Jordanian leadership styles have been described as paternalistic (Weir, 2003), but this simplistic interpretation is changing as Jordanian society becomes increasingly complex and in some ways more contested (Al-Kharouf and Weir, 2008; Mehtap et al., 2016). There is a relationship between paternalism and leader–member exchange (Scandura and Pellegrini, 2008) and it is suggested that loyalty by employees is exchanged for benefits provided by the leader/manager (Cunningham and Sarayrah, 1993; Hutchings and Weir, 2006). This could be linked to *wasta* as a mechanism to distribute 'favours' to loyal employees and family members which enables them to 'get things done' and which requires and constitutes in-group relations between those involved (Cunningham and Sarayrah, 1993).

Often, organizations in various sectors in Jordan are family-owned. In small organisations, the father typically is the owner/manager and the rest of family are employees. In larger organisations, the oldest male member of the family tends to assume the role of the Chief Executive Officer or General Manager (GM) and the management of different functions is allocated to immediate family members with a tendency to hire members from the 'in-group'; extended family, tribe or individuals of the same city or area of origin (Al-Rasheed, 2001). This also affects the way employees are selected in organisations, small or large, as many employees are selected on the basis of their relationship to the ownership/management of an organisation. Thus, many organisations are *tacitly* connected to certain families and tribes (Al-Rasheed, 2001).

This is particularly true in the Jordanian banking sector. Officially, banks are classified by the Central Bank of Jordan as national or foreign or based on their financial ethos as Islamic or commercial. Nonetheless, the majority of banks are tacitly viewed by Jordanians in terms of ownership as Christian,

Muslim, Palestinian or Jordanian where each bank is affiliated with the identity of the family or families who have majority ownership or control of the management of the bank. We must therefore assume that these tacit connotations of 'in-group' and 'out-group' have a substantial impact on the way these banks recruit and select employees. As such, this case study has set to explore how *wasta* practice 'plays out' in employee selection in banks operating in Jordan.

Insights From the Case Interviews

During the interviews, it became clear that most interviewees associated *wasta* with the ways people identify themselves and identify with others. Indeed, this was viewed to be so prevalent that even certain banks were associated with particular families. Interviewee A said:

> Actually, we have some banks in Jordan that are family business which is actually some kind of wasta, a couple of them actually.

This family and tribal identification was understood as having an extensive impact on the hiring practices of these banks. According to Interviewee C (female):

> Look, my manager is from one of the tribes in Jordan and I am from one of the tribes in Palestine but I as an HR keep distance from my family [in hiring] and I even notice that my manager does the same. Now sometimes there is a certain pressure. What I mean is that sometimes he comes to me and tells me . . . "[Manager C's name] we want that person." But not always. . . . What I see in other banks in a lot more.

Despite the acknowledgment of hiring based on familial relations in the organisation she works at, the interviewee seems to indicate that this is done on a very small scale and is due to pressure from her manager who acts as an intermediary for his relatives. However, it was felt that the interviewee may be distancing herself from *wasta* practices by downplaying the scale of *wasta* practice in the bank. This can be related to the negative implications of using *wasta* to hire candidates from the same family or tribe who might not merit the position given to them (Mohamed and Mohamed, 2011). This negative view from society and colleagues is not limited to the hired candidates who are viewed as not qualified for the job, but also extends to the organisation which is viewed as an unjust place where powerful association with in-group members precede qualifications in importance. Another reasoning for trying to alienate oneself from being associated with this practice is that it might be perceived as contradictory with Islamic work ethics (IWE) which call for transparency in business dealings and dictate that the most qualified person is the best choice to be hired (Ali and Owaihan, 2008; Abuznaid, 2009) rather than one with family and tribal associations.

Despite the negative view of society and religion on hiring based on such criteria, it appears that this method is still dominant in the sector and in the country. Indeed, it appears that it is not just limited to family and tribal ties but exceeds these to other forms of in-group association. Interviewee N (female) explains:

> If you go to some banks you would see most of them are Christians or if you go to the Islamic bank of Jordan you will see almost 100 percent of employees are Muslims. If you go to X bank in Jordan you would find that most of them are from Palestinian origin.

The interviewees detail a tacit practice of selection based on tribal and religious affiliation in many banks operating in Jordan, resulting in the majority of the organisation's employees sharing the same religious or ethnic background— which in turn shapes the 'identity' of the bank as a Muslim, Christian, East Jordanian or Palestinian Jordanian bank.

These statements also describe the different types of in-groups (e.g., Palestinian or Muslim) that form the basis for organisation's identification with the candidate. It seems that the shared identity acts as a criterion for organisations in their employee selection, linked with the process of categorical social identifications which are said to "derive from membership in larger, more impersonal collectives or social categories" in which members of such groups have a common value or characteristic but do not necessarily know each other on a personal basis (Brewer and Gardner, 1996). This type of social identity exists in social networks between homogenous groups of people. In these statements, the individuals identify a commonality with others: being from the same ethnic background (e.g., Palestinian Jordanian) or belonging to the same religious group (e.g., Christian). They also provide psychological motivation for individuals to accept acting as an intermediary or *waseet* for job seekers, despite not knowing them personally.

It is worth noting, however, that such use of *wasta* might be beneficial and have a positive impact for job seekers. Interviewee A (female) stated:

> *Wasta* is a way, it's a tool, and it's an entry . . . way to open the door. For example, if I know someone who has authority and who knows people and is well known . . . according to our culture there is nothing wrong if this person recommend[s] me to work in one of the banks.

This highlights the emic view of *wasta* as an acceptable way to try and secure a job through the recommendation of a respectable mediator.

Securing candidates through *wasta* also could be beneficial for the organisation, Interviewee A (female) stated:

> If I want to hire a branch manager. Basically, branch managers are known in Jordan [as] Jordan is a very small market and I don't need to look for

more than four or five banks in the main branches or the area branches, I want to hire in order to attract some people you know.

This highlights how *wasta* could benefit managers by securing an employee who they can trust and which reflects the importance of the long-term relationships for these managers.

The interview discussions also highlighted a description of *wasta* as a process in which power plays a vital role; namely, by securing employment for the individual who is requesting *wasta*. This view can be exemplified by the definition offered by Interviewee I (female) who was asked to define this process:

> Someone who push[es] something for another one . . . someone you don't know if he fits in the organisation, ok, but you use your power in order to get him on board, ok, this is a simple definition of *wasta*.

Here, some interviewees perceived *wasta* as a way to use an intermediary's high status or powerful position to influence a hiring decision. This reflects the important role of powerful members of the tight-knit closed social groups in securing *wasta* favours to other members which reinforces the group members categorical social identification with the group (Davis, 2014). Interviewee C indicated that she sometimes is forced by the GM to adhere to the request of *wasta* when hiring a particular candidate:

> The negative is when someone comes and you say 'No, this person is not good or competent', and tell the general manager 'Sorry, this person does not fit with us', and he says 'No, hire him.

This decision maker in the selection process, who is female, perceived that she was forced to hire the candidate despite holding reservations about their capacity to perform the job. In this situation, an individual seeking employment uses her/his social ties to reach out to an intermediary in a high position with the power to procure the appointment of a preferred candidate, even though s/he lacks the required skills and qualifications for the job, thus moving beyond conventional Western employee selection processes. This contradicts with the understanding of IWE as highlighted previously (Ali and Owaihan, 2008) and as such would be viewed negatively by colleagues and society, leading to the negative consequences discussed for all stakeholders involved.

Interviewee I affirmed the perceived importance of a job seekers using *wasta* when seeking employment, stating:

> You cannot limit the usage of *wasta* because it is built in our minds. So when people say '*bamon alek*' ('can you grant Me an "unspecified" favour'), they get hired in the organisation.

This interviewee, who is female, perceives *wasta* as something deeply engrained in the mindset of Jordanians. In explaining the perceived need for job seekers to use *wasta* to secure a job, interviewee C highlighted how such requests rely on the emotional value of the social ties between the intermediary and the decision maker. An intermediary who is seeking employment for a job seeker will play upon the emotional value that the decision maker attaches to the person in order to 'enforce' the hiring of the job seeker. This is highlighted in the interviewee's reference to '*bamon alek*', an Arabic dialect term in which somebody requests something because s/he perceives herself/himself as being emotionally valuable to the other person.

This perception of having some value can be linked with in-group favouritism as identified by Tajfel and Turner (1985). Social identity theorists argue that individuals will favour others whom they identify as members of their in-group to satisfy the expectations of group members. So our material suggests that in-group orientation tends to overcome the 'need' to comply with merit-based selection as viewed by Western management literature (Hutchings and Weir, 2006). It also overcomes the ambition to comply with Islamic work values transparency in business dealings and dictates that the most qualified person is the best to be hired (Ali and Owaihan, 2008; Abuznaid, 2009). Depending on context, the in-group might be understood as the family, tribe or ethnicity of origin; as Palestinian or Jordanian; as members of the same religion; or as Muslims or Christian.

From the insights provided from the interviewees and their statements discussed in this section, it seems that two aspects of *wasta* were of particular importance: namely, *wasta as identity* and *wasta as power*.

Wasta as identity denotes the role *wasta* plays is reflecting and strengthening in-group identities. Multiple in-group membership criteria, such as being Muslim, Christian, East Bank Jordanian and Palestinian Jordanian, play a vital role in a banks' management decision to hire a particular candidate and in the candidate's choice to apply to a particular bank. This creates tight-knit groups in which members support each other and help each other secure benefits but excludes people who are out of this group.

Wasta as power denotes the role of powerful members of a group enabling other members of the group to secure such benefits as getting a job while reinforcing this power in their hands. Indeed, this provides an insightful emic view as to why *wasta* practices still prevail in Jordan and its banking sector, despite being internationalised.

Power and CCM

The insights and statements from the interviews provide a much more balanced and emic insight into the practice of *wasta*. Indeed, when analysing the interviewees' statements discussed previously, it becomes apparent that *wasta* is not just a nepotistic practice which is mainly used in the hiring process as described by many Western researchers. Rather, it is mediation process in which mediation results in reaching an agreed outcome not just based on economic sense. It appears that *wasta* 'works' because society is already networked and that hiring decisions are not just based on merit but take into consideration the long-term outcome for the in-group.

However, there are also emic power implications to this practice. One might ask the question: who exactly profits from *wasta*? Based on the insight that every social setting is linked to formal and informal hierarchies, knowledge networks and frameworks of power, we therefore must also consider who is advantaged and disadvantaged by *wasta* practice. Loewe et al. (2007), for instance, conclude that *wasta* practice tends to further strengthen the *wasta* and the access to *wasta* of those who are already privileged in terms of *wasta*. They find, for example, that, in a paternalistic environment, men are more advantaged by *wasta* than women. Although these interviewees did not directly signpost gender as a source of insider–outsider access to *wasta*, it could be inferred that most interviewees who don't have access to *wasta* demonstrated a more negative stance to the practice which aligns with the arguments of Cunningham and Sarayrah, (1993) and Loewe et al. (2007). The access to *wasta* in this data set appeared to be more related to ethnic identity (Palestinian and East Bank Jordanian) and religion (Muslim and Christian) but, as highlighted previously, identity is multifaced; as such, *wasta* can be used in different in-groups, including gender-based in-groups, by the same individual. It is worth noting that although only six of the interviewees were female, they were the most 'outspoken' about wasta, which could reflect strong opinions about the topic.

These insights and findings are important to CCM research as they enable us to understand how *wasta*, as an example of a culture-specific concept, operates and is perceived in its emic setting. *Wasta* can have positive outcomes on the micro-level for individuals when mediating between parties helps a qualified individual secure a job though the mediation process. It is also beneficial to the organisation which can secure a qualified and loyal employee in a country where certain skills and qualifications are scarce because of the brain drain of Jordanian employees to the Arab Gulf countries (Loewe et al., 2007, 2008). However, it can have some severe negative outcomes on the macro-level, as it reduces organizational diversity and leads to reinforcing power pockets in particular groups. Another negative impact of this use of *wasta* is that it weakens the formal institution as it reduces trust in political and legal institutions (Loewe et al., 2007).

Reflexive Considerations

The data collected formed part of a PhD project aimed at exploring the impact of *wasta* on the employee selection process in banks operating in Jordan. This aim and the research concept stem from the background of one of the authors, who was born and raised in Jordan and who has worked as a recruitment officer in a bank in Jordan dealing with *wasta* on a daily basis both on personal and professional levels.

In targeting a 'networked' country as Jordan, researchers face several issues, particularly in attaining access to organisations in order to conduct data collection. Instead of relying on formal ways such as sending e-mails or phoning the targeted organisation, researchers need to rely on their social network (the use of *wasta*) to establish a connection. Using *wasta* to study *wasta* creates ethical and practical issues; centrally, *wasta* had to be used to secure access but at the same time may not be imposed upon the interviewee.

Interestingly, since the first author was a PhD student with limited work experience and connections in Jordan during the data-collection period, he had to rely on the social networks of his family and friends, who acted as *wastas* to secure the interviews. Most interviewees were Palestinian-Jordanians, which could be a reflection of the in-group connections of the first author but also could be due to the demography of the sample, since the private sector was predominated historically by Palestinian-Jordanians who were described as less tribal and in which women had more 'social access' to work (Cunningham and Sarayrah, 1993). Although the use of the author's *wasta* to collect data can highlight that the insights are more representative of Palestinian-Jordanian perspective, it is worth noting all interviewees—from both backgrounds, religions and genders—articulated a negative perception of at least some uses of *wasta*.

The authors had the benefit of being seen as both an insider and outsider at the same time. The insider perception was due to the fact that the first author is an Arabic-speaking Jordanian from Palestinian origins but is perceived as an outsider, having lived a considerable part of his adult life in the United Kingdom and conducting his research in a 'Western' institution. This affiliation, however, provided a certain perceived 'prestige' that was very valuable in the sense that the first author, who conducted the data collection, was well received by the interviewees, most of whom most of were happy to share their insights with him. The second author, while being a cultural outsider, has gained an insider status from working in and researching business and management practices in the Arab world over 40 years. This unique status of being an insider and an outsider proved beneficial in discussing the very sensitive topic of *wasta*, as many interviewees used Arabic expressions while perceiving that their statements would not affect them afterwards because the research is conducted in the United Kingdom. The inverse point can positively advantage "outsiders" who can pass as "insiders" (Hutchings and Weir, 2006). It also helped in avoiding the cultural embeddedness and outsider negativity in developing the 'complex' view of *wasta*.

Recommendations to Students, Researchers and Practitioners

For researchers and students, we recommend the following:

1. When researching culture-specific concepts such as *wasta*, it is important to understand them from their emic setting. *Wasta*, for instance, cannot be dealt

with adequately with a mindset that labels it from the outset as "nepotism" or "not-nepotism" and is construed in terms of Western cultural assumptions. *Wasta* networks mitigate the uncertainty pressure in any organizational situations by increasing the opportunity for basing business decisions on trust and mutual benefit rather than on considerations of cost and price only.

2. Although this research highlights some positive aspects of *wasta* on the micro level, such as enabling qualified individuals to attain a chance of employment and securing trustworthy and qualified employees for the organisation, it is also important to consider the negative impact of using this practice. There are, for instance, diversity and exclusion issues, and this also suggests that an emic approach to culture-specific concepts can never be free of power implications.

3. Practitioners are invited to consider how diversity and merit are not culture-free concepts; in fact, the recent prominence of these concepts owes much to the postmodern Western need to come to terms with a new understanding that the global world does not map securely onto the largely Western-dominated management literature. Managers therefore need to understand that what is considered good practice in different cultures should be balanced by the different cultural perspectives on what is considered 'good'. International managers are advised the following:

   a. In practical terms, *listening*, looking and asking open-ended questions are the drivers of communication for learning. *Wasta* is not a formal process and subtle signs may have great significance.

   b. Travel itself, backed by critical reflection and openness to learning, is indeed a great opportunity for understanding other cultures' practices and understanding that different social and business practices which might not work in some contexts work in others. The traveler may soon find that *wasta* can be achieved through the networking attained through travel.

   c. In both life experience and formal learning the practices of constant critique and self-reflexivity, almost as if one were conducting a personal auto-ethnography can be bases for cultural learning (Weir and Clarke, 2017). *Wasta* is not a static practice and the configurations of *wasta* networking are constantly evolving.

Acknowledgements

The first author would like to thank his PhD supervisors Dr Ani Raiden and Dr Susan Kirk for all their advice during his PhD. He would also like to thank his partner Dr Sophie Strecker for proof reading the different drafts. Finally, both authors would like to extend their gratitude to the editorial team for all the kind feedback they have provided on different drafts of this work.

References

Abuznaid SA (2009) Business ethics in Islam: The glaring gap in practice. *International Journal of Islamic and Middle Eastern Finance and Management* 2(4): 278–288.

Al Harbi S, Thursfield D and Bright D (2017) Culture, wasta and perceptions of performance appraisal in Saudi Arabia. *The International Journal of Human Resource Management* 28(19): 2792–2810.

Ali AJ and Owaihan A (2008) Islamic work ethic: A critical review. *Cross Cultural Management: An International Journal* 15(1): 5–19.

Ali S (2016) *Social Capital in Jordan: The Impact of Wasta on Employee Selection in Banks Operating in Jordan*. PhD Thesis, Nottingham Trent University, UK.

Al-Kharouf A and Weir D (2008) Women and work in a Jordanian context: Beyond neo-patriarchy. *Critical Perspectives on International Business* 4(2/3): 307–319.

Al Khayed LT, Zain SRS and Duasa J (2014) The relationship between capital structure and performance of Islamic banks. *Journal of Islamic Accounting and Business Research* 5(2): 158–181.

Al-Rasheed A (2001) Features of traditional Arab management and organization in the Jordan business environment. *Journal of Transitional Management Development* 6(1–2): 27–53.

Barnett A, Yandle B and Naufal G (2013) Regulation, trust and cronyism in Middle Eastern societies: The simple economics of "wasta". *The Journal of Socio-Economics* 44: 41–46.

BBC News (2018) Jordan Country Profile. Available at: www.bbc.co.uk/news/world-middle-east-14631981 (accessed 12 October 2018).

Branine M and Analoui F (2006) Human resource management in Jordan. In: Budhwar PS and Mellahi K (eds) *Managing Human Resources in the Middle East*. Abingdon: Routledge, pp. 145–160.

Brewer M and Gardner W (1996) Who is this "we"? Levels of collective identity and self representations. *Journal of Personality and Social Psychology* 71(1): 83–93.

Chua A (2018) *Political Tribes: Group Instinct and the Fate of Nations*. London: Bloomsbury Publishing.

Cunningham RB and Sarayrah YK (1993) *Wasta: The Hidden Force in Middle Eastern Society*. Westport, CT: Praeger.

Davis J (2014) Social capital and economics. In: Christoforou A and Davis J (eds) *Social Capital and Economics: Social Values, Power, and Identity*. London: Routledge, pp. 1–16.

Denis A (2008) Review essay: Intersectional analysis: A contribution of feminism to sociology. *International Sociology* 23(5): 677–694.

Hutchings K and Weir D (2006) Guanxi and wasta: A comparison. *Thunderbird International Business Review* 48(1): 141–156.

Jones D (2016) *Vitamin or Poison, Wasta and Politics in Jordan*. PhD Thesis, New Brunswick Rutgers, the State University of New Jersey, USA.

Leung K, Bhagat R, Buchan N, Erez M and Gibson C (2005) Culture and international business: Recent advances and their implications for future research. *Journal of International Business Studies* 36(4): 357–378.

Loewe M, Blume J, Schönleber V, Seibert S, Speer J and Voss, C (2007) The impact of favouritism on the business climate: A study on wasta in Jordan. *German Development Institute (DIE)* 30: 1–211.

Loewe M, Blume J and Speer J (2008) How favouritism affects the business climate: Empirical evidence from Jordan. *Middle East Journal* 62(2): 259–276.

Mehtap S, Jayyousi Y, Gammoh N and Al Haj A (2016) Factors affecting women's participation in the Jordanian workforce. *International Journal of Social Science and Humanity* 6(10): 790–793.

Mohamed A and Mohamed S (2011) The effect of wasta on perceived competence and morality in Egypt. *Journal of Cross Cultural Management* 18(4): 412–425.

Rowland J (2009) Democracy and the Tribal System in Jordan: Tribalism as a Vehicle for Social Change. SIT Graduate Institute/SIT Study Abroad, 1–47.

Scandura TA and Pellegrini E (2008) Trust and leader-member exchange: A closer look at relational vulnerability. *Journal of Leadership & Organizational Studies* 15(2): 101–110.

Sharp J (2012) Jordan: Background and U.S. Relations. CRS Report for Congress, 1–19.

Smith, P.B. Huang, H.J Harb. C and Torres, C (2012). How distinctive are indigenous ways of achieving influence? A comparative study of Guanzi, Wasta, Jeitinho, and pulling strings. *Journal of Cross-Cultural Psychology*, 43(1): 135–150.

Tajfel H and Turner JC (1985) The social identity theory of intergroup behaviour. In: Worchel S and Austin WG (eds) *Psychology of Intergroup Relations* (2nd ed). Chicago: Nelson-Hall, pp. 7–24.

Weir D (2003) Management Development and Leadership in the Arab Middle East: An Alternative Paradigm for the Mediterranean worlds, Leadership. In: *Management Theory at Work Series Conference*, Lancaster, UK, 14–16 April 2003.

Weir D (2018) The Arab Middle East: Diwan, Ummah and wasta: The pillars of Arab leadership. In: Western S and Garcia EJ (eds) *Global Leadership Perspectives: Insights and Analysis*. London: SAGE, pp. 11–18.

Weir D and Clarke D (2017) What makes the autoethnographic analysis authentic? In: Vine T, Clark J, Richards S and Weir D (eds) *Ethnographic Research and Analysis: Anxiety, Identity and Self*. London: Palgrave MacMillan, pp. 127–154.

Weir D, Sultan N and Van De Bunt S (2016) Wasta: A scourge or a useful management and business practice? In: Ramady MA (ed) *The Political Economy of Wasta: Use and Abuse of Social Capital Networking*. London: Springer, pp. 23–32.

6

SELLING CULTURAL DIFFERENCE

The Position and Power of Cross-Cultural Consultants

François Goxe

Introduction

Mainstream cross-cultural management (CCM) literature tends to focus on identifying national cultural differences and usually explains internationalization success or failure in *national* terms. This approach neglects other factors, power games and personal strategies that may affect individuals and organizations' behaviours and results. Against this background, the following case shows how some experienced actors on the global stage can manipulate the ignorance and prejudices of inexperienced ones for their own benefit. The case goes beyond the mainstream perspective that often considers CCM actors as benevolent mediators or as 'neutral' in terms of power and provides an example of how consultants and presumed 'experts' can take advantage of their position to run a profitable business. Therefore, this case invites us to contemplate whether 'neutral' CCM situations are possible and to reflect upon the possibility that every intercultural interaction or CCM context is linked to potentially divergent interests and motivations.

Specifically, this case presents a group of French small business owners and entrepreneurs trying to create or grow their business in China with the aid of consultants, public servants and peers. The first section introduces the main protagonists and relates the genesis of the case. The text then explains these people's unexpected culture shock when they went to China and finally provides a few elements to elucidate the reasons for such a surprise. The final sections discuss the critical implications of the case and provide some guidelines to develop more efficient and ethical CCM consulting services.

Methodology

The study is interview-based. It comprises 35 individuals working for organizations operating in various industries (confectionery, mechanics, furniture, architecture, consulting, and more). The author collected data using a semistructured interview guide focusing on three items:

1. Respondents' sociological background (education, professional background, national and international work experiences);
2. Respondents' personal networks (or people met and/or contacted during the internationalization process), views, opinions and perceptions of those networks; and
3. Respondents' self-assessment of internationalization performance.

In line with the social constructivist perspective, the author followed a reflexive pragmatist approach to qualitative interviews (Alvesson, 2003; Bourdieu and Wacquant, 1992). The aim was to disclose "sources of power" and reveal the reasons that explain social asymmetries and hierarchies. This implied challenging the interviewees and our own initial interpretations, confronting the interviewees with alternative views and challenging and reconsidering assumptions and beliefs of what data are about (Alvesson, 2003). Practically, this meant first asking "conventional" interview questions. The next phase was then either to ask respondents to rephrase the initial questions (in my words: rephrasing), or, as interviewer, to come back to a particular theme using different vocabularies to trigger more critical answers (in my words: restarting). The very issues tackled during interviews—the internationalization process and its actors—therefore were only a pretext for exploring the social mechanisms and power struggles that underpin the community under study (international entrepreneurs, managers and internationalization support providers). Out of the interviews, the author of this text constructed a case narrative that is presented here.

Case Presentation

This is the story of Christiane, Danielle, Emmanuel, Eric, Jean-Luc and Marc,[1] a group of French small- and medium-sized enterprise (SME) owners and managers who live and work in a suburban city in northern Paris (Saint-Fleury) and who decided to create or grow their business in China. This is also the story of Nathalie, Marie and Henri who brought the group there. This story takes place in 2010.

The Context of This Case

Saint-Fleury is a formerly industrial suburb of Paris. The economic crises of the 1970s and 1980s and more recent plant closures have severely shaken the city.

At the time of this story, in 2010, China was deemed a major investment location. For instance, President Nicolas Sarkozy had just come back from Beijing where he had announced the sale of 160 Airbus aircrafts and 3 nuclear reactors to China, as well as several contracts between French industrial flagships and their Chinese counterparts.

The mayor of Saint-Fleury, Claude Parnasse, declared the city should seize such opportunities and strengthen ties with China. He stated that neighbouring cities "now all have a Chinese sister city" and that some had managed to attract large Chinese firms. The city council thus established a task force to work on the promotion of China in Saint-Fleury and vice versa. The task force included Marie, a French "cross-cultural consultant"; Henri, the Chinese-born president of a French–Chinese association of managers specialized in international business development; and Nathalie, the Director of Saint-Fleury's Economic Bureau.

The Intermediaries

Marie, a French woman in her 40s, studied Mandarin in Taiwan, married a Chinese businessman and worked as his assistant until his death in 2008. She then went back to Saint-Fleury and now works as an independent consultant.

Henri is about 50 years old. Born in China, he has been living in France for over 20 years. After working as a manager for French companies, he started his own consulting business, acting as an intermediary between Chinese and French cities or companies.

Nathalie is 45 years old. She had always lived in Saint-Fleury. She used to work for multinational companies and now supervised business development in Saint-Fleury. When Parnasse told her he would like to build ties with China, she readily thought of her friend Marie, who had just returned. The mayor agreed and suggested to hire Henri, a consultant recommended by the mayor of a neighbouring city.

Henri offered some potential destinations, in particular the city of Sanzhou, where he claimed to have many "old friends". After a brief informal agreement between Henri and some officials in Sanzhou, the Chinese offered to host Marie for a month to prepare for Saint-Fleury's delegation.

The Chinese Endeavour

Nathalie often gathered a few friends who either ran their own business or worked for large firms. She created Saint-Fleury Business Club, which she calls a "friendly place for business people".

The China project first was presented at a "business breakfast". Nathalie briefly explained that the city will support a business trip to China at a very reasonable cost for participants. The one-week trip would introduce participants to "the complexities of doing business in China" but also would "give them the opportunity to meet Chinese entrepreneurs, politicians and diplomats" and to "experience China's rich cultural traditions".

'Small' by Chinese standards (600,000 people versus 50,000 in Saint-Fleury), Sanzhou is a coal-mining centre and a railway interchange between Beijing and Shanghai. Henri vaunted its "very dynamic industrial base", its "booming economy" and a "GDP of more than ¥30 billion". Besides that, he argued, "Beijing is close and national heritage temples and monuments only a stone's throw away". He also stated that "the Chinese are particularly eager" to meet the French delegation and to show them "what China and Chinese culture really are" and to "do serious business with them". However, back from Sanzhou, where she spent a month, Marie told a slightly different story.

Marie's Story

Marie recalled that "someone came all the way to Beijing airport" to fetch and drive her to Sanzhou's city hall, where she was hosted. Her room was empty "except for a single bed, a desk and a chair". At this point, Marie saw no offence as the city was, apparently, "not as wealthy as Henri said".

Marie was then introduced to a few people, employees working at the city hall, people with little or no responsibilities. She met the director for economic affairs a few days later. Albeit friendly, the director seemed to have little interest in her. Marie had a hard time communicating with the Chinese, as she was lacking in practice and the local language was different from the standard Mandarin Chinese to which she was accustomed. The director promised to provide her with a list of local companies, potential partners for Saint-Fleury's entrepreneurs.

Marie befriended a young Chinese woman, Mai. Mai offered to bring her along to buy some food and other things she might need to make her stay more comfortable. Marie was pleased until she understood that Mai was reporting her comings and goings to her supervisors. Later, Marie was kindly but firmly asked not to leave the building alone.

Marie resigned herself to staying in the city hall and focused on her task: finding partners or at least companies that would give a tour of their facilities to the French delegation. This proved particularly difficult, as Marie was seldom, if ever, in contact with the right people. The director remained elusive; his subordinates only provided Marie with incomplete or outdated lists. A few visits were finally scheduled after Marie complained to Henri.

The French Delegation

Meanwhile, in Saint-Fleury, Nathalie managed to gather a small group of entrepreneurs and managers.

Christiane, a woman in her late 50s, owned a small furniture company. She employed around 50 people and was a good friend of Nathalie. She had little interest in doing business abroad but thought it would be nice to go to China with Nathalie, which "could only help her business anyway".

Danielle, a woman in her 40s, worked as an independent interior designer. She used to work for clients in the Middle East and would like to know more about the Chinese market. A friend of friend told her about the China trip.

Emmanuel, a man in his 40s, held various positions as an engineer in large companies before creating his business to sell a technology he patented. Some of his customers recently went broke and he needs to find new opportunities.

Eric, a man in his 50s, is an architect and town-planner. He has worked for Saint-Fleury and other cities around. He does not expect much from the trip but the cost is low and going to China with Parnasse and SME owners "cannot hurt".

Jean-Luc, a man in his 50s, recently had serious health issues and had to quit his job in a large company. He was thinking about creating his own business and searching for potential customers.

Marc, a man in his 50s, has spent over 20 years working as a chemist. He got bored and now thinks about producing and selling chocolate ("It is just a matter of mixing ingredients together!"). He had just seen a TV show about China ("a French baker became a millionaire there!") when Nathalie suggested that he join the trip.

An Old China Hand

Henri was in charge of providing cultural training to the aforementioned group of entrepreneurs and organized a two-hour crash course in Saint-Fleury. Henry gave the participants a general presentation of China, Sanzhou province and Chinese people. He explained the importance of "*guanxi*" (personal and professional relationships governed by reciprocity, see Warner, 2010), "*mianzi*" (face) and other "Chinese values". He provided some advice and a list of do's and don'ts:

- Dress code: men and women should wear conservative clothes with subtle colours;
- Being on time is crucial;
- Bowing is the common greeting;
- Present and receive business cards with both hands;
- Introductions are formal, so use formal titles; and
- Personal contact must be avoided.

Not the Expected Culture Shock

The group went to Sanzhou one month later. Marc recalls that he "really enjoyed the trip" but he also found some Chinese behaviour "quite surprising":

Henri told us the Chinese are conservative, polite, on time, and so on . . .
One day they invite us to a factory. They tell us the company is similar
to ours. We go there early. The appointment is at 9 a.m., we get there
around 8:45. Nobody's expecting us, they all look quite confused. The
boss is not there. They offer us some tea, and we wait altogether in the
front yard. 9 o'clock. 9:15. 9:20 . . . A big black car arrives. We all line up
like toy soldiers. The boss (Mr. Wang) gets out of the car. I don't know
where he had been but he doesn't look wide awake, quite dishevelled, he
wears dirty jeans, and so on.

He goes to see one of his employees then he goes to Henri then to
us. One of us presents a business card . . . with both hands of course! He
looks a bit embarrassed. He searches his pockets and finds one to give us
in return. He gives it with one hand and the card is not even clean!

That was . . . funny! The guy was nice, he gave us a tour of the factory.
A 'small' factory with about a million people working in there!

Christiane continues:

What shocked me there was how they treated their employees. I mean . . .
They don't beat them or . . . but they call this a 'small' company and you
see endless assembly lines. The boss does not know anyone there. He does
not even consider them. They told us Chinese people cared for family,
the boss is like a father to his employees, and so on. Come on! I can tell
you the name of each of my employees, their children's; I know what they
did this weekend . . . I am much more Chinese than them!

Danielle adds:

I can't say I was disappointed . . . We saw incredible things. But the Chinese are different. Different from us for sure but also different from what
we were told. We went to the Confucius Festival. That was incredible but
not exactly how I imagined Confucius! There were acrobatics and Chinese opera performances, fireworks, and so on. We saw people dancing,
drinking . . . They're not dull or sad at all!

Jean-Luc admits that:

We can't blame Henri, Marie or Nathalie for that, but it's obvious that we
didn't know anything about China and the Chinese and the only things
we were told were wrong or very simplistic. They tell us: 'the Chinese
care for relationships, they're very close to their employees, they are this
and that . . .' The guys we met are just big business owners. They want
to make money.

Christiane agrees:

> When I told the one who made furniture that I was doing the same thing in France . . . I asked him how many pieces he produced a month, and he wasn't sure! When I told him we make perhaps 40 or 50 pieces he smiled then he went to talk to someone else! (He was not interested or disappointed).

Eric remembers:

> Henri and others told us that, in China, you need to work on listening and being more patient and understanding with local ways of doing business. Actually, they look much more hurried than we do. They want to get things done quickly, and on a large scale. I talked to a manager at the glass factory we visited on Thursday because I saw one guy jumping on a moving conveyor while the line was still running! He did not even understand what I meant! I tell him 'dangerous!', he tells me: 'no, not dangerous!'. If I ask a worker to do this in France, the day after, we're in court!

Marie reckons that Sanzhou was probably not the ideal destination for a first visit to China:

> I found it very paradoxical. On the one hand, the city council and the municipality were like China 30 years ago with rules, people who don't speak and so on. On the other hand, the people in the companies were even more modern than us. I still don't really understand why it was so hard to find those companies to visit. I think the city was not sure what image they wanted to present."

In the following years, no contracts were signed and no partnership of any kind was developed between Saint-Fleury and Sanzhou. Henri still offers his services to cities around Paris. Marie has left Saint-Fleury and is seeking new professional opportunities.

Henry's Role

Later that year, we met Marie again to ask her final thoughts about that experience. Marie had been quite puzzled. She had tried to understand why her Chinese hosts had been quite reluctant to open their companies to visits and why the Chinese behaved the way they did.

In her opinion, Henri was the key to this riddle. Discussing with people in Sanzhou, she discovered that Henri was well known there and working for both Saint-Fleury and Sanzhou's governments, promising both to provide highly profitable contacts and contracts.

Contrary to what Henri said, Saint-Fleury's people quickly understood that Sanzhou and its companies were much different from their hometown's. Conversely, the people of Sanzhou had never heard of Saint-Fleury before. All were told that Saint-Fleury was part of Paris.[2]

Marie also found out that Henri had offered a quick training on France and French people to the Chinese, mirroring what he had done in Saint-Fleury.

One of the Chinese entrepreneurs, Mr. Wang, revealed what had been going on. An assistant to the director for economic affairs had called him a few weeks earlier. The assistant explained that Sanzhou needed volunteers to present their companies to potential French investors. Foreigners interested in Sanzhou were few and the City had made it a priority to attract some. The assistant also explained that French investors owned large firms and could invest in Mr. Wang's business. Besides, a Chinese man born in Sanzhou and now working in France would guide the visit and provide some cultural training. Mr. Wang accepted and took part in the training. Mr. Wang did not remember much about it except that "Westerners don't like to be too formal" or "French people are always late. It is polite to be late". He also recalls he was disappointed by the French delegation as he realized that they were neither potential investors nor large business owners.

Marie also understood what had happened during her stay. According to an employee who spoke more freely after she went back to France, "the guys at the Economic bureau were told she was someone important, that they should take care of her". There are no foreigners in Sanzhou and those they saw worked for multinational companies. There is an implicit "respect given to them, and Chinese people do not want to directly oppose them". Marie also believes Henri certainly told some friends he preferred they kept her away so that she could not reveal anything incriminating.

A member of Saint-Fleury's city council confessed that he "believes after some extensive research and discussions that Henri's association is actually a 'disguised company'":

> At first sight, one may think that those people are not only interested in making money, that nothing too bad can happen there . . . But it's still about big money. People think: 'If it is not-for-profit, it is harmless' but this is a smokescreen.

Also,

> [T]here are abuses. Some begin to speak of an 'associative mafia' with members of such and such association, president of association X, secretary of association Y, etc. to whom good salaries are paid, who

recommend each other to companies, public organizations, and so on claiming they're experts in their field or that they have a good address book.

Position, Power and CCM

Mainstream scholars and practitioners readily consider national cultural differences as the main source of conflict between individuals or groups. Individuals and organizations thus often hold national cultural differences responsible for their failures overseas. Many seem to forget that internationalization does not take place in a social vacuum. Individuals belong to different social groups, each with its own values, knowledge, beliefs, rules of conduct and so on. Conflict across cultural boundaries thus can occur at different levels of social grouping. Here, various groups or fields are intertwined. One specific actor, Henri, masters the 'rules' of many fields and is the only person connected to all. He can thus take advantage of his 'bridging' position between at least two fields. The intersecting fields and the position of Henri (and Marie) can be graphically represented as in Figure 6.1:

We distinguish two groups or fields among French actors:

- Government officials, state, region or city representatives; and
- Entrepreneurs and managers (Christiane, Danielle, Emmanuel, Jean-Luc, Marc and so on).

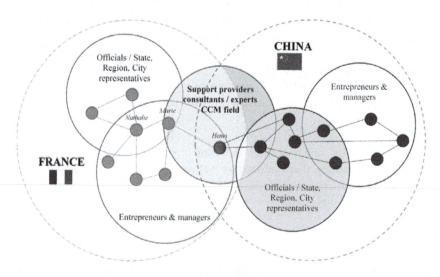

FIGURE 6.1 Fields and Positions of Some Major Actors

Chinese participants also belong to at least two fields:

- Government officials, state, province or city representatives; and
- Entrepreneurs and managers.

Nathalie, Marie and Henri's positions are more complex, as they belong to at least two fields:

- Nathalie acts in-between two fields (officials and entrepreneurs): her job consists in connecting local entrepreneurs, managers with the Region and City representatives and vice versa;
- Marie is located in-between three fields: French officials, French entrepreneurs and managers and an intermediate field connecting the French with the Chinese, typically together support providers, consultants and so-called cross-cultural experts; and
- Henri works as both an entrepreneur and a consultant. He is also connected to Chinese officials.

Marie and Henri are "Interculturalist" (Dahlen, 1997) professionals working with the theme of cultural differences or cultural diversity. In sociology and social network research, their positions are called "structural holes" (Burt, 1992). Marie and Henri act as "gatekeepers" (Tushman and Katz, 1980) or "boundary-spanners" (Aldrich and Herker, 1977), bridging a gap between two groups of individuals otherwise separated but who have complementary resources and interests. A lot of research in CCM has thought of boundary-spanners' action as positive, (e.g., Brannen and Thomas, 2010) but neglected the fact that such positions also provide individuals like Henri, cross-cultural managers, consultants and experts with significant power as they can manipulate information and knowledge, maintain asymmetry, reciprocal ignorance, cultural prejudices, and turn them into various forms of capital. In other words, such individuals have the potential to bridge gaps but do they want to and do they span boundaries in a 'good' way?

Henri is active in many fields and competes for clients with other 'experts'. To maintain his position or grow his business, he uses culture and real or fantasized differences as strategic resources. He focusses on business etiquette guidelines and stresses on superficial cultural differences while keeping the French away from more strategic business concerns (the importance of finding a reliable and experienced partner for instance) and his own business. He seems to deliberately simplify and "otherize" (Fougere and Moulettes, 2012) Chinese culture and behaviours to French people and vice versa. Othering is a process of making others more culturally alien than they actually are, and CCM knowledge (for instance, the bipolar character of cultural dimensions or the use of some specific terms such as *"guanxi"*), contributes to such othering (Romani et al., 2018: 12). By doing so, Henri (and, to some extent, Marie) legitimates his presence and action. In other words, Henri and other cross-cultural actors orientate and manipulate cross-cultural knowledge for strategic purposes to maintain their intermediary position. This echoes with and complements previous studies on similar professional communities dealing with the topics related to culture and cultural differences—the "Interculturalists" (Dahlen, 1997), for example, "Entrepreneur"-type interculturalists, oriented towards corporate clients and "Activist"-type interculturalists, "oriented towards public clients such as municipalities or various NGOs" (Romani and Szkudlarek, 2014: 180). Both types "must find a way to combine their agenda and that of their clients" (*ibid.*) and need to "sell" national cultural difference: the more they sell it, the better they can position themselves as the 'experts' to overcome it. When both sides (French versus Chinese) finally meet and the intermediary's strategy is revealed, they first experience cognitive dissonance, an uncomfortable feeling of conflict when two sets of cognition or perceptions are contradictory or incongruent. They seek to reduce dissonance arising from the discrepancy between their initial prejudices, consultants' subjective representations of reality (adding up to their initial prejudices) and experienced reality. To do so, they can blame other participants (Henri, Marie and their Chinese counterparts) or more cultural misunderstandings. Cross-cultural consultants can then further emphasize such differences and the need for further advice.

In Henri's defence, we notice that the French participants all have a certain number of prejudices about the Chinese: for instance, Marc recalls established discourses about the Chinese, such as working like ants, military drill and no individual freedom in the 'French' sense, and Christiane and Marie adopt some form of developmentalist discourse ("the people in the companies where even more modern than us!"). Henri actually only adds another layer of 'othering'. Could Henri have sold modern China to the French? By doing so, he would certainly have sold the 'right difference' but still would not have helped the delegation to make sense of it and to not look down on the developmental stage of China.

The case illustrates that CCM and intercultural interactions are inseparable from power and power effects, here, the position and strategies of some individuals bridging structural holes in-between groups of French and Chinese entrepreneurs, managers and politicians. Research on 'boundary spanners', individuals spanning various organizational, cultural and national boundaries to accomplish day-to-day demands of work, is not new (Aldrich and Herker, 1977), even in an international setting (Brannen and Thomas, 2010). However, a lot of research in CCM has thought of boundary-spanners as positive (e.g., Brannen and Thomas, 2010) and the traditional, mainstream perspective often considers the actors of CCM as benevolent mediators. What we show here is that consultants and other self-claimed experts can actually take advantage of their position. The case also shows that, in order to understand cross-cultural interactions and their outcomes, one must consider various contextual elements including the actors' social positions regardless of their culture of origin. In general, it contributes to a critical management research agenda (Alvesson and Deetz, 2000; Alvesson and Willmott, 2003) as it draws attention to the social context and the strategic implications of CCM.

Reflexive Considerations

To be reflexive, we must interrogate the assumptions and routines upon which we found knowledge production (Alvesson et al., 2009: 11) and thus investigate the assumptions that support our views on culture and actors under study. This also involves the understanding that a critical CCM cannot exist independently of those involved, including the researcher (Mahadevan, 2017). As a researcher, my approach is guided by two dimensions (Bourdieu, 2000): the adoption of a critical posture aiming to reveal how power and domination are exercised and a self-reflexivity. I see research as means to reveal the structure of reality by disturbing the tenants of the established order and to reveal relationships of domination, hidden by nature and internalized by agents. I also believe that understanding social mechanisms, highlighting social determinisms, structures of domination and so on can eventually help to free others and ourselves from these factors.

In the meantime, unveiling dominations and power effects means facing a number of obstacles. Researchers are often blinded by their own situation. I grew up in the environments or fields I analyse: France, China, 'global managers', support providers, diplomats and politicians. I have been educated among them and now, as a lecturer, I contribute to train participants to those fields. Familiar with such environments, I certainly tend to deny cultural differences and to consider that social borders matter more than (national) cultural ones. This approach also leads us to downplay national cultural impact and to consider individuals' international trajectories as the result of some kind of social determinism that no one can finally escape from.

Recommendations to Students, Researchers and Practitioners

What if everything you were told about how other people will behave turn out to be wrong? What if the Chinese shake hands when you try to bow, exchange business cards with one hand and show either too much or not enough emotion from what you would expect? How do you know what is personal, what is cultural, and what is in-between? For many business people in foreign territory, cross-cultural consultants lead the way, tell the do's and don'ts, introduce local partners, solve all kinds of unexpected problems and so forth. The only familiar faces abroad, they are also the only trusted partner. However, some may be tempted to take advantage of their intermediary position and information asymmetry.

The case shows the need for an intersectional, more socially and strategically embedded approach to culture. Mainstream academic and practitioners' literature tend to present culture as a fixed element that needs to be tamed, with CCM trainers as benevolent mediators helping others to make the world their oyster—but explaining cultural differences and bridging gaps between people with different cultures is their livelihood. Therefore, it seems natural for them to withhold some information, stress potential culture shock and keep control over their contacts in the destination country in order to defend their business.

Their clients, observers, analysts and scholars should not be fooled and should consider cross-cultural consultants' depiction of culture in a larger business and social context. Culture and cultural differences can be a strategic resource and we provide an example of how consultants and other self-claimed experts can actually take advantage of their intermediary position to run a profitable business.

Yet, despite the meagre results obtained here, the latter group should certainly not relax its efforts to provide such training to companies and people who are usually neglected. Indeed, as intercultural knowledge and practice becomes a source of competitive advantage, this source is typically available only to those corporations that have the access and financial resources necessary to run intercultural training programmes. Consequently, intercultural training contributes to maintenance or even increasing of power inequalities (Szkudlarek, 2009: 981). Provided that the recommendations suggested here are followed, the initiatives described in this case can certainly contribute to reduce those inequalities.

As for cross-cultural consultants, trainers and, perhaps, ourselves, we should certainly reflect more generally on our work and the complex and ambiguous aspects of cross-cultural interactions. First, the case shows the uncomfortable position of small business owners and entrepreneurs, less familiar with the international stage and more likely to be manipulated. Improving cross-cultural training may also mean first improving clients, trainees or students' business or strategic skills and their ability to analyse the context they (want to) join. Second, we should also wonder whether they really train culturally sensitive leaders, who will help to shape the open-minded, tolerant and responsible corporate citizenship of tomorrow or, instead, contribute to the development of highly sophisticated but ruthless manipulators who apply their intercultural communication skills to pull the wires of international business and politics, without due consideration to the disturbing consequences of their actions? (Szkudlarek, 2009: 977).

Notes

1. This is a true story, but all names (individuals and cities) have been changed to ensure anonymity.
2. Although the idea of a city being a unit consisting of several towns may not be common in France, it is the norm in China.

References

Aldrich H and Herker D (1977) Boundary spanning roles and organization structure. *The Academy of Management Review* 2(2): 217–230. DOI: 10.2307/257905.

Alvesson M (2003) Beyond neopositivists, romantics, and localists: A reflexive approach to interviews in organizational research. *Academy of Management Review* 28(1): 13–33. DOI: 10.5465/AMR.2003.8925191.

Alvesson M, Bridgman T and Wilmott H (2009) *The Oxford Handbook of Critical Management Studies*. New York, NY: Oxford University Press.

Alvesson M and Deetz SA (2000) *Doing Critical Management Research* (1st ed). London and Thousand Oaks, CA: SAGE.

Alvesson M and Willmott H (2003) *Studying Management Critically*. London: SAGE.

Bourdieu P (2000) *Pascalian Meditations*. New York: Polity Press.

Bourdieu P and Wacquant L (1992) *An Invitation to Reflexive Sociology*. Chicago: University of Chicago Press.

Brannen MY and Thomas DC (2010) Bicultural individuals in organizations: Implications and opportunity. In: Brannen MY and Thomas DC (eds) *International Journal of Cross Cultural Management* 10(1): 5–16. DOI: 10.1177/1470595809359580.

Burt RS (1992) *Structural Holes: The Social Structure of Competition*. Cambridge, MA: Harvard University Press.

Dahlen T (1997) *Among the Interculturalists: An Emergent Profession and Its Packaging of Knowledge*. Stockholm: Coronet Books.

Fougere M and Moulettes A (2012) Disclaimers, dichotomies and disappearances in international business textbooks: A postcolonial deconstruction. *Management Learning* 43(1): 5–24. DOI: 10.1177/1350507611407139.

Mahadevan J (2017) *A Very Short, Fairly Interesting and Reasonably Cheap Book about Cross-Cultural Management*. Thousand Oaks, CA: SAGE.

Romani L, Mahadevan J and Primecz H (2018) Critical cross-cultural management: Outline and emerging contributions. *International Studies of Management & Organization* 48(4): 403–18.

Romani L and Szkudlarek B (2014) The struggles of the interculturalists: Professional ethical identity and early stages of codes of ethics development. *Journal of Business Ethics* 119(2): 173–191. DOI: 10.1007/s10551-012-1610-1.

Szkudlarek B (2009) Through western eyes: Insights into the intercultural training field. *Organization Studies* 30(9): 975–986. DOI: 10.1177/0170840609338987.

Tushman ML and Katz R (1980) External communication and project performance: An investigation into the role of gatekeepers. *Management Science* 26(11): 1071–1085. DOI: 10.1287/mnsc.26.11.1071.

Warner M (2010) In search of confucian HRM: Theory and practice in Greater China and beyond. *The International Journal of Human Resource Management* 21(12): 2053–2078. DOI: 10.1080/09585192.2010.509616.

7

CONFIGURATIONS OF POWER AND CULTURAL EXPLANATIONS

The Case of a Chinese–Pakistani Mining Project

Qahraman Kakar and Jasmin Mahadevan

Introduction

The way in which the order of today's international business has developed,\ is not the only development that could have emerged. Actual historical events contributed to it, such as colonialism and imperialism or the Cold War, all of which affected countries and peoples all over the globe (Cairns and Śliwa, 2008; Westad, 2011). These developments also created established hierarchies in today's world order.

For example, the world's most powerful multinational corporations (MNCs) have emerged from the countries and cultures of former colonizing nations, and from Western capitalist systems, and these are also the nations that are the most powerful players in today's supranational institutions (Cairns and Śliwa, 2008). Within this order, the Anglo-American world has emerged as the most prominent center of world business today, with English language as the established global lingua franca (Cairns and Śliwa, 2008). Recently, however, we can see 'ruptures' in this order: nations such as China now claim their seat at the table of supranational institutions and globally successful MNCs emerge from these countries.

Activities of MNCs beyond their country of origin are cross-cultural by default because representatives from different national cultures interact. What happens in MNCs is therefore a classic CCM context, and it is also a major focus point of comparative CCM to analyze relative national-cultural differences in this setting. However, we argue that some perceptions of cross-cultural difference in MNCs are not actually cross-cultural; rather, they are a result of corporate configurations of power, intersecting with how power is configured in today's world order.

Focusing on a Chinese mining corporation in Pakistan, we show how these archetypical configurations of power lead to a sense of difference and mutual distrust. These issues are then *culturalized* by those involved but they are not 'cross-cultural' in origin.

Out of this insight, implications emerge. On corporate level, this suggests that a change in the country of origin of a MNC does not change the organizational patterns of how power relations are interpreted with the help of national–cultural categories: in terms of corporate configurations of power, it just replaces one dominant and presumably 'better' cultural category with another one (e.g., Anglo-American with Chinese). On global level, our case suggests that power in world business will become more kaleidoscopic than it used to be: countries such as China now claim to be another global centre of today's world order (whilst still being part of the global periphery to which Anglo-American and Western countries offshore), and this means that a future CCM needs to consider less-binary and more-complex configurations of power.

Context of Our Case

The specific Gold-Copper mining project upon which we focus lies close to the Iranian border in the extreme Northwest hinterland of Pakistan, in the highly resource-rich province of Balochistan. Investment there is highly attractive to foreign MNCs despite the high entry risks that are due to the volatile political situation in the region (Akhtar, 2007). For a foreign employee working on such a project, this is a 'hardship post', with a risk of personal endangerment.

In our case, the investing company, a Chinese MNC, had been granted a first lease by the Pakistani governmental institution in charge in 2002. Since then, the contract has been renewed twice. It was the first time in Pakistani history that such an important lease was granted to a Chinese company. The Chinese MNC had won the original bidding against two Australian MNCs, both with a strong history of investment throughout South, Southeast and East Asia, this being a first. Generally and historically, Australian companies are the common investors in the region.

Methodology

The first author conducted 29 in-depth qualitative interviews with 14 Chinese (eight managers and nine operational staff; eleven of them male) and 15 Pakistani (six managers and nine operational staff; all of them male) at the Pakistani mine. The interviews were mainly conducted in English; some of those with Pakistani interviews in Urdu. The interviews focused on perceptions of each other, ways of work, the challenges faced when working together and individual strategies to overcome these challenges.

About one year after the actual research, both authors started a reflexive process of making new sense out of the material. The second author provided the outsider perspective to develop interpretations and also introduced an intersectional, critical and power-sensitive framework to the material. By questioning initial interpretations in such a way, it became visible that the interviews were actually about much more than cross-cultural differences in the national cultural sense, which was the focus point of the original research. Also, as it became clear when the first author explicated the conditions of his research towards the second author, he was used by some Pakistani managers for their own empowerment; we reflect upon this later.

So, although the first author is the one who collected the actual data, the second author took the lead in writing and framing this text. For the purpose of this chapter, our joint methodology is critical, which means that we wish to reflect upon historical imbalances of power in contemporary CCM (see also Mahadevan, 2017: 101–126), and intersectional, which means that we examine the power effects of the researcher's standpoint while doing research and of the way he was perceived.

Case Presentation

During the interviews, it became notable that all employees categorized their experiences in terms of 'the Chinese' and 'the Pakistani'. For instance, Pakistani employees would ascribe acts of Chinese management which they perceived to be unjust, inhumane or simply stupid to 'Chinese culture' and thus paint a negative picture of a 'Chinese leadership'. Likewise, Chinese managers would ascribe actions by Pakistani employee—namely those which, to the Chinese, signified laziness, low performance standards or an inability to meet the expected standard of work—to a certain 'Pakistaniness', thereby creating the image that the Pakistani were unable to get the job done due to 'Pakistani culture'. Thus, it became clear that all employees categorized their experiences predominantly in terms of 'the Chinese' versus 'the Pakistani' and also ascribed difficulties in working across these categories to the negative effects of the other group's national culture. However, in line with our perspective as introduced at the beginning of this chapter, we did not take these categories and descriptions at face value, but looked into the content of what was actually described by the national–cultural labels 'Pakistani' and 'Chinese'. Out of this emerged numerous aspects of how power inequalities create perceptions of difference and contribute to a general sense of distrust. These are discussed in the following pages. Whenever we use the terms 'the Chinese' and 'the Pakistani', we understand them as categories which were constructed by the interviewees to make sense out of their experiences and not as factual reality.

The Chinese View

From Chinese perspective, Pakistani managers and coworkers were perceived as performing worse than the average Chinese person in the same position. Phrases used during the interviews to describe the Pakistani included "lazy", "cannot think on their own", "we need to monitor them" and "lower standard of work". Sometimes, the Pakistani did not even qualify for comparison with the Chinese. In the words of one Chinese manager: "The Pakistani know nothing." Out of this followed that, from the Chinese perspective, the Chinese needed to constantly check the work of the Pakistani. In the words of a Chinese manager:

> Whenever a task is assigned, we have to give them every detail and check their work. They want spoon-feeding. On the other hand, when Chinese are given a task, they stick to their work and get it done. But Pakistani employees are only concerned about their pays, leisure, and most of the time they drink tea and do not care about the goals and objectives of the project.

In this logic, the Pakistani perform worse than the Chinese *because of culture*, and it is the Chinese's responsibility to make sure to monitor the Pakistani closely. For, if left solely under the influence of their own culture, the Pakistani would surely perform inadequately ("not care about goals and drink tea").

This "tea drinking" of the Pakistani, signifying lack of motivation and an inferior way of work, was a topic frequently raised by Chinese interviewees. Interestingly enough, "tea drinking" as practiced by the Pakistani (black with milk and sugar) shows the influence of the former colonizing nation, England, on Pakistani culture today, wherein "tea time" signifies cultural refinement. So the last statement can be interpreted as resistance against the historically learned world order (with the Anglo-American world at its centre) from the Chinese side.

This points to the existence of wider frameworks (e.g., historically learned normalities of 'world order') that influence how culture is perceived within the corporation. We also find this in the quote of a Chinese manager, who said:

> The Pakistani must concentrate on producing professional managers to compete with us, they must learn from us. For example, Saudi Arabia is dependent on the oil economy, if oil finishes, what are they going to do . . .? Same for this project: What will the Pakistani do after these mines are exhausted? The Pakistani should travel and open their eyes, they should learn from us, from the West, or from the developed world.

In this quote, the Chinese manager seems to create a world order wherein China equals 'the West' or 'the developed world' but Pakistan remains inferior. Also in a quote by another Chinese manager, there is the idea that China is culturally superior to the Pakistani. He said:

> [The] Chinese have a future-oriented view, when we Chinese make decisions by looking at the future, we foresee the future. Initially, the Pakistani would refuse the decision we take, but after discussions and communication, they agree on our decisions.

It seems that this quote constructs the Chinese as being simply 'better' in making long-term decisions than the presumably 'short-sighted' Pakistani who, in the end, nonetheless bow to the Chinese superior decisions which 'foresee the future'.

Chinese managers also expressed that they, as individuals, are part of a wider change in today's world order. One Chinese manager voiced how he, and the corporation for which he works, are representing China's progress, development and emancipation. He said:

> We are here and representing our country . . . we must save the reputation of China. . . . And we make them realize that it's about the future of Pakistan. My father was born in 1947, two years before independence, to feed us he used to ask and beg for food, but after Chairman Mao we made progress dramatically.

From this logic, it then becomes the Chinese's responsibility to help the Pakistani achieve the same ("make them realize that it's about the future of Pakistan"), just like 'Chairman Mao' helped the Chinese to realize this. In this worldview, Chinese managers are representing the economic and political system of the People's Republic of China which, as it is assumed, will prove to be equal to the West or, potentially, superior.

These new claims also bring new challenges. One Chinese manager said:

> [Because of the importance of] this project, the company has changed the management style; here, we do not have the same organizational structure as we have in China. We are operating in a cross-cultural team, so management must check and balance more.

In the previous quote, the Chinese manager labels the situation which he experiences as 'cross-cultural' in the national-cultural sense. He also creates a certain logic around this interpretation: 'cross-cultural' is perceived as more difficult than 'non-cross-cultural' and, because of the importance of the project, management needs to prevent that working across cultures leads to inferior results. The root cause for any potential inferior outcome is identified in the work of the Pakistani employees (a thusly constructed 'Pakistani culture'). It then becomes the responsibility of Chinese management to control the Pakistani ("to check" upon their work) and to make up for whatever the Pakistani employees are incapable of, both in terms of culture and in terms of actual work ("to balance" any inadequacy of the Pakistani employees).

In contrast to the Pakistani, the Chinese were perceived as loyal. To quote a manager who talks about how the Chinese are different from the Pakistani employees:

> We are working away from our country and treat each other as one family. We discuss every problem with our seniors. We put forward suggestions, and let the leader decide for us. We have chosen our leader in every section and would never question their decisions; we understand the importance of listening to our leader which is good, both for us and for the company.

Conversely, the working style of the Pakistani was perceived as arbitrary, recalcitrant and sometimes even dangerous. One Chinese manager, for instance, spoke about the attitude of Pakistani employees towards safety rules. He said:

> They [the Pakistani] don't act the way I want them to act. They would do it the way *they* want it. They will never ask questions which creates ambiguity and frustration when they do it wrong. Sometimes, it could lead to fatal accidents. Life is not a joke, and they don't care about their lives. Whenever I assign any task to an employee, I always ask myself: 'Should I trust this man or not?' A minor mistake can risk the lives of many workers. I have to double-check his task.

This quote illuminates how groups of people, in this case: 'the Chinese', construct presumed realities about 'other cultures', in this case: 'the Pakistani', by means of generalizing small observations of actual behavior at work. Via this process, 'how Pakistani employees work' is generalized on the level of a wider idea of 'how the Pakistani are' in terms of culture. The socially constructed logic that emerges is: 'due to culture, the Pakistani seem incapable of understanding what is at stake at work—therefore, it is the Chinese management's responsibility to check the Pakistani employees' work'. We can also see how a certain way of work and how to interact with one's superiors is interpreted along the lines of trust. This then creates and further affirms a sense of distrust, not only in the Pakistani way of work but also in the Pakistani in general. For example, another Chinese interviewee said: "I've never seen somebody honoring his word. I lost my cell phone during working hours [and nobody reported to have found it or gave it back to me], and I am of the view, you cannot trust any [Pakistani] employee here."

The Pakistani View

From Pakistani perspective, 'the Chinese' were described as "authoritarian" and "autocrat". Statements to this effect were, for example: "they [the Chinese] have complete control over the decision making" or "the Chinese have all the power; it's a kind of established fact . . .".

The 'Chinese' management style was perceived and rejected as random dominance. One Pakistani interviewee, for example, said: "The Chinese treat the Pakistani employees like flock of sheep . . . Chinese masters would herd them [the Pakistani] wherever and whenever they want". The previous quotes suggest that Chinese dominance is perceived as totalitarian and unjustified: From the Pakistani point of view, the Chinese make decisions and lead not because they are better at doing so, but because they have the power to do so.

From the Pakistani perspective, there was clearly an unequal distribution of formal power in the organization. One Pakistani manager said: "The Chinese occupy all key positions in the organization". Another said: "They [the Chinese] are the bosses here. Most of the top-level managers are Chinese so they have complete control over the decision-making".

A related theme was the lack of transparency and involvement. One Pakistani manager stated: "the Chinese do not involve us [the Pakistani] in decision-making, and they only want us to do counting and shuffling or doing labor work". A Pakistani engineer said: "Pakistani senior management does not know about the monthly production target or the decisions taken by the company". Also, the Pakistani vice president stated that:

> They [the Chinese] know every detail about this project, from production to hiring new employees. Meetings regarding production targets are only attended by Chinese whereas we [the Pakistani] are neither invited nor told about the daily or monthly production.

The power to make or influence decisions was not perceived as being based on actual skills and competencies. In the words of a Pakistani worker: "Decisions made by a Chinese, even a Chinese worker, are more influential than those of the Pakistani's top management." Many Pakistani were of the opinion that their own qualification did not match their position. One Pakistani, for instance, said:

> I am a mining engineer, but Chinese management has appointed me as a clerk. . . . I asked Chinese management to appoint me somewhere in the production plant, but I got an answer that I will be fired if I refuse.

Many Pakistani interviewees stated (in the words of a Pakistani engineer) that "the Chinese don't trust anyone; they are not willing to trust the task we perform". Yet, whereas the Chinese view was that the Pakistani were simply incapable of making decisions (and that there were therefore good reasons not to trust them), the Pakistani viewpoint was more differentiated and involved the idea that any Pakistani contribution was unwelcomed by the Chinese and might even have negative consequences for oneself. Another Pakistani engineer working as an operator described the rules of the cooperation as follows:

> Here, you must remain dumb and say 'yes' to everything, if you start ask-
> ing questions or give suggestion in a professional way, they start disliking
> you, and you could lose your job, they discourage the technical Pakistani
> staff who have leadership skills.

In this statement, the Pakistani engineer refers to a universal standard of 'profes-sionalism', so, he stresses his ability to do the job. Yet because of the 'random dominance' which is ascribed to Chinese management by the Pakistani, he feels that this professionalism will even be to his disadvantage should he show it.

Getting fired was dreaded by all Pakistani interviewees, and this is why many choose to "play dumb". In the words of another Pakistani engineer: "Day to day conflicts are part of the project but . . . I must compromise because of fear of losing my job . . .". When explaining the need to remain employed, many Pakistani stated that the present situation in Balochistan was precarious and that they therefore could not afford to go against Chinese decisions. Inter-viewees referred to how virtually all Pakistani workers were the sole breadwin-ners of large families. To them, staying employed was crucial, no matter what. A Pakistani manager said: "There is a sense of fear in every worker".

This suggests that the Chinese perspective that the Pakistani are not asking crucial questions (e.g., regarding safety) is linked to the Pakistani's fear of get-ting laid off, which again seems linked to the Pakistani's distrust of the Chinese because of their exercising 'random dominance'. Unfortunately, this then seems to prove the Chinese's side distrust in the Pakistani, and we can understand this as a vicious circle of distrust.

Pakistani managers also often stated how their salary was much less than the salary of even lower-ranked Chinese employees. So, a classic effect in MNCs— expatriates are often paid home country salaries and even more when abroad whereas local employees are paid local wages—was interpreted as yet another aspect of unjust Chinese leadership. Another frequent theme was, in the words of a Pakistani interviewee, that "there are no Pakistani employees in the Finance Department." This was linked to the often expressed feeling that the Chinese had full control over all financial aspects of the operation and could therefore deny the Pakistani workforce their due payment. Pakistani managers and workers alike complained that the company did not even provide workers with the original pay slip. They perceived this to be in violation of Pakistani labor law wherein pay slips serve as the tangible proof of payment being paid or due. In the words of a Pakistani worker:

> [Now,] we cannot claim our right even if the company refused to pay us, nobody is going to believe that we are the employees of this company without the original pay slip with the company's monogram.

This suggests that, for the Pakistani workforce the issue of 'pay' also signifies the larger issue of trust, or, more specifically the distrust that the Chinese would ever act in the interests of the Pakistani. Conversely, the Chinese perception that "the Pakistani employees are only concerned about their pays" (see previous subsection) fails to grasp this trust issue and rather constructs this 'interest in pays' as proof for the Pakistani's inferior work ethos.

The question of whether one should trust the Chinese was often linked to the wider frameworks of the cooperation: many Pakistani stated how the Chinese exploited the country, how they, the Pakistani, had to bow to the Chinese, and how their own Pakistani government did nothing to stop them being exploited by the Chinese. Some also mentioned how Balochistan was disadvantaged within Pakistan, because profits went to the central government, and the local population did not benefit from the richness of their soil. To quote a Pakistani mining engineer:

> I don't want foreign investors and companies to take our resources; [I don't want a situation wherein] I am subservient to them in my own land. It's unfortunate that we are unable to initiate and run a project like this by our own. In my opinion, *we* are the ones losing these resources without gaining much. If some foreign company wants to invest they must work *here* under *our* [Pakistani or Balochistani] terms and conditions, but it is opposite in this project.

This suggests that the whole situation, far beyond Chinese managers supervising Pakistani employees—with whatever means and in whatever way—is perceived as unjust and against the interests of the local Pakistani population; there is more to the conflict than a simple Pakistani–Chinese divide within the organization. Rather, it is also about Balochistan versus the Pakistani central government, despite the conflict being framed in terms of 'Pakistani' versus 'Chinese': again, 'world order' comes into the picture, but on a regional level.

Likewise, within the company itself, the perception of unjustified Chinese dominance over the Pakistani goes much further than mere managerial or work-related interactions. Rather, it was inferred from a variety of large and tiny aspects. Regarding 'large dominance', there were separate canteens, hospital wards and sleeping facilities for Chinese and Pakistani, and the Pakistani often commented upon how the Chinese food and facilities were much better and how they were denied such amenities. Regarding perceptions of 'tiny dominance', a Pakistani engineer referred to how the bell-tones signifying shift rotation sounded "Chinese". He stated: "Look, we must even listen to Chinese ring tones, they imported everything from China, from food to a cleaning duster, and this is how it works here".

Also, we can infer first acts and statements of resistance against such dominance: there are the Pakistani statements of the need to "play dumb", there is the idea that the Pakistani *could* perform better, *could* contribute more, *could* work as qualified engineers instead of mere clerks or machine operators—if only the Chinese would let them. Another frequent theme for all Pakistani was "the Chinese speaking bad English" (in contrast to the Pakistani, as it was said), and the purpose of this idea seems to be to place Pakistan within existent global hierarchies: English is the lingua franca of today's world order because of a specific past which made England the largest colonial empire of recent history (see Cairns & Śliwa, 2008). When constructed as speaking 'better English than the Chinese', the Pakistani and Pakistan are affirmed as being much closer to the centre of world power, in comparison to the Chinese and the People's Republic of China.

Power and CCM

Macro-cultural categories such as 'the Chinese' versus 'the Pakistani' are often the means by which individuals make sense of their experiences of difference in an MNC. Yet, as this case suggests, this is not the issue to be managed. We can also see that inside and outside interpretations of both groups never match. Interpretive CCM would thus make the point that this case is about a vicious circle of distrust, and we also identified and shed light on this issue.

Yet, stopping at this point fails to answer the question of *why* both sides fail to overcome difference (as routinely happens in other, similar contexts). Power as such is not the major point here (it is always present): whenever there are headquarters–subsidiary relations, one side has more power, and one side also has to make the decisions of how to exercise this power. This is 'normal', and we can understand both positions (headquarters versus subsidiary) as archetypical roles which are present in every MNC: headquarters hold formal power and have to exercise it, and subsidiaries have the power to resist, change or subvert. These roles are not only archetypical to MNCs, they have been present in other systems, such as colonialism or imperialism, and this is why MNCs have often been understood as neo-colonial or neo-imperial spaces (overview in Mahadevan, 2017: 102–126), with headquarters representing the centre of power and with the subsidiary representing the periphery.

But how and why is this power allocated? In this case, the Chinese company won the bidding against two Australian companies. It could be that the Pakistani government preferred an investment from outside the Anglo world, or it could be that the Chinese company was really better (as the Chinese need to believe to affirm their suitability to play their current role). In any case, what might have been intended as an emancipation strategy turned out not to be one: the only thing that has changed is that, now, the Chinese continue to play the role which otherwise an Anglo-American or Australian company would have played. This insight brings us closer to the root of the problem. Since colonial times, the existence of an Anglo-American or 'Western' MNC has been, on an overall scale, more common than a MNC that is neither 'Western' nor Anglo-American. In this case, the Chinese company is both, so corporate centre and learned world order diverge in both ways.

This is a new experience, and it is difficult for both sides: for the Chinese, having this kind of power is comparably new—they might be less experienced in how to exercise it. One could argue, for instance, that those who can be considered the old centers of power in the existing world order—e.g. Anglo-American or French—might have had the time to reflect upon past mistakes in the role of 'colonizers' during colonial times and in their postcolonial relations to former colonies. On the other hand, one could also argue that the Chinese still operate from the position of tabula rasa (that is, a blank slate): there is no 'Chinese' history of colonization in Pakistan, no established picture, no risk of being held responsible for past mistakes. Still, we do not know yet into which direction this cooperation is going to develop; at present, it does not seem that power relations have changed for the better, based on the perceptions of those involved.

It might not only be that some are more experienced in occupying the centre-stage: it might also be that those being ruled from the centre are more used to the 'old' rulers (and also more familiar to them in terms of culture, because their cultural histories have already crossed paths). For instance, in this case, the Pakistani view the lack of English-language fluency from the Chinese side as a sign for the Chinese claim to power being unjustified. Also, the Pakistani drink tea 'like the English', and the Chinese comment on this trait very negatively. A 'Chinese' bell tone is identified as such by the Pakistani and commented upon as being a proof for unjustified dominance. Yet, it is difficult to imagine that an 'Australian' or 'English' ring tone would have been identified as culture-specific and as proof for cultural dominance. One might even wonder how to identify an 'Anglo-American' ring tone at all—it most likely sounds like a ring tone that seems 'normal' from a global perspective, because it represents the dominant global cultural history. So, could it be that Pakistani employees would not have rejected the claim to power by an Australian company that much? Also, why does a 'bell tone' becomes a prominent 'power signal': how is such a huge meaning attached to it?

From a critical perspective, the crucial point regarding power is that there is no equilibrium of forces, not even a hierarchy that is accepted by all. The

Chinese want to lead because they have invested in the project; they are now in the formal position of power. The Pakistani do not accept it: they consider the Chinese to be inferior because they do not originate from the learned historical centre of the established world order. Because of this, otherwise small phenomena such as a certain 'Chinese bell tone' or the way in which someone drinks their tea suddenly become huge and significant. To the Pakistani, these phenomena mean that the Chinese claim to power is not justified, and to the Chinese, the same phenomena are the proof for the Pakistani not accepting the Chinese as leaders. As a result, the Chinese feel the need to shut out the Pakistani from decision-making and to force their will upon them, which again justifies the Pakistani perspective that the Chinese are not suited to rule and dominate by sheer force. In the end, we have a situation wherein one side (the Chinese) has the responsibility but the expected 'followers' (the Pakistani) do not follow. So, what else—besides (actual or perceived) dictatorship or, at the other extreme, upheaval and revolution—could be the result?

In summary, it seems that, on corporate level, a change in the country of origin of a MNC does not change the patterns of how archetypical corporate power relations are interpreted with the help of national–cultural categories. On the level of world order, our case suggests that some might be more experienced in claiming the power of the world centre, or at least their claim to this power might be more accepted by those subjected to it. Our case also represents a recent trend in global corporate relations wherein corporate centre and the historically learned centre of today's world order are less likely to match. This suggests that power in CCM becomes more complex than it used to be, and also more contradictory for those who are experiencing it. The result is an ongoing struggle of forces compared to the stable equilibrium associated with accepted hierarchy. Whether this change will be to the better or worse, or simply different, remains to be seen.

Reflexive Considerations

The first author who conducted the actual fieldwork is originally from Pakistan and could not avoid being categorized as 'Pakistani' during the research. He also was a male researcher interviewing mainly male interviewees in a male environment. At the same time, he was also perceived as an outsider, being affiliated with a university in Paris.

Upon arrival in the field, the first author was received by the Pakistani vice president and then accommodated in a block specified for Pakistani managerial-level employees. There, the employees told the author that the Chinese are reluctant to be interviewed, and the Pakistani vice president and a Pakistani manager offered to help in arranging the interviews. The Pakistani manager then introduced the researcher to other potential interviewees, also from the

Chinese side. When doing so, the manager stressed the interviewer's identity of being a "master's student from Paris", thereby positioning him beyond the "Chinese–Pakistani" divide.

This process highlights how organizational research often involves "studying-up" (Nader, 1972). In order to gain access and establish trust, the researcher needs to let themselves be 'utilized'. In the given case, the most likely interpretation is that Pakistani management wanted 'their side of the story' to be told, and the first author was a means of doing so.

The second author of this text is a German citizen of partly Indian descent. When working on this case, she was reminded of how she herself has experienced power-plays and the culturalization of difference along national–cultural lines when doing ethnographic research in several MNCs. To her, power and history are therefore inseparable from cultural categories, as are organizational boundary conditions and individual interests.

Recommendations to Students, Researchers and Practitioners

Our case suggests that there are no 'cross-cultural facts' which are free of standpoints. When analyzing any cross-cultural cooperation, we should thus bear in mind that perceptions of difference are not (only) a cross-cultural reality. Power—as equilibrium or ongoing struggle—is part of the situation. We therefore need to investigate relations of forces by asking questions such as:

- Which are the cultural explanations used by whom, against whom and to what ends?
- Who occupies which corporate role in terms of power?
- How are these corporate roles related to the learned roles of the present world order?
- How is power exercised and how is it resisted?
- Which intersections can we see across these processes?

Furthermore, the researcher's standpoint needs to be reflected upon and explicated. Instead of aiming at 'power-free' research and 'writing themselves out of the story', researchers should understand power as inseparable from the act of researching cross-cultural contexts and to acknowledge this as a source of 'valid' data on power in relation to cultural categories (Mahadevan, 2011). So, again, the previous questions need to be asked so that we can better understand how the researcher is positioned in terms of power.

References

Akhtar AS (2007) Balochistan versus Pakistan. *Economic and Political Weekly* 42(45/46): 73–79.

Cairns G and Śliwa M (2008) *A Very Short, Reasonably Cheap and Fairly Interesting Book about International Business*. London: SAGE.

Mahadevan J (2011) Reflexive guidelines for writing organizational culture. *Qualitative Research in Organizations and Management* 6(2): 150–170.

Mahadevan J (2017) *A Very Short, Fairly Interesting and Reasonably Cheap Book about Cross-Cultural Management*. London: SAGE.

Nader L (1972) Up the anthropologist: Perspectives gained from studying up. In: Hymes D (ed) *Reinventing Anthropology*. New York: Pantheon Books, pp. 284–311.

Westad OA (2011) *The Global Cold War: Third World Interventions and the Making of Our Times*. Cambridge: Cambridge University Press.

8

CULTURAL RHETORIC IN ONSHORE/OFFSHORE PROJECT WORK

How Swedish IT Consultants Talk About 'the Indian Team' and What This Means in Terms of Power

Helena Fornstedt

Introduction

When studying virtual teams, the notion of culture has traditionally been an explanation model that rationalizes much of the interaction within the teams (e.g., Hofstede, 1983; Holtbrügge et al., 2011). However, this understanding of culture can be seen as simplistic and other scholars have found that the concept of culture might actually function as a deflective shield, concealing other agendas and rationales. Cohen and El-Sawad (2007) highlight that the concept of culture can be used to excuse existing behaviour and avoid any discussion on alternative ways of handling matters. Another example is the study by Jensen and Nardi (2014) that concluded that the *rhetoric of culture* was used as a closure mechanism that was invoked to explain the failure of Danish employees when working with their department colleagues in the Philippines. This chapter is a continuation of the exploration behind the curtain of what might appear to be cultural differences. Using the case of a Swedish branch office of a multinational company working with the Indian branch office of the same company, this chapter shows that intersections of the *construction of the 'way of work', organizational setting, power proximity* and *technical infrastructure* may be concealed beneath the notion of cultural differences and that those intersections are relevant to how Swedish consultants construct the identity of both themselves and their Indian counterparts. The main purpose of this chapter is to show how power, not culture, is the root cause of how the onshore/offshore team is interpreted and perceived. For this, multiple intersections of power and their contribution of how people make sense of themselves and others in interaction need to be acknowledged.

Methodology

The study was carried out from 2014 to 2016 and consists of 13 intensive interviews (Czarniawska, 2014, pp. 28–30) with IT consultants with experience of working at a multinational IT consultancy firm. The interviewees remain anonymous and all names have been altered. The interviews loosely followed a set of questions, but deviations from these were welcome when the discussion led to new, interesting paths of inquiry. The interviewees were chosen based on their experience of onshore/offshore project work and were initially found through the author's personal connections and, later, through snowball sampling (Goodman, 1961). Nine interviewees had around three to five years of work experience and four had more than five years of work experience. On average, the interviewees had experience of three different onshore/offshore projects stretching from a few months up to two years. The interviews were recorded and lasted around one hour each. Eleven of the participants had only worked onshore, and two had worked both offshore and onshore. I refer to them as "Swedish" or "Swedish personnel" because this category—like the opposing category, "Indian" or "Indian personnel"—was constructed based on employment contracts rather than ethnicity (holders of Swedish employment contracts were considered to be Swedish, even if they were ethnically Indian). Related to both terms are 'the offshore team' and 'the onshore team', which were additional markers of difference. This case presents the Swedish personnel's perceptions of their own collaboration and work with their Indian colleagues. The one-sided 'onshore' perspective could be said to be limiting, since the Indian personnel have not been given a chance to give their views, and the way they construct themselves and their Swedish counterparts has not been analysed. On the other hand, this setup has enabled a deeper analysis of the Swedish perspective and rendered their construction of their Indian colleagues visible.

Case Presentation

The Swedish Branch Office of an IT Consultancy Firm

The consultancy firm employing the Swedish project workers in the study is a large American consultancy firm with branches all over the world. The interviewees had been involved in projects where the project teams were set up so that one team was placed onshore and one offshore. Both teams worked for the same IT vendor company but were employed by the branch offices in their respective countries (Sweden and India), which also gave them different terms in their employment contracts (remuneration and other benefits being less in India than in Sweden). In all the projects in which the interviewees had participated (around 30 in total), the nature of the tasks assigned to the onshore and offshore teams were different. Planning, structuring, coordination and client meetings were assigned to the onshore teams while the operational work was assigned to the offshore teams. At the start of a project, the onshore teams were normally more involved because the initial phases of a project require leadership-related tasks typically performed by an onshore team. During subsequent project phases, the work of the offshore teams progressed or the teams grew while the onshore teams diminished. During the implementation phases, Swedish personnel checked the quality of the offshore work regularly and as new tasks appeared, they set up elaborate instructions for the offshore teams. The onshore personnel made regular checks to ensure that the quality of the offshore delivery was good enough.

Narratives Indicating Connections Between Cultural Explanations and Power

Many interviewees described the difficulties they encountered when communicating with their Indian colleagues in terms of cultural differences. Greta put it like this:

> The cultural difference is the big challenge. They interpret things in a completely different way, they think completely differently and react completely differently.

At face value, this seems to support the notion of national–cultural difference, which is the traditional focus of comparative CCM. However, if we take a closer look, much of what the Swedish personnel describes can actually be understood in terms of the intersections of way of work, organizational setting, power proximity and technical infrastructure. This will be elaborated upon in the following sections.

A 'Swedish' Versus 'Indian' Way of Work

In the interviews, there was a collection of ideas—about the how the project work should be carried out—that was shaped by the Swedes, taken for granted and perceived as 'best'. Interwoven with the Swedish personnel's perception of themselves and their Indian colleagues was thus a note of superiority. One interviewee stated that people at the Swedish branch office viewed themselves as "superhumans" and that the Indian personnel were regarded as "some sort of pet". There was even a sense of personal ownership. For example, the Indian personnel were commonly referred to as "our Indians" in a possessive way and in a more formal setting they were referred to as "resources". There was a general idea that since the client was located in Sweden, it was 'the Swedish' way of working that was the proper one, and that the Indian personnel were expected to understand that. One example of this is Nina, who says:

I think, it is a process, if you work together during a longer time period then [the Indians] understand that it is okay to think egalitarian, then they start to change their behaviour.

In this quote, we can see how a certain idea of 'the Swedish' way of work is constructed by the interviewee, namely the idea of an 'egalitarian' way of work (which is not the 'Indian' way). However, there were also critical perspectives on the same matter. Sam, for instance, said:

[Swedish personnel] are bad at giving instructions and don't understand that they're trying to force a Western mindset on to a non-West nation.

Still, some of the onshore personnel *did* indeed believe that the Indian teams did not meet the same high quality standards as they did themselves. Greta, for example, says:

[The Indians] never question things that you do. As a Swede you are brought up to question and we are thought this. Always. To look at it, how will I do this, one, two, three. No, this seems strange. 'Are you sure that I should do this'? That is the natural reaction but that is not the way they [the Indians] do it . . . [The Indians] do not take initiatives, they do not question.

Some interviewees talked about how they appreciated the exotic nature of engaging with Indians while at the same time speaking approvingly of Indians that had adjusted to Western culture and saying that they found that it was easier to work with them. Magnus, for instance, said:

The ones I've interacted best with are the ones who have explicitly said that they want to be a little bit more Westernized. Then it becomes easier to work with them and I don't know what's causing that but it's surely a cultural factor (. . .) you understand each other in another way and move forward more naturally.

Greta also said:

We have one super good guy, we used to say that he doesn't feel like 'an Indian' because he . . . well, he's lived in the U.S.A. for a long time I think and he's been to Sweden a lot, so he isn't like your typical Indian.

Greta also described one project that became very difficult to manage because of communication difficulties and because the onshore team was not taking the time to get to know and understand their Indian colleagues. At one point, she even heard her Swedish project manager refer to their Indian colleagues as "boneheads". After that project, she joined another one where the situation was completely different. Here, the project manager put a lot of emphasis on the teams getting to know one another—she made sure, for example, that all the team members (both onshore and offshore) met at the start of the project for one week to work together at the same site as well as to socialize in the evenings. Throughout, the project manager stressed the importance of viewing the projects as consisting of one team rather than two (onshore versus offshore). Greta reflected that this manner of working was a success factor for the entire project, making it a lot more effective and pleasant to work on.

Greta's reflection was that, in her first project, it was actually the Swedish project manager who had performed poorly and had managed the Indian team 'badly' in the sense that he had not enabled the formation of a common team spirit and thus facilitated the transfer of crucial knowledge to the remote part of the team (see also Mahadevan, 2011). Moreover, he had put the blame on the Indian team ("boneheads"), thus linking their underperformance to presumed 'Indianness'. This way, an organizational root cause was 'culturalized' and ascribed to presumed macro-cultural traits. Furthermore, the blame was put on the thus constructed cultural other and not on the cultural 'self'. At this point, Greta had had no alternative experience of onshore/offshore work, and she had believed her first project manager's description, even though the way he had worded it had made her feel uncomfortable. Nonetheless, she had believed that the Indian team had performed poorly, whereas she could now to some extent differentiate organizational reality and cultural rhetoric which helped her to avoid negative culturalization.

Organizing the 'Indian Factory'

One interviewee (Valter, who also was the department manager) had been driving the setup of the offshore work in his department. According to him, the starting point of the journey was a situation where the Swedish team asked the Indian personnel to do occasional work. However, he developed this way of work into a more (as he called it) 'industrialized' process, in which the Indian team worked according to well-defined standard instructions. The reason for initiating 'the industrialization process' was to cut costs and subsequently manage the projects so that the corresponding cut in quality was minimized:

> Depending on the area you're talking about, it's more or less manual intervention from our side, but in the best of worlds, [the work of the offshore team] is really rather like a machine.

A well-functioning Indian team was thus described as working 'like a machine' while the Swedish engineers described their own work quite differently. As Erik said:

> [The offshore team's] starting point is that they should be a production line, a factory that really will deliver a pretty commercialized and packaged service . . ., while our starting point is that we should coordinate, project manage, use them as a resource in a way. . . .

Another interviewee described it as "the offshore team is almost like factory workers . . . the brain is onshore". The company way of organizing the projects were described by the interviewees as predominantly giving the offshore team low-status tasks that were "well-defined and technical" as well as "well-defined, mundane and repetitive". The interviewees described the use of an offshore team as beneficial when 1) technical expertise was needed at a lower cost, 2) many people were needed who had a specific area of technical expertise that was hard to find onshore, 3) there was a need to conduct what were perceived as repetitive boring tasks. The interviewees described their management of the Indian team as very different from the way they managed their onshore colleagues, as well as the way in which they liked to be treated. One example of this was when Greta described her reaction when being subjected to the same treatment as her Indian coworkers:

> I worked on a project with an Indian manager and he treated me that way, he wanted follow-ups on things almost every day, and I went completely mad.

Furthermore, it seems that the Indian personnel were measured in a different way to the Swedish personnel. In Sweden, the emphasis was on soft values like leadership, creativity, problem-solving and management, and every employee was encouraged to continuously find ways to improve the efficiency of their team and their work. In India, on the other hand, the focus was on econometric values, such as the number of applications or tests completed during a certain time period. As one interviewee put it: "You don't use qualitative measurements in a factory". Another interviewee (Jonathan) pointed out that if the Indian teams had been measured differently, then the Swedish team would have seen different qualities in them, such as creative thinking:

> [In Sweden,] you have to have drive and come up with new ideas [to get a favourable evaluation], but in India that's never a factor. Instead you have to deliver on time, deliver the right amount and be predictable.

As described previously, the organization at the Indian branch office was structured in a way that did not allow for much flexibility. A few of the Swedish consultants had reflected upon this and thought that it had to be hard to be creative in the offshore teams, and neither the Indian company structure nor the onshore teams typically encouraged that. Some interviewees felt that difficulties in working together were rooted in the hierarchical structure of the company that did not encourage Indian personnel to take initiative and question people whom they perceived to be their leaders. The process of culturalization is still present in their statements, however. Erik, for instance, said:

> I think that it's the cultural differences that are the reason why they behave like they do [don't take initiative and are hesitant]. It's a hierarchical culture.

This is consistent with Upadhya and Vasavi (2006) who argue that the rigid top-down hierarchy of 'offshore' organizations effectively works against the ideal of autonomous workers. There is, however, a discrepancy between how the Swedish and Indian management groups set up the Indian teams and the wishes of the collaborating Swedish teams. The Swedish personnel became frustrated when they encountered 'machine-like' behaviour in their Indian counterparts, and they then requested behaviour resembling more their own way of working. At the same time, the majority of the tasks assigned to the offshore teams were well defined and did not encourage creative or autonomous thinking. To a certain extent one might say that the Swedish employees demanded autonomous creative Indian workers who had agreed to mundane and repetitive tasks that the Swedish themselves would not have wished to perform. The Swedish personnel thus expected both subjugation and autonomy from their colleagues in India while struggling with this paradox. When viewed in this light, the Swedish personnel created 'the inferior Indian' who is incapable of performing as well as a Swede (similar processes of constructing 'the inferior other' have been described by Mahadevan, 2011 and Metiu, 2006).

Some interviewees believed that many of their onshore colleagues had prejudices that determined which tasks they assigned to the offshore teams. One interviewee (Holger) thought that the Indians themselves were not the most important reason why they were given these kinds of tasks. He assumed that it was rather the Swedish personnel's idea of the raison d'être of the Indian team:

> I can imagine that there's a cultural difference but I don't think that it's the biggest . . . I think that it's the culture that prevails here internally at [the Swedish branch office], I mean what do you have an [Indian] team for, what should they contribute? . . . in the [offshore] teams that I've worked with, I have nevertheless recognized that they've had well . . . a greater capacity than we . . . than we've used the team for.

This suggests that the potential of an offshore team is deemed to be greater by some interviewees, and Anjali, who had also worked in an offshore team, had actually experienced that her competence was better used when she started to work onshore. This is consistent with Ridgeway and Berger (1986) who argue that, when group status differs in a group, the expectations concerning the people in this group tend to mirror the status hierarchy. Members subsequently develop expectations for high- or low-valued positions given their referential belief of what position they should have.

Power Proximity and Technology

The two locations were designed as center and periphery, which is apparent from their names 'onshore' and 'offshore'. The onshore teams were close to the client, and that was also where the project manager was based; in other words a great deal of power was situated onshore. The client had hired the teams and therefore the focus was on delivering and making sure that they were pleased with the achievement of the teams. Thus, the client had a great deal of power and the Swedish personnel benefitted from being close to them. This also gave the Swedish teams a considerable advantage over the Indian consultants especially due to their control of the flow of information between the Indian team and the client(s). The Swedish personnel saw themselves as cultural translators since, as one interviewee put it, "The clients think in a Swedish way". Since the Swedish personnel were close to and often spoke the same language as the client (who ultimately controlled the project), they often became the unofficial leaders of their Indian colleagues. As Erik said:

> . . . While I was a very junior and new member of staff and did not know that much, I was . . . since I was onshore, in some way or other I became their [the Indian colleagues'] client and the one who ordered things from them, even though they were so much more experienced and good at their jobs and . . . and sometimes it was perhaps apparent that they didn't like that balance of power and I would sort of . . . I didn't really deserve it [the power].

Erik, the Swedish junior consultant was also close to another powerful actor, namely the project manager. On the Swedish site, there would be a project manager supervising a team leader of two to three consultants. This gave the junior consultants in Sweden a position of power vis-à-vis their peers and seniors in India. Greta said:

> Since I'm the one who knows what should be done, I informally become the one who says what should be done, which turns into an informal leadership position. I have to admit that I'm on the same level as many of my colleagues in the [offshore] team but people often think that I'm the one who should tell them what to do. I also work with colleagues in the Indian team who are more senior than I am and even then, I sometimes need to tell them what to do.

Another aspect of the Indian personnel being further away from the centre of power is that they then become invisible to the clients. As one interviewee reflected, this might also be the reason for why clients do not view Indians as 'human beings' but rather as "a machine that can work five nights in a row". So, it seems that the Indians are made invisible in two ways; they are physically made invisible (from working in another country than the client) and in addition to this their humanity is made invisible (since they are compared to a machine). This invisibility is seemingly interlinked with inferior status. Metiu (2006) argued that the high-status groups (e.g., onshore personnel) can try to enhance their status using geographical distance as an excuse for not learning about and interacting with the offshore team. The Swedish personnel were aware of this to some degree. Some of them even acknowledged that they had a duty to use their position of power to make the Indian colleagues visible.

Another difference in the situation of the two teams could be found in the characteristics of their physical working location. Almost all of the Swedish interviewees had spent one or two weeks in India, normally in the beginning of a project and then after officially becoming team lead. Greta recalled her first impression of the conditions of work in the Indian open offices:

> They sit there in their cubicles. That's really how they sit! They sit in long rows with one person in every cubicle, like at the beginning of 'The Matrix'. And it's noisy and they have very bad phones and really bad internet connection. It's shocking, and it irritated me. Before I went there I just couldn't understand what the problem was. Why couldn't we hear what they said on the phone? Why did it take so long for them to go online? And then you go there and see. Okay, it's because they have shitty phones and really slow Internet connection. And then you really understand why things don't work.

Greta was surprised when she learnt about the bad technological infrastructure of the Indian site. This could be seen as her taken-for-granted view on 'normal conditions for office work' being challenged. Through this visit she realized that the poor infrastructure contributed to the communication difficulties and made it more complicated for the Indian team to decipher what the Swedish team, and ultimately the client, wanted. This suggest that the technological divide, too, adds to the power differential inherent in onshore/offshore work.

Overall, this quote suggests that Greta perceived working conditions in India as inferior. However, there is more to it: When making her point, she refers to a movie ('The Matrix') which is also about the technological future of the world and its negative effects on human beings. So, it might also be about a certain anxiety in relation to this world. At the same time, the organizational layout which Greta describes in her quote (open offices, single-person cubicles) is quite common in North America, the region from which the whole industry has originated. However, Greta fails to see the possibility that the Indian office might be more 'Americanized' than the Swedish office (wherein consultants work in open offices without single person cubicles).

Power and Cross-Cultural Management

This chapter shows how cultural explanations and power are inseparable in onshore/offshore projects. Whilst this is not a new insight in itself, this chapter sheds further light on *how exactly* this is the case and how factual conditions of work and ideas about work add to the emergence of certain images of 'Swedish' and 'Indian' which they also sustain.

As this case suggests, there was ideas about a certain 'Indian way of work' amongst the Swedish personnel. For instance, performing in a manner that was flexible, independent and creative was not perceived as 'Indian'. Typical deficits attached to 'the Indian way' were Indians as not taking initiative, as not questioning tasks, and as not acknowledging when they did not understand something. However, it also was considered a possibility that one might teach them how to become more 'egalitarian'. The latter was then, implicitly, constructed as the 'more modern' 'Western' way which 'the Swedish', in their own perspective, already represented.

Out of the ways in which 'Indian culture' and 'the Indian way of work' was constructed, we can infer the self-image of a 'Swedish way of work' which was, constructed as superior. Part of these effects can be understood as being rooted in the organizational setting: It lies in the nature of offshore/onshore work that the onshore team is closer to the centre of power (e.g., corporate headquarters or clients). This creates imbalances in terms of status and visibility, both of which add to each other and which also contribute to the 'dehumanizing' aspects of offshore work. Secondly, it is also somewhat to be expected that one's own way of work is perceived as superior (Muhr and Salem, 2013). However, there might also be wider frameworks contributing to the self-image of 'the Swedish way of work', such as the idea of project work being implicitly modern and global, with underlying values such as egalitarianism, teamwork and individual initiative (Upadhya, 2008).

Ultimately, none of these aspects are 'cultural' in the mainstream cross-cultural sense: rather, cultural explanations are given to aspects of work which might not be cultural. Examples from this case are, for instance, the bad technological infrastructure at the Indian delivery centre or the effects of difference in power proximity as related to the invisibility of the Indian team.

For instance, out of the dehumanizing aspects of offshore work and the dominant expectations regarding a certain 'modern' way of work, a paradoxical situation emerges: on the one hand, the Indian personnel were expected to show their 'Swedishness' (as constructed by Swedish personnel in the aforementioned sense), on the other hand, the structure wherein they worked further constrained their scope of action to 'functioning as part of the machine'.

Furthermore, it seems that 'the Indian personnel' were caught between two somewhat contradicting expectations: on the one hand, the individual Swedish consultants expected them to be egalitarian and prone to taking initiatives in their daily work. On the other hand, the conditions of working offshore (bad technological infrastructure, lack of proximity and thus status, a dehumanizing perspective on them and thus quantitative measures of performance) prevented them from working as expected. So, the only way in which they could counteract dominant ideas about 'how they work' was to a large extent not accessible to them. This then further contributed to dominant cultural ideas about a 'Swedish' and 'Indian' way of work.

It is worth noting that the construction of 'the Swedish way of work' as superior, the Indian team being organized as "a machine", the Swedes' power proximity and the poor technical infrastructure at the Indian site put an individual Swede in a position where it is very hard to *not* contribute to the imbalance of power. So, despite individual consultants showing reflexivity regarding these matters, it can be expected that the underlying power mechanisms of onshore/offshore projects will remain in place.

Reflexive Considerations

The starting point of this study was the personal contact that I gained while working in a similar environment to the one described in the case. As a Swedish woman with experience of the Swedish side of an IT project, I was able to make my interviewees trust me and possibly speak more freely than they otherwise would have done. My initial curiosity concerning cross-cultural teamwork originated from my own work in a similar context in which I realized that I was being treated as superior to my colleagues in India. I was both pleased and uncomfortable with that. Pleased, because I enjoyed being a leader, and uncomfortable, because I realized that my level of expertise did not justify my position. I could therefore relate to the interviewees' narratives very much. At the same time, I tried to avoid imposing my own experiences onto them.

Recommendations to Students, Researchers and Practitioners

This chapter shows how the organizational setup, power effects and cultural explanations come together in onshore/offshore work. Out of this insight, the following recommendations to CCM students, researchers and practitioners emerge for the context of global or virtual teams:

- Be aware of the mechanisms by which you and others construct prevalent ideas about certain 'ways of work'. Especially, if these are formulated in terms of national or societal culture (e.g., 'Swedish' versus 'Indian') reflect upon them critically and try to question any taken for granted hierarchy between them.

- Reflect upon the power structures wherein work takes place. In particular, pay attention to power proximity and how it further affirms the invisibility and the dehumanization of the 'offshore team'.
- To avoid the culturalization of work aspects which are not cultural, look for 'simple explanations' for presumed 'profound cross-cultural differences' (e.g., bad technological infrastructure at the offshore site, quantitative measurement of performance).
- Finally, reflect upon how you are positioned in terms of power and experience and ask yourself whether and how you contribute to affirming negative power effects. Use these insights to work against the prevalent regime and to challenge the cultural assumptions which others might have in mind.

The purpose of all these recommendations lies in their aim to contribute to a process of 'micro-emancipation', understood as a key element of any critical CCM (Romani et al., 2018), which can change the position and perspective of individual actors, e.g., in an onshore/offshore context. This might not change the whole system but improve the conditions under which individuals work. Ultimately, joint individual efforts and many small adjustments may have large systemic effects.

Acknowledgements

I wish to thank all my interviewees for generously sharing their time and experience with me. I would also like to thank the editors for their constructive comments on earlier versions of the manuscript. Finally, I would like to extend a special thanks to Jasmin Mahadevan for her encouragement and guidance through the entire process of writing this chapter.

References

Cohen L and El-Sawad A (2007) Lived experiences of offshoring: An examination of UK and Indian financial service employees' accounts of themselves and another. *Human Relations* 60(8): 1235–1262.

Czarniawska B (2014) *Social science research: From field to desk*. London: Sage.

Goodman LA (1961) Snowball sampling. *Annals of Mathematical Statistics* 32(1): 117–151.

Hofstede G (1983) Cultural dimensions for project management. *International Journal of Project Management* 1(1): 41–48.

Holtbrügge D, Schillo K, Rogers H and Friedmann C (2011) Managing and training for virtual teams in India. *Team Performance Management: An International Journal*, 17(3/4): 206–223.

Jensen RE and Nardi B (2014) *The Rhetoric of Culture as an Act of Closure in a Cross-National Software Development Department*. Tel Aviv, Twenty Second European Conference on Information Systems.

Mahadevan J (2011) Engineering culture(s) across sites: Implications for cross-cultural management of emic meanings. In: Primecz H, Romani L and Sackmann S (eds) *Cross-Cultural Management in Practice*. Northampton: Edward Elgar Publishing Limited, pp. 89–100.

Metiu A (2006) Owning the code: Status closure in distributed groups. *Organization Science* 17(4): 418–435.

Muhr SL and Salem A (2013) Specters of colonialism: Illusionary equality and the forgetting of history in a Swedish organization. *Management & Organizational History* 8(1): 62–76.

Ridgeway CL and Berger J (1986) Expectations, legitimation, and dominance behavior in task groups. *American Sociological Review* 51(5): 603–617.

Romani L, Mahadevan J and Primecz H (2018) Critical cross-cultural management: Outline and emergent contributions. *International Studies of Management & Organization* 48(4): 403–418.

Upadhya C (2008) Management of culture and managing through culture in the Indian software outsourcing industry. In: Upadhya C and Vasavi A (eds) *In an Outpost of the Global Economy: Work and Workers in India's Information Technology Indutry*. New Delhi: Routledge, pp. 101–135.

Upadhya C and Vasavi A (2006) *Work, Culture, and Sociality in the Indian IT Industry: A Sociological Study*. Bangalore: Indo-Dutch Programme for Alternatives in Development.

9

LIVED ETHNICITY

Two 'Turkish' Women in Germany

Jasmin Mahadevan, Esra Cetinkaya and Dilara Özer

Introduction

This chapter is about the lived ethnicity of two women, who, at this point, will be described as 'middle-aged Turkish-German'. Ethnicity involves ideas about culture and race, and, depending on the ethnicity concerned, also of religion (Rahman, 2017); it might be identified, for instance, via language, history, behaviour and dress. Thus, ethnicity is not about a clear content, rather, it is an identity mechanism by which *certain* groups—but not *all* groups—are socially constructed as different or might construct themselves as a distinct 'ethnic group' (Barth, 1969).

In our chapter, we differentiate between lived ethnicity and ethnic images. With lived ethnicity, we refer to how individuals experience their ethnic identity. We understand ethnic images as perceptions of 'this is how ethnic group xyz people are and behave'. They are formed and filled with identity expectations regarding role, behavior, values, interactions and other cultural forms. It is also assumed that individuals associated with a certain ethnic identity will stay within the boundaries of the ethnic image (based on Barth, 1969). Ethnic images are present in many societies (Eriksen, 2010), both mono- and multi-ethnic.

Ethnic images constrain the identity options of those who are placed into them and make it difficult to view individuals as anything else than representatives of what has become the 'normal' content of a certain ethnic identity (Barth, 1969). Often, hierarchies are attached to ethnic images (Barth, 1969). At work, these effects might hinder companies to recognize and manage talent (Mahadevan and Kilian-Yasin, 2016).

On the other hand, those who do not fit into existent ethnic images, e.g., descendants of migrants, or bicultural and third-culture individuals, might have more cultural options if they are aware of their identity possibilities (Eriksen, 2010). Thus, as ethnic diversity increases, it becomes more relevant to CCM to understand the life experiences of ethnic minority individuals—including life experiences that are constructed as inferior by the ethnic image—beyond simplified generalizations. To do so, we need to examine the intersections of multiple identity markers, such as gender, ethnicity, religion, age and so on, all of which come together to shape lived ethnicities.

Against this background, this chapter traces the lived ethnicity of two German residents to whom the ethnic image 'Turkish-Muslim migrant woman' is ascribed. It enables us to approach individual life experiences beyond dominant pictures of ethnic difference, and, this way, view them as 'more' than or 'different' from the ethnic image and its expected features.

Methodology

Our chapter is based on informal in-depth interviews with two female middle-aged Turkish-German citizens who immigrated to Germany in early adulthood. The names of all individuals and places have been changed. The interviews were conducted by the second and third author, both German citizens of Turkish descent. The interviews took place in the interviewees' homes, in Turkish, of which all interview participants are native speakers. They were documented via memory protocol (in German and Turkish) which was extended and typed immediately after the interview. Later on, the notes were checked with the interviewees for accuracy and further insights. For the purpose of this publication, excerpts of the interviews were translated to English by the second and third author. The first author helped frame and interpret the material, and provided the outside perspective required for reflecting upon interview process and outcome.

What the two interviewees have in common is that they immigrated to Germany from Turkey in their early adulthood to join a spouse who was already settled in Germany, and that they have built a life in Germany since around 1990. Both have kids in Germany, both are professional women and both self-identify as Muslim. One of the interviewees has chosen to wear a headscarf, the other has not.

Case Presentation

Nurdan's Story

Nurdan lives in Germany, works as a machine operator in a company, and speaks German with a Turkish accent. She fits the image of the 'traditionally religious Turkish guest worker's wife', performing unskilled manual labour, presumably because of material family needs and a lack of access to education (this picture being a prevalent ethnic image in Germany). However, for Nurdan herself, an important anchor of her identity (in addition to having raised her children), is having graduated with a degree in dental medicine. Her story unfolds in the following section.

"If You Have the Opportunity, Then Go and Seize it"

Nurdan was born in 1965 and raised in Ankara, the capital of Turkey, and she proceeded to study dental medicine there for five years. Her parents had grown up in a village, with poor access to education. Conversely, Nurdan and her two older brothers went to university. "I was born into a family with an enthusiasm for knowledge . . ." Nurdan said. Her parents told her: "We could not go to school, so, if you have the opportunity, then go and seize it", and she followed their advice. For instance, those completing high school in Turkey needed to take a nationwide exam, and the rank in this exam determined their higher education options. Nurdan said: "I was amongst the best 1,500 students [nationwide]"; she was admitted to one of the top institutions.

"I Never Questioned It Before"

In her second year at university, in 1984 at age 20, Nurdan got engaged. Her future husband, Melih, had been introduced to her by her father (both were working in the same German city at that time). Melih was the son of a Turkish guest worker;[1] he had migrated to Germany at the age of 16 and was now employed as a skilled industrial worker in a technical company. To Nurdan's father, Melih seemed to be a prospective match.

During her studies, Nurdan had a long-distance relationship. Right after graduation in 1988, she got married in Turkey. In February 1989, Nurdan and Melih moved to (West) Germany together. When being asked how the decision to move to Germany was made, Nurdan said: "I've never questioned it before . . . you are young and don't know it all. My husband was living there. This is how it was, and I agreed to it".

"The Biggest Disappointment in My Life"

Shortly after her arrival in Germany, Nurdan investigated how she could practice dental medicine in her new home country. However, her degree was not recognized, and Nurdan was told that only two years of her five-year education would count. So, she would have to study for three more years at the nearest university, in University Town.

Several reasons withheld Nurdan from taking this path. First of all, she didn't know any German: "I was using gestures and hand signs to communicate with my neighbours or other people. To be on the safe side, I was carrying a small

dictionary with me". Secondly, not being familiar with her new surroundings—
for instance, means and regulations of public transport—created the impression
that University Town was further away than it actually was. All in all, it seemed
to be impossible to her. For instance, Nurdan thought that she would have to
move there, when in reality—as she now knows—it would have been a com-
mute of approximately 1.5 hours one way: a strenuous and time consuming
journey, but potentially feasible.

Obtaining a professional permit as a dental assistant was the second option
that Nurdan had. Regulations at that time specified that, in order to obtain this
permit, one had to be a refugee, a German citizen or married to a German citizen. Nurdan didn't fulfill any of those requirements. "To get the German citizenship you had to be living in Germany for nine years [according to German law
at this time]. This was the only requirement I would have been able to fulfill.
Therefore, this was the only option for me".

After nine years, she applied for the German citizenship, but the process
took another two years. Afterwards, she got a temporary professional permit—
eleven years after her application. Now, Nurdan had to find a dentist who
would let her work for one year as a dental assistant, upon which she could take
an exam, which she would then have to pass to obtain her full permit. However, a lot of things had happened in between.

"The Most Important Thing"

Nurdan took her first German language course in May 1989, just two months
after her arrival, but being a university graduate and having highly developed
study skills, she was dissatisfied with the course, which she took together with
some others who had only rudimentary schooling.[2] She perceived progress
as "too slow", and having paid a relatively high amount of money, she had
expected to learn more.

Nurdan and husband Melih did not have anything when they came to Germany. Melih's salary before marriage had always gone to his father, and there
were no savings. Now, Nurdan also wanted to contribute by earning money.
She started working in a record shop owned by a Turkish immigrant. Most of
the customers were Turkish: she did not need any German language skills.

A few months passed, and Nurdan got pregnant for the first time. Yet, to
her and Melih's dismay, she had a miscarriage. Therefore, when Nurdan got
pregnant for the second time, she stopped working immediately, because she
was afraid of losing this child, too. In 1991, the first child, Hatice, was born.
Nurdan said: "I told myself: 'You can start working at any time again, but now
the child is the most important thing'." Two more children were born in 1993
and 1995.

During the interview, Nurdan went through her documents. She also found
her translated degree: "Look, it says March 1989. It is a proof that I directly

started to do some research" [of how she could be able to work in her profession in Germany]. Nurdan is still keeping all the documents, letters she wrote or received, and more ready in a folder. By checking the dates, it was possible to see that she always had been going to great lengths to get her education recognized. The only recognizable gap is between 1991 and 1995, when her children were born.

"I Was Missing Home"

Nurdan did not see it coming. Living in a foreign country, having difficulties with learning the language, not being able to stay in contact with the wider family in Turkey, not being able to work in her profession despite having earned a degree and having a miscarriage: together, all of this was hard on Nurdan, and she became very homesick. Nurdan said: "I believe that . . . everything happens for a reason. So, I thought that this is my trial in life". She searched for meaning in her hardships, and found out that her Muslim faith helped her.

"Praying for the Atheist"

It was in 1996 when Nurdan decided to wear a headscarf very spontaneously. As she told the interviewer, she was supposed to meet friends for breakfast one day. She had just said her morning prayer at home, and for this purpose, has covered her head, as required. Nurdan recalls: "Afterwards, I was looking at myself in the mirror and just thought: 'this headscarf suits me very well'." Thus, Nurdan decided not to take the headscarf off. She left the house wearing it, and has worn it ever since.

According to Nurdan, this decision influenced her professional opportunities. After Nurdan had finally received the temporary permit to work as a dental assistant, she applied to many dentists and even offered to work without payment. Nurdan recalls: "You go in there full of hope. But as soon as they see you, their expression reveals that they are despising you". But one dentist was different: he told her that he would let her work under the condition of removing the headscarf. To her, this was a kindness, and she says: "He was the only one who actually listened to me and treated me with respect, not looking down on me. He said: 'I don't belong to any religion, I am an atheist. So, I want to be honest with you. No one will let you work with a headscarf. But if you remove it, I will'." As his offer was contrary to what she believed in, she rejected it, but she still includes him in her prayers.

"My Reward"

Not being able to find work, Nurdan was a housewife for many years, taking care of her three children. She also gave her friends' children extra lessons in mathematics, and, finally, when her youngest child was 14 years old, she did not want to stay at home anymore.

Nurdan says that she has "never considered herself too good for anything". Because she did not find work as a dentist, not even as a dental assistant, she decided to apply for a job as a machine operator in the company where her husband works. She started working there in 2010, and she engaged in learning activities offered by the company (e.g., English language courses). "It is destiny and luck, some are successful without going to university, and others are not, despite of it", Nurdan said when looking back at the past years.

The only thing she regrets is not attending university in University Town. Even if she feels sad about it, she believes that she made the best out of her life. Nurdan finishes the interview with the words: "Although, I could not work in my profession, I am still proud. Proud of raising my children. [They], my children, are my reward".

Fatma's Story

Fatma's story seems to start with a stereotype; namely, a young woman from a village of several hundred inhabitants in rural Turkey who is married off by her grandfather at the age of 16 to one of his relatives, Kemal, who was then living and working in Germany. At first sight, this story fits the label of Turkish 'import-brides' (*Importbräute*), which is a known ethnic image in Germany. It emerged during the 1990s in German media and suggests that men of Turkish descent born and living in Germany 'import' presumably 'traditional brides' from their country of origin. The image is associated with 'forced marriage' (*Zwangsheirat*) which, in public perception, is attached to the idea that these 'import-brides' are subordinated to traditional patriarchic cultures from which they should be 'emancipated'. Still, whilst also fitting to the image, Fatma's story, too, is much more than the story of a woman to be 'freed' by others—rather, it's about she herself worked towards gaining independence and what she calls 'becoming an emancipated woman'.

"Difficult Beginnings"

Fatma was born in rural Turkey in 1975 to a French mother and a Turkish father. Her early childhood and adulthood were by no means as supportive as the surroundings experienced by Nurdan: she never formed a relationship with her biological mother, her biological father died after having been imprisoned for many years and, after having lived with her grandfather until the age of twelve, Fatma was forced to move to her stepmother. There, she was a kind of housemaid, not being accepted as an equal family member, neither by her stepmother nor by her stepbrothers. She recalls that even though she always tried hard to be a part of the family, the only thing she got to hear was "it is not the same as your own daughter". During the interview, Fatma said that she had always felt that she never belonged anywhere and that she did not "taste the feeling of being loved and accepted". It was therefore all the more important to Fatma to create her own "happy family" which, to her mind, is characterized by "esteem, respect and love".

It was also never Fatma's plan to come to Germany. It happened as a consequence of her grandfather choosing Kemal as her future husband. Kemal, then aged 19, was the son of Turkish parents; his father, like Melih's, had come as a guest worker to Germany. Fatma says that her grandfather had no bad intentions: It was all about giving his grandchild to a family he knows and trusts and providing Fatma with a financially secure life. Fatma says: "Well, all he wanted was to see his grandchild happy". She also believes: "Respect is being written with big letters, being against the opinion of my grandfather would have been disrespectful".

After the marriage ceremony in Turkey, Fatma stayed with her parents-in-law in Turkey for two years while Kemal was in Germany. In 1993, at age 18, Fatma came to Germany to live with Kemal in a small village, not far away from where Nurdan could have resumed her studies. In the consecutive three years, Fatma gave birth to three children, and a fourth one was born in 2005.

"Feeling Alone"

In the beginning, Fatma felt very alone in Germany, and German life was not as "perfect and peaceful, without any financial problems" as she had imagined it to be. Because her husband worked full-time, Fatma was the one responsible for the household. However, she did not know any German. Her husband, Kemal, tried to solve this problem by not allowing Turkish television in their home. His idea was that, by being exposed to the language, Fatma would learn it. Yet, to his disappointment, she did not, and Fatma felt even more cut-off—both from "home" (the Turkish language) and from her husband.

Today, Fatma believes that if her husband had practiced with her instead of "throwing sentences at me like: You cannot speak German, you are not able to speak German, you are too dumb to learn German", she might have had more courage at that time. To enroll in a German course, like Nurdan, was unimaginable to Fatma, whose schooling was sketchy at best.

Whenever Fatma left their flat, she felt very uncomfortable and perceived the people as "cold". For about one year, she only left the flat when accompanied by her husband. Not being able to speak German, she feared that people would then make fun of her and thus avoided to be spoken to. As she recalls now, this fear reflected her dependency, which also Kemal seemed to be frustrated with. Still, Fatma made attempts to take up responsibilities such as grocery shopping, despite her fears. She wanted to be accepted "as equal" by her husband. However, as she recalls, she also lacked the courage to reach out and seek social contacts, and she now believes that this was the reason why Kemal was hard on her and pushed her even more.

"Friendly Neighbours"

Things changed when Fatma gave birth to her first child in 1994, at the age of 19. Now, she felt that the baby "was a kind of backing" and a reason to go out and meet other people—mothers, for instance. Nonetheless, Fatma was still "not strong". When, for instance, her neighbour came to pick up her child, after the kids had played together, Fatma did not dare to talk to her, and the only thing she said in German was "hello" and "goodbye".

After a few years in Germany, Fatma and her husband moved to another village. There, she met some "friendly German neighbours". For the first time, Fatma was exposed to German language and culture beyond public interactions. Also, for the first time, she started perceiving language and cultural differences as something other than an "obstacle" causing her difficulties and problems. To the contrary: she actually started to enjoy exchanging thoughts on these differences and to learn. Her landlord, in particular, gave Fatma the support and help she needed. She encouraged Fatma to speak German and corrected her gently and not in what Fatma perceived as Kemal's harsh ways.

"Speaking Up"

Fatma's first experience of taking courage in public was in the town hall. It was the first time that she dared to say, "Could you please speak slowly, and with no dialect, I cannot speak German fluently." When those working there reacted in a very friendly way, took time to tell things again very slowly and after each sentence asked her if she could follow, Fatma was surprised. From this experience onwards she recognized that "people are not that cold", but that they "can be polite and helpful if they know what you want". From then onwards, she started nearly each conversation with unfamiliar people saying, "I cannot speak German very well, please speak slowly and without a dialect, so that I can understand you."

This way, Fatma experienced small successes and improved her German language skills, which made her grow confident and, by that token, more independent. Believing more in herself led Fatma to recognize that she was "not too dumb for Germany or too dumb to live like other emancipated women". As she said during the interview, she "wanted to show to everyone out there who did not believe in me, that I am equal to them, as humans are all equal in front of God".

Because she had promised this to herself, she then kept learning German, got her driver's license and started to work. She made herself meet the requirements of what she calls "being an independent woman". However, the more she became independent, the less she asked her husband for help, for instance, to escort her for grocery shopping or to the city. In his "harsh way", Kemal continued to support her in gaining independence. For instance, when she asked him to escort her, he would answer with a curt: "The keys to the car and the banking card are yours". But, instead of feeling encouraged to just take both and leave the house alone, Fatma felt pushed away. After a while, Fatma felt that she was too exhausted to ask anyway. So, slowly and over the years, the two of them grew apart. Ultimately, the marriage ended in divorce.

This influenced Fatma's life very much, in particular financially. She was by now solely responsible for her four daughters, and, without any formal education, had to resort to low-paid unskilled work. She also did not receive any financial support from her husband and encountered hard times financially. The only thing she had were her children, and she was "ready to sacrifice herself in order to see them happy". Also, she now felt that she had found inner peace: "Even if we did not have as much money as before, we were happy."

So, was it worth it? Fatma says that she does not regret anything. She believes that everything happens for a reason. But she also believes that if she had had the experience and knowledge of today, she would have had more courage, realizing that she had nothing to lose. She ended the interview with the words that "every change starts by changing yourself".

Power and CCM

Lived ethnicity emerges from the intersections of multiple influencing factors. For instance, when Nurdan's degree is not recognized in Germany—as it would have been in Turkey—she cannot uphold her professional identity as a dentist. She still tries to maintain it, but, at a certain point and, maybe, also as an act of protest, she seems to choose alternative identifications (e.g., family, religion) over it. When not accepting her only employment offer as a dental assistant under the condition of removing her headscarf, she also rises above the categorical thinking of those who are not able to see behind this symbol and their assumptions of what it might mean. On the other hand, one could also argue that Nurdan's own ideas of 'religiosity' do not allow for changing her ways. Yet, it could also be questioned whether this should be demanded from her.

Whereas ethnic images are static, lived ethnicity allows for change, as shown in particular by Fatma's story. She discards virtually all previously held assumptions about life and shapes herself outside the ethnic image, as a professional woman and a single mother of four. This way, she shapes herself to the image of the 'emancipated Western woman' and also defines herself in these terms. Thus, the German majority might wholeheartedly applaud her for having 'freed' herself of the restrictions of what the ethnic image assumes 'the Turkish woman' to be. Yet, this neglects the perspective of Fatma's husband, Turkish-German

Kemal, who was 'hard on her' in order to achieve just that—to make Fatma become more independent, which to her, a recent immigrant from rural Turkey with not much of an educational background, was unfathomable at that time.

Moreover, we need to investigate the hierarchies involved: The ethnic image that is projected upon Nurdan and Fatma constructs them as inferior, backwards and traditional. This is not the case for the 'ethnic image' which Nurdan and Fatma held in mind about 'Germans'. For instance, Fatma expected them to be 'cold', but this ethnic image contributed to her own sense of inferiority and affirmed 'German ethnicity' as superior. This suggests that certain ethnic images lead us to undervalue some individuals more than others and to question, for instance, their modernity more—as it is the case with the ethnic image of 'the Turkish woman' in Germany.

Ethnic images, in particular those that construct 'inferiority', unify and cancel out the particularities of lived ethnicity, and this is their power effect for CCM. This process is totalitarian, because it subsumes all differences: it neglects change and variation, it only considers individuals in relation to the ethnic image. For instance, Nurdan and Fatma each had an arranged marriage which they did not question. The ethnic image takes this as 'proof' of their passive adoption of traditional forms of society, which are seen as inferior to German modernity. However, this arranged marriage *meant* different things to each of them, and, to both, its *lived* meaning is different from what the ethnic image ascribes.

In CCM, it has been suggested that key intercultural competencies such as the ability to access multiple cultural schemas, to empathize with others or to switch between different cultural codes can be more easily developed from a bicultural life experience, if this experience is reflected upon by bicultural individuals themselves and others (Brannen and Thomas, 2010). Also, the requirements of successful international assignments might be similar to the challenges faced by bicultural individuals throughout their lives (Lee, 2014). These assumptions have been extended to ethnic minorities to whom inferior status is assigned, so-called "marginals" (Fitzsimmons et al., 2012). If we link this insight to Nurdan's and Fatma's life stories, we can start to understand how their lived ethnicity involves intercultural competencies which are not acknowledged by the ethnic image. This way, also a presumably 'marginal' ethnic minority life experience might be an asset yet unrecognized by CCM (Mahadevan, 2017: 94–100). Yet, CCM can only uncover the resources of presumed marginality if it moves beyond the etic ethnic image and approaches lived ethnicity from the inside.

Reflexive Considerations

All three authors of this text are female German citizens. The second and third author are Germans of Turkish descent and have experienced the ethnic image of 'the Turkish woman'. They are also aspiring and highly educated in the area of management and engineering, which is profitable and much sought after in terms of money and career. This way, they have resources beyond the ethnic image, and the further they proceed in this way, the less the ethnic image will fit their lived ethnicity. This bears the possibility that the ethnic image might change.

However, there are also paradoxical combinations and dominant expectations: for instance, the second author's sister has chosen to wear a headscarf, whereas the second author has not, and this seems to be puzzling for some members of the Turkish community, as well as for ethnic Germans. As the second author recalls, her sister's belonging in Germany is questioned more often than her own (that is, the second author's). To the second author, this shows how close the 'ethnic image' is and how one small decision, such as wearing a headscarf, might result in a stronger ethnic image being projected upon a person.

The first author has no other link to Turkish ethnicity besides being a citizen of Germany, a country wherein Turkish immigrants and their descendants constitute the largest ethnic minority group. Ethnicity in general is of interest to her, potentially, because her own ethnicity is mixed. In her own life, she has experienced an ability to evoke, change or avoid ethnic images, for instance, by making a more or less 'ethnic' choice of hairstyle, dress or accessories, and she has pursued this as a research methodology.

Recommendations to Students, Researchers and Practitioners

Ethnic images unify and cancel out the particularities of lived ethnicity. We thus need to be aware of such stereotypical generalizations and their power effects in CCM interactions involving ethnic minority and majority members. This requirement applies to both ethnic minority and majority members: both groups need to challenge their assumptions of what ethnicity (their own and those of others) 'means' to them and how they have learned to 'see' ethnicity. They should pay special attention to the symbolic markers of ethnicity which seem self-evident to them and to which they ascribe deep and significant meaning (e.g., wearing a headscarf). Also, they should keep in mind that a person is never just 'ethnic': there are always alternative identifications and possibilities (e.g., professional identity) which might be shared across a presumed ethnic divide and which might be different for members of the same ethnicity. If we understand this, we can figure out how we are not only different or similar but actually related in multiple intersecting ways. We can then investigate alternative possibilities, for instance, how Nurdan is a 'city woman' and a 'dentist' and not only a 'religious person'. We can also allow for more complex ethnic images and lived ethnicities to emerge, for instance, a 'Turkish' family wherein one daughter wears a headscarf and the other does not.

We should also keep in mind that both ethnic images and lived ethnicity are dynamic and context-specific. In another societal context, Nurdan's wearing a headscarf would have been interpreted differently, and she herself might have made another choice. In another time, the headscarf meant different things in 'the West'. For instance, the great film-divas of another era routinely accessorized their outfit with an elegant headscarf not dissimilar to a style which is now understood as 'modern Muslim'. Also, the headscarf was banned in public institutions in Turkey when Nurdan attended university in Ankara, and it is in light of this context that wearing it can mean a 'free choice' to her in Germany.

When changing cultural contexts, we should thus bear in mind that lived ethnicity and ethnic image might change as well and pay attention to these processes. We should also investigate our own assumptions in light of the time and the context from which they emerged. This way, we can move beyond the limitations of our own ideas about ethnicity.

Notes

1. The mainly male Turkish guest workers (*Gastarbeiter*) were recruited to work in Germany between 1961 and 1973, due to a shortage in low-skilled production workers. It was assumed that they would leave again, but in reality, family often followed, and their descendants remained in Germany.
2. Remark: the standard German language courses do not consider the participants' prior level of education, e.g., whether they have studied any other foreign language previously, or their literacy.

References

Barth F (1998 [1969]) *Ethnic Groups and Boundaries: The Social Organization of Culture Difference*. Long Grove: Waveland Press.

Brannen MY and Thomas D (2010) Bicultural individuals in organizations: Implications and opportunity. *International Journal of Cross-Cultural Management* 10(1): 5–16.

Eriksen TH (2010) *Ethnicity and Nationality* (1st ed). London: Pluto Press,.

Fitzsimmons SR, Lee YT and Brannen MY (2012) Marginals as global leaders: Why they might just excel! *European Business Review* November–December 2012, 7–10.

Lee HJ (2014) Identities in the global world of work. In: Gehrke B and Claes MT (eds) *Global Leadership Practices: A Cross-Cultural Management Perspective*. London: Palgrave MacMillan, pp. 85–101.

Mahadevan J (2017) *A Very Short, Fairly Interesting and Reasonably Cheap Book about Cross-Cultural Management*. London: SAGE.

Mahadevan J and Kilian-Yasin K (2016) Dominant discourse, orientalism and the need for reflexive HRM: Skilled Muslim migrants in the German context. *International Journal of Human Resource Management*: 1–23. DOI: 10.1080/09585192.2016.1166786.

Rahman M (2017) Islamophobia, the impossible Muslim, and the reflexive potential of intersectionality. In: Mahadevan J and Mayer C-H (eds) *Muslim Minorities, Workplace Diversity and Reflexive HRM*. London: Taylor and Francis, pp. 35–45.

10

FAMILIAR STRANGERS

Two 'Turkish' Employees in a Danish SME

Heidrun Knorr

Introduction

This chapter focuses on how 'naturalization' renders two male ethnic-minority Turkish employees working at a Danish small- and medium-sized enterprise (SME), referred to here as ESAG, 'familiar strangers'. In simple terms, Bourdieu (1977, 1991) conceptualizes naturalization as a process of identification in which powerful actors identify individuals as belonging to a more general group, for example a given ethnic group. In so doing, the powerful actors silence these individuals' 'individualities' and substitute them with a group identity. Hence, naturalization ascribes a more or less homogeneous identity to *all* group members and thus it is assumed that *all* group members show identical traits and behaviours. Consequently, not only group identity is naturalized but also its members' range of legitimate actions. The process of naturalization thus leads to simplified and stereotypical understandings of, in this case, 'Turkishness' and 'Danishness', including their interaction structures, legitimate practices and status of power.

The reduction of individual actors' unique identities into a common group identity can be understood in terms of Simmel's concept of the 'familiar stranger' (Simmel, 1950). In brief, Simmel (1950) understands the 'familiar stranger' as a social actor moving from one sociocultural context into another. Therefore, the 'strangers' are always outside some aspects of that society, but also become part of it in other aspects; hence, they are close and far simultaneously. "The stranger is close to us, insofar as we feel between him [sic] and ourselves common features of a national, social, occupational, or generally human, nature. He [sic] is far from us, insofar as these common features extend beyond him or us, and connect us only because they connect a great many people" (Simmel, 1950: 406). Thus, despite being in the same space with 'the stranger', 'familiarity' is not "based on the commonness of specific differences [typical for] the relation to more organically connected persons" (Simmel, 1950: 405). Rather, 'familiarity' is based on all-encompassing identities such as working at the same company or simply being a human.

In this case, naturalization is the critical mechanism by which minority individuals are rendered 'familiar strangers' and denied inclusion into the majority group. As a result, ethnic Turks struggle with moving up the corporate ladder and their competencies remain unseen and undervalued, which can lead them to withdraw from the company. For an intersectional CCM, this is relevant, because companies are primarily based on the logic of merit-based promotions. However, if false pictures about certain groups of people hinder those in power to see their potential, corporate talent is lost.

To make this conclusion, I focus on how one German and one Danish citizen, both of Turkish descent, experience practices of withdrawal in a Danish SME. As a result, this chapter highlights how organizational practices 'naturalize' ethnic difference and national culture (in this case the perceived 'Turkish' culture and its expected behaviours, that is, "how Turks *are*"). Thus, this chapter shows how the process of 'naturalization' renders ethnic identities *and* their expected behaviours as 'fixed' and 'natural' (in this case expected 'Turkish' traits and behaviours, such as "being overly family-minded", "being less educated than 'Danes'", and "being less efficient"). I show how naturalization of ethnic identity includes the naturalization of expected behaviours, that is, behaviours that are perceived as being "unchangeable and stable"; consequently, differences become 'fixed'. The withdrawal of two employees with Turkish backgrounds becomes a process based on a variety of perceived, intersecting differences of which ethnicity is only one.

Methodology

This chapter is based on a longitudinal qualitative case study of a Danish SME, ESAG. This company employs about 150 people at its Danish headquarters (almost all of them of ethnic Danish origin) and about 50 people at its four sales subsidiaries in Europe. ESAG works within the so-called ethnic food sector, with its main focus being on Turkish inspired food products. ESAG's main customer groups are ethnic-minority Turks living in the European Union; the company's sales department catering to this customer group is named 'Ethnic Sales', and, except for its headquarters (HQ) division, all sales subsidiaries dealing with 'Ethnic Sales' are staffed by ethnic-minority Turkish employees. Within 'Ethnic Sales', the German, Austrian and Dutch markets are the most economically important ones, as several million ethnic-minority Turks live in these countries. In this chapter, I draw on observations, interviews and informal conversations with two male ethnic-minority Turkish employees and their ethnic-majority Danish superiors conducted over a period of two and a half years. One of the employees, who I call Yusuf, was employed at a sales subsidiary in Germany, and the other, who I call Ahmet, worked as a trainee at ESAG's headquarters in Denmark. The interviews with Yusuf were conducted in German, which is my native language, while those with Ahmet were conducted in Danish, which I speak fluently. In addition, I wrote numerous pages of field notes, some of which are in Danish, others in German or English. The interviews ranged from exploratory and open-ended to semistructured, with a special focus on intercultural collaboration practices. The interviews took place in the workplace; they were transcribed verbatim and interpreted in a reflexive manner (Alvesson and Sköldberg, 2009).

Case Presentation

This chapter presents how the process of naturalization constructs two ethnic-minority Turkish men as 'familiar strangers' in the sense that their ethnicity is perceived as 'fixed' and 'natural' by the majority of their ethnic-Danish managers. However, the stories told by these two men reveal that their experiences at ESAG are influenced by more sociocultural categories than the Danish mangers' construction of their ethnicity as 'Turkish males' might suggest. All names, including the name of the company, have been altered.

The Story of Yusuf: So Far and No Further

Yusuf is a man of Turkish descent. He holds dual Turkish–German citizenship and lives in Germany. He speaks German with a mixture of a slight Turkish accent and a distinct accent from the region of Germany where he grew up. With his dark hair, dark eyes, a height of almost 1.90 meters and tendency to use a lot of body language while speaking in a rather loud voice, he seems to fit into the stereotypical category of the Turkish male who dominates interactions. But Yusuf understands his identity to be fluid in terms of ethnic belonging, and perhaps the most important parts of his identity are his bachelor's degree in economics from a German university and his successful role as key account manager at one of ESAG's fastest growing sales subsidiaries in Germany. Yusuf was responsible for generating new sales and developing and maintaining productive long-term relationships with smaller supermarkets, supermarket chains and wholesales throughout the southwestern regions of Germany. Even though Yusuf had been working with ESAG for several years, HQ personnel and especially his superiors at HQ hardly knew him; in fact, he had never been to HQ and had never met the head of 'Ethnic Sales'.

"If It Doesn't Work, It Doesn't Work"

Yusuf was born in former West Germany in 1975, where he also grew up, attended school, and went to university. His parents came to Germany as so-called guest workers. Both of his parents worked, but both became unemployed right after Yusuf received his bachelor's degree in economics. This meant a major change to his future: "I had to assist my parents. I had the bachelor's degree, but then I couldn't continue. And this you can only grasp when you're part of this situation", Yusuf said.

Leaving his studies, he continued in various student jobs until he was finally offered a full-time position. "There I worked full-time while also taking some hours on the side at the companies I worked for when I was a student. And then eventually I ended up at ESAG", Yusuf told me.

"Building Personal Relationships is Very Important"

When Yusuf started at ESAG, he worked primarily in what he calls "CRM, customer relations management" of small supermarkets. However, over time, he succeeded in building up his own key accounts. In order to do so, Yusuf had to establish and maintain personal relationships with each supermarket owner, because, even though they sometimes went bankrupt, they often survived and established a new business. "And therefore it is very important to maintain personal relationships because we will meet each other again. In the ethnic food market it's extremely important to build personal relationships in order to secure the future", Yusuf pointed out. During the interview, Yusuf mentioned several times that he understands himself as a very loyal, hardworking, and engaged regional sales manager who often goes to great lengths to enhance his customers' and ESAG's profits. Yusuf gave the following example: "I fight to get the best out of our products. Even products that are very close to their best-before date or even have reached that date, even there I try to make some money out of that." Thus, Yusuf developed a strong position within ESAG's sales subsidiary in Germany by drawing on his prior education, working long hours and building and maintaining personal relationships with ESAG's customers.

"Taking on a Key Position as Bridge Builder"

When I asked sales managers at HQ why ESAG's entire sales personnel at the subsidiary level was of Turkish descent, they explained that this was for strategic reasons: Since ESAG's customers are primarily of Turkish descent, they argued, only sales personnel who understand Turkish norms, values, and rites and the Turkish language could reap the highest profits and enhance ESAG's share of the ethnic food market in Europe. In addition, HQ managers expect their sales personnel to share knowledge gained in the ethnic food market with HQ. Yusuf makes sense of his key position in the following way: "Our cultural background is important for the company's success. Our target group is mainly Turkish. I am Turkish and I can handle them. A Dane is less suited or not at all. We always position Turks between HQ and consumers. In that sense we take on key positions".

However, even though Yusuf seems to hold a key position as a bridge builder between HQ and ESAG's consumers, his experiences, knowledge and competencies seem not to have been recognized, shared or implemented by HQ personnel. And although Yusuf and I were told that ESAG's ethnic minority sales personnel are very important to ESAG for enhancing sales and providing insight into effective marketing strategies, in reality, personnel and mangers at HQ do not listen to the sales personnel's experiences, knowledge and ideas. On the contrary, HQ mangers seem not to consult them at all, but rather manage to them in a top-down fashion. In addition, almost all HQ managers seemed to devalue non-Danish education; for instance, this was conveyed when a Danish sales expert from a well-known Danish business school was hired to provide a sales course for ESAG's ethnic-minority Turkish employees. The sales course took place in Germany, was taught in broken German, lasted for three days and addressed rather simple sales theories. This course totally underestimated the educational backgrounds and knowledge of ESAG's sales personnel. Just a few hours into the course, several of them, including Yusuf and especially Ahmed, made clear that they already knew about the concepts 'taught' by the course facilitator. Additionally, they vehemently pointed out that most of the approaches mentioned by the Danish expert would not work within the context of ethnic food sales. During the first break, I spoke with the course facilitator about his impression so far. He said: "Obviously, ESAG misinformed me about the sales knowledge gathered here".

"We Are the Stepping Stones for Their Careers"

Throughout his employment at ESAG, Yusuf worked hard and used his educational, cultural, and social competencies to build long-lasting and successful relationships with ESAG's customers. He hoped to be considered for promotion and perhaps become a subsidiary leader. Yet, his hopes dwindled over the years and he felt stuck: "We will never move on; we sales people will always stay sales people and that's it". When asked to elaborate on why he had developed this impression of being stuck, he mentioned that no one had ever been interested in his suggestions as to how ESAG could improve its sales; even when he started mailing them to his superiors, they would not respond. When speaking about his superiors, he mentioned that they had changed often over the past six years. While telling me this, he suddenly arrived at the following quite powerful explanation for why he felt stuck and how HQ was taking advantage of him: "It seems to be . . . yes, they make their career, . . . they make their path on top of us. We are the step-stones; they step on us, move one step further, step on us, move one step further. And my suggestions are not heard or are heard and then presented as their own. It is as if my work isn't honoured".

Sometime after my interview with Yusuf, his erstwhile superior, Mikkel, told me that Yusuf had left the company and had found himself another job in sales. This was considered to be a loss, but Mikkel remarked: "When Yusuf asked for promotion, there was nothing we could offer him".

The Story of Ahmet: ESAG's First Ethnic and Religious Minority Employee at Headquarters

Ahmet was the first trainee at HQ with an ethnic-minority background at the company. He was born and raised in Denmark, is a practicing Muslim, holds dual citizenship, speaks Danish without any Turkish accent and, according to him, speaks Turkish with a slight Danish accent. Ahmet has dark hair and brown eyes. He is rather short, about 1.70 meters in height, and he often speaks in a low voice. He studied business at a business school close to his parents' home and received an A on his final thesis, in which he used ESAG as a case company. At first glance, Ahmet's story does not seem to be very different from those of Danish business school graduates. In March 2014, shortly after his graduation, he started his traineeship at ESAG HQs. However, even though Ahmet's story seems to be one of a typical Danish youth, he did not identify himself as a Dane; rather, he positioned himself in a variety of intersecting identities, all of which expressed his wish to stay close to his Turkish roots.

"They've all Been Very Nice to Me"

Ahmet described the first days and weeks of his traineeship as 'fantastic'. He felt very welcome and, since asked about it during lunch breaks, he was eager to talk about Islam. He got the impression that he had managed to settle down and work effectively much earlier than expected of a trainee. Ahmet felt accepted and experienced a "desire and enthusiasm" for his position.

This desire and enthusiasm made the future look bright. He could easily see himself working as a 'bridge builder' who would facilitate ESAG's various business connections. But he also could envision himself in a top-management position at ESAG headquarters. Thus, Ahmet clearly felt that he had the skills, knowledge and competencies to make it all the way to the top. The only thing he needed to get there was to be a successful trainee and learn the rules of the game.

"He's Been Assimilated, What a Pity"

Although ESAG's managers, Ahmet's coworkers and Ahmet himself considered it a huge advantage to have a bicultural background, living between identities also proved to be challenging, especially when others would prefer that one fit into a fixed identity. Ahmet himself felt torn between identities: he loved Denmark; however, he could not identify as a Dane. Rather, he tried to uphold his

Turkish roots, which he considered to be an essential part of him as they made him different and special and thus would enable him to take on special tasks such as being the bridge-builder he envisioned becoming.

But Ahmet felt that Danish society would prefer all foreigners to be assimilated, an idea which he strongly disliked: "I do know many [ethnic-minority Turks] who no longer speak Turkish or only some Turkish, and here you can say, 'Look there, he's been assimilated, what a pity, how aggravating'. . . . I do also often get this: 'If we hadn't heard your name, we would have taken you for a Dane'. [But] I don't want to be considered to be Danish". Ahmet made clear that he would never be 'assimilated', even though at times it hurt to be different. Thus, Ahmet felt that he had to hold onto his Turkish roots while at the same time learning to play the game of business and life in the Danish context. It was therefore rather important for him to practice his Turkish language and rites which, in his view, included the practicing of Islam.

"Something Inside Me Shattered"

Ahmet's appreciative use of Turkish language, rites and Islamic practices marked the beginning of his struggles at ESAG headquarters, however; only three months into his traineeship, Ahmet's superior, Malene, started to challenge his work attitude. During the second evaluation meeting, Malene said the following to Dan, the company's head of human resources: "Ahmet is an asset to us. However, you are still quite slow in handling your tasks, Ahmet. Another issue is that we of course wanted you to introduce yourself to our Turkish employees in Turkish. But now it happens far too often that you speak Turkish on the phone". To this, Ahmet answered: "Well, I will get faster in the future, I am confident about that. In regard to my phone calls in Turkish; you know I will soon get married, and therefore, I sometimes call my bride to be, and then I do of course speak Turkish". Malene continued: "Yes, and that's another issue. You really speak with her often, and I rather would like you to keep private and business-related aspects apart". Dan supported Malene's concerns: "There is a kind of balance you have to find, Ahmet. You have to find the balance between speaking Turkish, Danish and German. And the same goes for mixing private and business-related issues".

Because Ahmet had experienced his first three months quite differently than they were portrayed by Malene, he was surprised and felt utterly misunderstood. "I don't get this. During work, Malene told me that I am doing a good job and then she comes up with a lot of negative things. . . . And I thought it's a big advantage to speak Turkish and now it's suddenly a problem. I don't understand these stereotypes and fear about Muslims". When I asked him, how this made him feel, Ahmet answered: "From that moment, things changed. Something inside me shattered".

"There are Invisible Barriers"

Ahmet's struggles with Malene influenced his relationship with his Danish colleagues at HQ. He felt alienated and misunderstood; in his view, Danes would focus too much on efficiency and too little on building relations: "Working together with Turks is very different from working here. We are good at building relations, becoming a family. . . . You build relations easily and this continues after working hours. But here in Denmark, colleagues don't see each other after work", he explained.

He continued his traineeship at ESAG's sales subsidiaries in Germany and Austria, where he felt "much more at home" because he had the chance of working together with fellow ethnic-minority Turks. Upon his return to HQ, he continued his traineeship in the department for South Asian sales. When I asked him, if he thinks that, one day, he would become a member of the so-called 'ESAG family', he remarked cautiously and with some hesitation: "I doubt it. There are some invisible barriers, invisible obstacles. And even if you ask me what it is, I don't know".

When I heard from him again, he had left ESAG.

Power and CCM

Based on the case description, one could argue that Ahmet and Yusuf choose to leave ESAG because they were unable to adjust to ESAG HQs' work culture. Yet, in taking a critical approach to CCM, the underlying rationales and power issues leading to Ahmet and Yusuf's decisions become far more apparent. In this very case, relevant questions to ask and answer could be *why and how* certain actors are more successful in defending or even strengthening their current positions of power and thus, are able to restrict the actions of others.

On the one hand, ESAG's organizational structure explains ESAG's distribution of power. As is the case with many international organizations, ESAG is divided into headquarters and subsidiaries; HQ exercises power over the subsidiaries, as decisions are made at HQ level and then implemented at subsidiary level. This power relationship can be considered 'typical' for any HQ–subsidiary relationship. In the case of ESAG, however, the differences in power coincide with differences in ethnicity. At ESAG, power is primarily exercised by ethnic-majority Danes holding powerful positions at headquarters, while ethnic-minority Turks at the subsidiary level have the freedom to react to this power. In addition, interactions between HQ and subsidiary personnel were very restricted. For instance, no common intranet existed and only few managers had regular face-to-face or telephone contacts with the subsidiaries. The result of this rather restricted HQ–subsidiary relationship was that HQ personnel perceived ESAG's subsidiary personnel to be a rather 'faceless' and 'nameless' group of employees, and vice versa. Thus, in this case, being employed by the same company turned out to be the only feature Yusuf and Ahmet had in common with ESAG's entire workforce; they did not share particular qualities with ESAG's HQ personnel and therefore were perceived as far more different and distant from HQs than, for example, Mikkel, one of the ethnic-Danish subsidiary leaders.

On the other hand, more subtle practices and processes can explain how those in relatively higher-power positions (top and line managers at ESAG HQ) created and sustained ESAG's configuration of power in such a way that Ahmet and Yusuf decided to leave ESAG. In order to make sense of Ahmet and Yusuf's withdrawal from ESAG, I suggest employing the concepts of 'naturalization' and 'familiar stranger' as they address issues of power as an inherent part of any social interaction.

In this case, one way of defending ones positions of power happened through keeping others on distance which at ESAG simply occurred due to the (unconscious) restricted interactions between HQs and subsidiaries, addressed earlier. Consequently, most HQ personnel, including management, had never met with their ethnic-Turkish coworkers. Instead, they had however heard many stories on "how Turks are" and "how Turks work". These stories were told by those few managers, who had frequent telephone or personal contact with ESAG's sales subsidiaries. In general, this ethnic identification portrayed ESAG's ethnic-minority Turkish workforce as "very different, exotic, and family-minded, less educated, impulsive and less efficient"; hence, very different from how ESAG's ethnic-majority Danish workforce talked about themselves. The ethnic-Danish majority at headquarters constructed thus a rather negative stereotypical understanding of Turkish ethnicity, which was projected on *all* employees of Turkish descent, including Yusuf and Ahmet. The ethnic-Danish majority had the power to ascribe differences in educational and work identity as a 'natural part' of *all* employees of Turkish ethnicity. In so doing, particular and individual features of these employees' identities are silenced and the only identity ascribed to these employees is that of a common group belonging, namely, that of 'being a Turkish employee'. Hence, Yusuf is perceived as 'working at ESAG and being of Turkish origin'; thus, the only feature he has in common with ESAG HQ personnel is his employment at ESAG. This is a rather all-encompassing feature of commonness which renders Yusuf as 'familiar stranger', who, even though he is present in a certain group, is distant, because he is not perceived as an individual with whom other group members could have particular features of identity in common (Simmel, 1950). In addition, the way in which he conducted his job is acontextualised and, even though his approach to sales seemingly fitted the context best, the powerful identify these practices as illegitimate and unsuitable.

Ahmet finished his master's degree in business studies in Denmark, and was the first Muslim and ethnic-Turkish trainee at ESAG HQ. He started his work experience from a far more privileged position than Yusuf: he had a higher relevant education and, most importantly perhaps, his education was taken in the Danish context. Therefore, it could be the Danish managers had no or less difficulty in comparing his grades with those of ESAG's other personnel at HQs. In addition, Ahmet was fluent in Danish, English, German and Turkish and, from the outside, he was often identified as a Dane; he did not appear to be that different from them, except for his name and his religious beliefs which he practiced and spoke about openly.

Thus, Ahmet seemed to have had all prerequisites for pursuing his career at ESAG. Ahmet did, however, behave in ways which did not fit ESAG's work culture: he not only dedicated most of his lunch time to explaining what it means to be a Muslim, he also continually used his work time for private issues, on the grounds of which he was identified as a 'Turk', and thus, no longer as a fellow ethnic-Danish colleague. Once he was labelled in an ethnic way, all other identity markers he portrayed, such as being a thorough learner and being proud of his education, were silenced by the ethnic-Danish majority. Instead, as was the case with Yusuf, Ahmet's identity and his particular behaviours were conceptualized as being a 'natural and fixed' part of Turkish culture and thus different and distant from Danish culture. In the case of Ahmet, it seems fair to assume, though, that he never wanted to be identified as a Dane as he had constructed a more negative than positive stereotypical understanding of 'Danishness'. Nevertheless, Ahmet aimed to become an accepted and powerful employee at ESAG HQs.

In sum, both stories exemplify how naturalization functions as a mechanism of power that puts people into fixed identity categories, that is, categories defined by the powerful (Bourdieu, 1977). In so doing, the perceived distance in culture and power between majority-ethnic Danes and minority-ethnic Turks is legitimatized and maintained. Furthermore, a certain range of expected and legitimized actions (Bourdieu, 1991) is ascribed to the members of each group (the way Turks *behave*); thus, the powerful actors tacitly construct an order of hierarchy and power into which each sociocultural group is placed. Consequently, members of certain groups remain a kind of 'familiar stranger', labelled according to their 'fixed' ethnic identity and possessing no individual characteristics. They are present at ESAG, but they are not identified as individuals with particular identities; they are supposed to visit but are also expected to leave again (Simmel, 1950). This means Ahmet and Yusuf are understood to be visitors who should not expect to get offered positions of power and influence within that group, they happen to 'visit' (ibid.). Yet there also is some acknowledgement from the 'Danish' side that its own perspective is limited; thus, Ahmet and Yusuf's withdrawal not only has negative effects for the Turkish side but also for the company and the majority.

Reflexive Considerations

The author of this chapter is a female German, who experienced stereotyping when she relocated to Denmark and thus became part of the German ethnic minority group in Denmark. In comparison to, for example, the Turkish ethnic minority in Denmark, however, the author's appearance resembles those of ethnic Danes. Thus, she is not easily identified as 'different' from the ethnic majority. In addition, in comparison to Yusuf and Ahmet, she has an even higher level of education.

Nevertheless, before she got her current university position, she was often labelled as 'familiar stranger'. For example, despite friends assisting her, she had a hard time finding employment in the Danish job market. And when she was invited to job interviews, she had to face stereotypical understandings of 'being German'.

These experiences have influenced her as a person and researcher. During her field work for this case study, she often found herself taking sides with the ethnic-minority Turkish employees; after all, she shared their experiences of 'struggling for respect and belonging' and being labelled as 'different', which was based simply on her nationality.

Recommendations to Students, Researchers and Practitioners

This case suggests that no interactions are free of power struggles. In addition, power and the struggles over power are not only part of social interactions but *simultaneously* of the structures created by these very interactions. Therefore, we should consider any structure, be it groups, departments, cultures or entire organizations, as socially constructed sources for power *and* as spaces in and across which social actors struggle for enhancing their power positions. In order to analyse and make sense of cross-cultural practices, we thus ought to analyse interactions as a place of 'power struggle' in which practices of (cultural) identification unfold between certain actors and contexts. The following questions may assist in discovering existing power struggles in organizational contexts:

- In which ways and how do organizational members identify themselves and others in relation to sociocultural categories?
- Which positions are available and which ones are taken by whom in a certain organizational context?
- How are these positions ranked in terms of power?
- How is power used by those occupying the given positions?
- How are the different positions of power and the way power is exercised related to sociocultural identification processes?

Seeing that this case suggests power to be part of any interaction, research as well is part of a power game. Therefore, as mentioned and practiced in this chapter, any research—and perhaps especially research addressing struggles of identity—ought to include the researchers' reflections on the assumptions, role and influence they have had on their research (Alvesson and Sköldberg, 2009).

References

Alvesson M and Sköldberg K (2009) *Reflexive Methodology: New Vistas for Qualitative Research*. London: SAGE.

Bourdieu P (1991) *Language and Symbolic Power*. Cambridge: Polity Press.

Bourdieu P (1977) *Outline of a Theory of Practice*. Cambridge: Cambridge University Press.

Simmel G (1950) The stranger. In: Wolff KH (ed) *The Sociology of Georg Simmel*. Glencoe, IL: The Free Press, pp. 402–408.

11

THE ETHNICIZATION OF IDENTITY

Chidozie Umeh

Introduction

In this chapter, I take the reader on a journey through the ethnocultural experiences narrated by two employees (the subjects) in a formal (Western-styled) organization in a culturally diverse and developing country—Nigeria. I resist the lure to present my subjects' accounts through an arguably convenient and simplistic view of ethnic identity as merely culture-oriented and value-driven as in mainstream cross-cultural management (CCM) literature (Hofstede, 1980; House et al., 2004; Trompenaars & Hampden-Turner, 2004; Schwartz, 2006). Such views (mis)represent ethnic identity as essentially linear, bounded and predictable. Rather, the subjects' experiences evidence more critical perspectives, which show how cultural identity is fluid, transient, contingent, and negotiated (Primecz et al., 2011; Mahadevan, 2017), culturally constructed (Mahadevan, 2001; Eriksen, 2002) and intersecting (Holvino, 2012).

But there is more to uncover based on the subjects' narratives. Here, three key terms come into play. First, I use the construct 'ethnicized identity,' which I have coined retrospectively and reflexively, to show how identity can be *mutiplexic* and *multisecting*. Second, I use the term '*multiplexic*' to denote multiple identities which underlie individual contextual identity adoption, and the term '*multisecting*' to indicate subject identity assertion, based on intersecting individual, ethnic, organizational, negotiated, hybridized and other identities.

Identity here as *multiplexic* and *multisecting* is not merely who one is in relation to others—Hall's (1990) idea of ascription and self-referencing—but also "who one is not" (Weedon, 2004: 19). The subjects' (ethnic) identity is *who we want to be seen as, even if we do not see ourself as such, in relation to who we see ourself as, which we do not want others to see*. In Nigeria, the subjects suggest, ethnicized identity is an outcome of *negotiation* (Mahadevan, 2017: 88) and *assertion*; the contextual legitimation of individual action and inaction through the endorse-ment of (in)significant others. Here, the power of individuals' claims to be lies in the in(accurate) perceptual endorsement of others.

This chapter is part of a wider study of two Nigerian banks, Bank Alpha and Bank Beta (I have anonymized original names for confidentiality), and 20 employees whose responses were collected through a qualitative research methodology using interviews over three months. The insights from the narra-tives of two employees—Ugo, a bank officer, and Ola, a manager (not their real names)—illustrate the shifting ethnocultural landscape in multiethnic Nige-ria and indicate specific areas of research which are theoretically fundamental but remain largely unexplored in mainstream CCM. These include, but are not limited to, evolving dynamics of group affiliation in ethnically diverse contexts, the shifting basis for determining ethnic identity in organizations in these settings and the diversity management implications thereof, as well as the instrumentality of ethnocultural symbols and meanings in uncoupling, not just intersecting, but also *multiplexic* and *multisecting* identities. Although some stud-ies, admittedly, broadly examine cultural influences on identity in the Global South (Jackson, 2013, 2017), scholars do so on a level of analysis entirely dis-tinct from the contextual drivers of ethnicity as experienced by ethnic affiliates in organizations in culturally diverse countries like Nigeria.

Methodology

There are two main approaches to understanding identity. One perspective treats identity as objective: here, ethnic identities are seen as socially and geo-graphically determined (Hofstede, 1980; Barth, 1994; House et al., 2004). The other perspective, however, treats identity as subjective. Here, emphasis is placed on individual creation of symbols regarded as fundamental in main-taining ethnic identity (Cohen, 2013). Both approaches have advantages and shortcomings. For instance, the objective view, although it is associated with self-identification of affiliates with the group, it is accused of introducing rigid cultural boundaries and essentializing culture. The study of culture then is reduced to cultural perceptions rather than culture itself (Bader, 2001). For now, though, I focus on the subjective approach and the social world of my subjects. Consequently, I accept that the boundaries between individual, orga-nizational, institutional and social milieus remain fluid and sometimes indis-tinguishable because identity is constantly constructed and reconstructed by individuals based on symbols and meanings generated through language and culture, as we shall see in the subjects' narratives.

Case Presentation

In this section, I first describe the wider sociohistorical context of the inter-viewees' experiences. This involves overviews on ethnic groups in Nigeria and indigenous Nigerian banks. I then focus on Ugo and Ola, and their experiences as ethnicized identities.

The European scramble, partition of and ultimate conquest of Africa was driven by capitalist industrialization. Between 1870 and 1900, Africa faced European imperialist hostility, military incursions and offensives, and eventually colonization (Cairns and Sliwa, 2008), driven by a pressing need at the domestic front for assured and cheaper sources of raw materials, guaranteed markets and profitability. By the early twentieth century, much of Africa had been colonized by European powers such as Britain, France, Germany, Belgium, Italy, Portugal, and Spain. Although Ethiopia and Liberia are said to be the only African countries never to have been colonized, Italy had a brief military occupation of Ethiopia from 1936 to 1941. Specifically, within British West Africa, in the territory now known as Nigeria, the British colonial administration amalgamated what was then the Northern and Southern protectorates along with Lagos in 1914. This was done to ensure cost-effective and efficient control over that territory of fragmented tribes, tongues, and ethnicities.

Although Nigeria formally became one entity in 1914, many members of different social groups suddenly discovered that their kin, friends, and neighbours were outside Nigeria's new political boundaries. People in the precolonial geographical region now occupied by Nigeria and her neighbours—the Republic of Benin, Chad, Niger, and Cameroon—were not only linked by blood or ancestry but also by commerce and by associations of friendship and conflict. Therefore, one could not speak of modern Nigeria as a society with a "national culture." Indeed, colonialism brought with it ethnic polarisation along with its consequent contradictions, relationships, conflicts and divisions (Mustapha, 2006).

In postcolonial Nigeria, ethnic groups were occasionally fusions created by intermarriage, intermingling, and assimilation over time. In such unions, the cultural constituents maintained a limited individual identity. Groups were composed of smaller groups, but differences within and between even these smaller groups abounded. Still, these groups formed inseparable parts of Nigeria, as each was encapsulated in a wider network of social relations within the State. Although some uniqueness remained, however, some ethnic values and associated identities were typically *Nigerian* and common among groups, including respect for power (status, influence, wealth, affluence) and age, kinship and brotherhood, traditionalism and collectivism. Therefore, Nigeria's ethnocultural history is so complex that although some scholars focus on real ethnic boundaries as a way of differentiating at least 371 ethnic groups, others have sometimes described such distinctions as artificial (Mustapha, 2006).

Since Nigeria's independence in 1960, however, successive Nigerian governments, consistent with the colonial heritage, have differentiated between ethnic groups based on certain markers. These include an association of each group with a specific geographical part of the country and certain unique ethnocultural indicators such as language and normative behavior. This depiction of ethnic groups by the Nigerian government has been debated though because even within mostly *similar* groups (occupying the same geographical area and broadly speaking the same or similar dialect, for instance), polarisation still abounds (Otite, 1975). This further highlights the challenge of applying mainstream views of cultural identity, which assume in-group/out-group dichotomy, in these contexts (Tajfel and Turner, 1986). The point is that relations among Nigeria's ethnic groups are multifaceted and multidimensional, as social and ethnic frontiers can also be shifting and fluid, which informs the contention among scholars regarding the number of ethnic groups in Nigeria.

Some scholars claim more than 250 groups, some more than 374 (Otite, 1975) and others more than 470 (DFID, 2006). Despite these differences, there seems to be some general agreement that Nigeria has a largely *tripolar* ethnic structure because the three 'major' ethnic groups make up over 68 percent of the population (Mustapha, 2006). The Hausa-Fulani of Northern Nigeria (29%) speak *Hausa*. The Yoruba of the Southwest (21%) speak *Yoruba*, and the Ibos of the Southeast (18%) speak *Igbo*. Other presumably autonomous 'minority' groups, many with their unique dialects, largely cluster politically, linguistically and culturally around these major three (Mustapha, 2006: 5).

The question of ethnicity in Nigeria, therefore, is complex. It seems to involve both dynamic ethnic heterogeneity and inherent core-value homogeneity. It also encompasses the extinction of some groups and the evolution of new ones over the centuries. This suggests that ethnicity is not characterized by a 'fixed' content but by an essentially fluid and shifting category of meanings (Barth, 1998).

Indigenous Nigerian Banks: An Ethno-Historical Overview

In 1929 a group of African businessmen set up the first indigenous bank in Nigeria as a protest against perceived oppressive colonial policies (Ayida, 1960). When the bank went into liquidation barely a year later (because it could not meet liquidity requirements such as demand deposit obligations to its customers), its insolvency was traced to the personal enrichment and fraudulent activities of the managing director (see Paton, 1948: 7). Consequently, at its early stages of development, the practice of banking in Nigeria, underpinned by Anglo-Saxon and American business values—such as trust, neutrality, impartiality, and egalitarianism—conflicted with certain shared core ethnic values. These include inequality, wealth, influence, and affluence, all indicative of class differentiation and power.

The second indigenous bank, the Nigerian Mercantile Bank, started in 1931 and wound down in 1936. However, one of the bank's directors happened to be the fraudulent ex-managing director of the collapsed Industrial and Commercial Bank. Indeed, this second attempt at indigenous banking marked the beginning of a challenge that would eventually plague Nigerian banks pre- and post-independence—mismanagement for personal enrichment. In 1954 alone, 16 indigenous banks failed (Newlyn and Rowan, 1954). In postcolonial Nigeria, this trend continued. From 2004–2009 the Central Bank of Nigeria removed the top executives of eight banks for infractions linked to the fraudulent diversion of bank funds for personal enrichment (Sanusi, 2011). Some authors have referred to these failings as reflective of symbolic elements within shared Nigerian ethnocultural values which, in the context of formal Western-styled bureaucratic business norms and practices, reveals what Ayida (1960: 31–32) quite bluntly termed the *"inherent dishonesty and lack of integrity of the African businessman."* Although this generalization is inappropriate, the point remains that symbolic power and status as elements of ethnic identity, however acquired, govern the needs of management, employees, and customers. Fry (1976: 116) reports how loans availed to Africans in business and meant for working capital frequently were diverted into building houses, symbolic of status, wealth, class and power.

Ethnicized Identities of Ugo and Ola

What seems to go unnoticed among scholars is the way in which ethnic identity and symbols leaked into the otherwise egalitarian banking industry in modern Nigeria and how this can be linked to ethnicized identities revealed by the subjects discussed here, Ugo and Ola.

Ugo

When I sat down to speak with Ugo, an employee of Bank Alpha, he immediately projected Ibo ethnic identity to me after he told me his name. I could comprehend the *Iboness* of Ugo's name because I am from the Southeast region of Nigeria (see reflexive considerations). However, although Ugo's parents are Ibo (like mine), Ugo does not speak the *Igbo* dialect (as I do). Throughout much of his childhood, Ugo lived in Northern Nigeria; his father was a railway worker, but Ugo does not speak *Hausa*, the main ethnic tongue of that area. Ugo speaks the *Yoruba* dialect fluently (but I don't) because his family moved to Southwest Nigeria after his father retired when Ugo was 12 years old. Ugo is married to a Kanuri (a 'minority' ethnic group from Northern Nigeria).

The Bank prohibits employees from speaking any Nigerian vernacular in the workplace, as this is considered 'traditional' and 'backward,' a vehicle for segregation along ethnic lines, reinforcing values such as inequality and favouritism. Only the (colonial) English language is allowed for communication and interaction because (paradoxically) it is associated with equality, formality, trust, and equity—which are all bank values. Ugo speaks the *Yoruba* dialect with his manager, who is himself Yoruba, but he speaks English with his Regional Head (RH), who is Ibo. Ugo is, however, a member of the Ibo town union, of which the RH is chairman.

Ugo lowers his gaze when he talks to his manager, and bows and observes a 'respectful distance' when he talks to his RH. The Bank approves first-name address only across hierarchies, but when Ugo speaks to both his manager and his RH, he uses prefixes (sir) or synonyms (BM, RH). Sometimes, Ugo remains silent. Ugo says his manager is hard working, but he softly confided to me: "I don't know why they [bank management] are still keeping that man [RH]." Still, Ugo says he *"deeply respects"* and is *"loyal"* to both manager and RH. He says only loyal employees get rewarded with good appraisals, which Ugo sees as job security and assurance for career advancement.

Ola

Ola, a manager in Bank Beta, seemed irritated when I asked his ethnic group. I could sense some sarcasm when Ola replied: *"Yoruba, obviously."* Ola was born in Northern Nigeria, speaks *Yoruba* and English, but says he cannot understand a word of *Hausa*—the main ethnic tongue of the North. Ola married a Yoruba woman and had five children. Marrying an ethnic affiliate and raising a large family is part of familial obligation, Ola says, although this has become financially demanding. Ola owes rent and children's school fees, and his wife just lost her job.

Nevertheless, Ola recently rejected a job offer with pay from another company which almost doubled his current salary. The reason Ola gave for his decision to forgo higher pay was for him simple: the new job will not have the designation 'manager' though it will pay more cash. Ola reasoned that if he accepted the job, it would effectively strip him of his status because the title 'manager' would go. People respected him because of it, and he was called 'manager' even outside the bank.

Experiences as Ethnicized Identities

The subject's narratives of their experiences evidence a unique portrayal of the changing dynamics of identity construction in Nigeria. These narratives question certain notions in mainstream CCM literature regarding ethnic affiliation that present ethnic group membership as socially bounded. The subjects seem to suggest that more widely acknowledged ethnic markers, such as name and language, have been de-emphasized by individuals for markers such as body language (bowing, lowered gaze, spatial proximity). Specific ethnic symbols have been woven and contextually applied when the need arose for subjects to assert a specific or a hybrid of identities making ethnicized identity all at once a craft, a performance, a contextual disposition, and a cocktail of social and other identities.

Ugo evidences *mutiplexic* identities or multiple identities, which underlie his contextual identity adoption. For instance, Ugo is Ibo, speaks *Yoruba*, is married to a Kanuri, and is also a banker, town union member, manager loyalist, regional manager allegiant, and husband, amongst others. Also, Ugo evokes, negotiates, and asserts several of these sometimes-contradictory identities simultaneously and contextually without losing the essence of any. By being open to mixing similar or dissimilar identities (I would call this *hybridizing*) and asserting the outcome of that mix based on subjective perception of context, Ugo also evidences *multisecting* identities.

Ugo's ethnicized identity then is manifested in how he transits and navigates sometimes dissimilar ethnic, traditional, and sociocultural and professional boundaries by being Ibo (by name), Yoruba (by ethnic tongue), and Hausa (by marriage) while remaining husband, tribal union member, and yet Western-styled banker. Furthermore, Ugo cares about his career because it also gives him a voice and image in society—a status enabler and enhancer. The organization is, therefore, Ugo's stage where he weaves a performance of identity by manipulating ethnocultural symbols of identity within an otherwise egalitarian organization. For instance, rather than equality (as required by the bank's values), Ugo legitimates and reinforces inequality with his superiors through actions (using prefixes and pseudonyms) and inactions (not speaking at all). How his superiors see him—that is, their expectations of him—matters as he navigates identities differently between each.

The point is Ugo manifests not just intersecting identities (in which multiple identities are frequently interlinked) but also *multiplexic* and *mutisecting* identities, in which the need to sometimes negotiate and assert conflicting and inconsistent identities, the hybridity of identities, and the (identity) outcome of the mix contextually subsists. Indeed, while Ugo identifies as a banker, the bank values of equality and neutrality are antithetical to ethnic values of respect for status, power, and wealth—inequality. Still, Ugo also sees a match in this outright inconsistency between the required bank identity and his ethnic values. To Ugo, the bank values of *respect* for the individual (esteeming everyone highly) are consistent with ethnic values of respect for (the status of) a person. So, Ugo *respects* his Yoruba manager, of whom he seems fond, as much as he *respects* his Ibo RH, whom he seems to most resoundingly despise.

Ola's identity seemed to affirm his *Yorubaness* through his expectations of others like me. For starters, he expected me, as a *fellow* Nigerian, to know he was Yoruba through his *obviously* Yoruba-sounding name, even though I am Ibo (see reflexive considerations). As we will see later in this section, this expectation—consistent with sharedness of core ethic values—underpinned Ola's ethnicized identity, but there was more that emphasized the multidimensionality of the construct. Firstly, Ola evidenced *mutiplexic* identities based on his need to adopt and negotiate multiple identities. These include personal identity, characterized by accruing debts, nonpayment of school fees for his five children, and his wife's unemployment. Professional identities, symbolized by workplace positional authority—manager, ethnic identity, family-approved marriage to a Yoruba woman, family, required child-bearing obligations, and language. Secondly, Ola evidenced *multisecting* identity based on the need to also assert identities such as societal identity, rank bestowed based on perceptions of relative power by ethnic and nonethnic affiliates, and (in)accurate perceptions of status, through symbolization of power by significant and insignificant others.

Ola's financial status, however, was inconsistent with the identity he wished to project to the wider society and, in essence, the expectation he had of others. The family had power over Ola's choice of a wife and even how many children he had. He needed their approval, so he carried out their bidding at considerable personal financial inconvenience. Ola also needed societal legitimation and endorsement by others outside the bank by projecting a managerial image as symbolic of status and power, since people equated Ola's managerial designation with societal title and rank. Even when the managerial identity he asserted and its symbolic representation with status was irreconcilable with his present financial circumstances—his personal identity—he asserted the former.

Ola evidenced that negotiation and assertion between ethnic and other identities are not merely based on how individuals (essentially) see themselves, but how they want others to (sometimes inaccurately) see them in order to ethno-symbolically endorse them. Consequently, the need to negotiate and assert identity by Ola had an overtly ethnic overtone: each outcome had to feed into ethnocultural expectations, *obligatedness*, endorsement, and approval of others even if they were not ethnic affiliates.

In all, Ola and Ugo show how ethnic identities can be fluid, transient, unpredictable, and contextual. They also show how one identity can evoke other similar and dissimilar identities and how hybridized identities are not just interlinked identities but even are contradictory. Indeed, this shows how the exploration of people's experiences of identity—the meaning they ascribe to elements in the construction of identity and how they symbolize these elements—clearly are a missing element from mainstream CCM. For instance, the construction of ethnicized identity is manifested in both subjects' experiences through ethnocultural symbolization of gain and loss, cost and benefit, relative power, and the accurate and inaccurate perceptions of others.

Power, Ethnicized Identity, and CCM

Although mainstream CCM views identity simplistically as an individual's sense of self, more critical perspectives refer to both the outcome and process of identity construction and the relevance of the group thereof. Thus, through a two-way process—ascriptions made by others and self-referencing (Mahadevan, 2017)—identity construction is linked to the social, evidencing social identity (Turner et al., 2006), or collective identity (Baumann, 2002). In essence, individual identity construction is linked to the idea that identity is (also) *learned* through others (Barth, 1998).

However, going back to the narratives of Ugo and Ola, we see that there is a need to uncouple not just elements within identity construction, but the symbolic meaning of these elements to the individual—including, for instance, when how one sees oneself is inconsistent with what one wants to project to others and when ascriptions by others contradict self-referencing or one's sense of self, based on one's present circumstances. As already clarified through ethnicized identity, Ugo and Ola reveal that how people see themselves (based on clear and real conditions and the effects thereof) may not be how they want others to see them and consequently are not consistent with the identity they project.

Ethnicized identity then is linked to perceptions of relative power to assert or to legitimize sometimes inaccurate self-referencing to reinforce sometimes inaccurate perceptions by others through shared symbols, which validate this implicit illegitimacy. In essence, a further preoccupation of more critical CCM research should be individual meaning-making through symbols in identity construction and the positionality of power in both the process and outcome. For instance, does the individual and others have equal power in the process and outcome of identity assertion? Here, the place of ethnocultural symbolization of relative power in identity construction becomes even more fundamental in uncoupling this under-researched phenomenon.

Further, the focus of critical studies on the relationship between power and identity traditionally lies in individual perceptions of group differences (Eriksen, 2002). We see from Ugo and Ola, however, that power is manifested in the reconciliation of differences through a focus on areas of identity convergence. In essence, to be meaningful, power must be represented through shared (ethnic) symbols. This is not novel. Through Bourdieu's (1984) analyses of cultural classes, we see power defined *symbolically* rather than literally, and identities of parties in a relationship underpinned not just by systems of social hierarchies and distribution of power, but by individual and group symbolism of such power through ethnicized perceptions of status, as is the case with the subjects.

For instance, how the manager and RH perceived Ugo was important because he needed to advance his career in order to project a powerful image in the wider society. Ola's managerial position was important not for itself but because it distinguished him as powerful to others. Although the job paid poorly relative to Ola's financial needs, here, power was not characterized by material benefits alone. That's why he refused the higher-paying job offer. Ola remained *powerful* as long as people saw him as 'the manager,' a symbol of status and power outside the organization. Indeed, as Mahadevan (2017) argues, identity construction is a power-infused mechanism, by which differences and similarities are subjectively, constructively, and contextually asserted by individuals.

Reflexive Considerations

It took some conscious reflection to see that my experiences had some resonance with the accounts of Ugo and Ola. After talking to the subjects and reflexively going through their narratives, I realize that their experiences are typically Nigerian. Ethnicized identity is a performance of *multiplexic* and *multisecting* identities. Ola and Ugo challenged my views, validated by Eriksen (2002), that how individuals are integrated into their societies is only through culture and that culture is not simply a socially constructed shared heritage but rather a shared system of communication. I find that my view seems to detach culture and its various forms, such as ethnic culture, from its constitutive elements. However, as a Nigerian from the Ibo ethnic group, a former banker, and a scholar, my life reflects the struggle to transit and to walk through, on, and in between boundaries of identity, which are frequently indistinguishable.

I struggled to come to terms with the depiction of ethnicized identity by my subjects because I have never really given it a conscious thought. I have always believed that ethnicity was all about social and geographical boundaries. For instance, I see myself as Ibo, because my name is derived from the *Igbo* dialect and my parents are also from Southeastern, Ibo-speaking Nigeria. However, based on the narratives of Ugo and Ola, there is a new perspective worth exploring further. That is, culture is manifested through a shared system of communication or language, and the symbolic ascription of meanings are developed experientially and situationally. Ethnicized identity, like culture, is a social construction and can be analyzed on a social, organizational, and individual level or in an intersecting manner, showing how each level influences and is influenced by the other. In essence, a description of the value system of Nigeria's ethnic groups does not suggest that those values determine the individual identity of its affiliates. This statement is true of Ugo, Ola, and, indeed, myself.

Recommendations to Students, Researchers, and Practitioners

The narratives by Ugo and Ola reveal some implications for increasingly globalized organizations operating in culturally diverse contexts and employing a multiethnic workforce. Organizations need to reassess approaches to managing based on how employees construct identities. I have summarized some implications arising from this research based on what may be termed the 'outsider' and the 'insider' perspectives, although I do admit the possibilities of overlap between the two approaches. The 'outsider' perspective is directed at managers from a mono-ethnic background in the main, who frequently do not see 'ethnicity' but 'national identity' and who see Nigerian employees as homogenous. The insider perspective is focused at managers (like me) from a multiethnic background who view 'ethnic identity' as a boundary-related concept and who may need to see 'ethnicity' differently while managing in diverse contexts.

1. For the 'outsider' manager, there is a fine line between managing identities through Western management models in developed as opposed to

ethnoculturally diverse contexts. Frequently, one is reminded that in countries like Nigeria, organizational understanding of employee identities is based on national government–defined labels. The question is, do ethnic labels equate to how individuals see themselves or want to be seen? Do common historical experiences and outcomes (like colonialism and geographical boundaries) always induce common identities? Managing in these contexts may demand an understanding of how individuals, as ethnic affiliates, project themselves and how this may be inconsistent with predetermined identity and ethnicity labels.

2. For the 'insider' manager, the meaning of hierarchies, positions, power, status, and even job tasks and roles to an employee will manifest in how they navigate real workplace situations. Managers must not focus only on the actions and overt practices of employees, but also on *inactions*. Rather than rely on predetermined organizational value statements, it may be worthwhile for managers to understand what organizational imperatives mean to employees through actions and inactions. Managers could, for instance, reflect and report on subjective meanings in everyday workplace interactions and how this is consistent or inconsistent with organizational meanings. Employee experiences may not always conform to organizational stereotypes, which make them valuable. Unless managers understand what organizational labels mean and their identity implications, the organization may be ill-prepared to meet the changing dynamics of managing diversity in these contexts.

3. Lastly, for both "outsider' and 'insider' managers, rather than concentrate only on group culture, managers could (also) focus on the employee as a representative of multiple and intersecting social and other identities in organizational settings. My focus on the individual (Ugo and Ola) revealed what we might not ordinarily know from a group setting, that is, the shifting basis for determining, negotiating and asserting identities. Managers could focus on the individual as mirroring the group, since concentrating on the group itself may not succinctly reflect how individuals see self and how they want to be seen by others. Managing by focusing on a group identity alone may then be counterproductive.

In concluding, even when scholars admit the existence of ethnic heterogeneity across countries like Nigeria, scholarly works frequently evidence a presumed homogeneous 'African' identity. What I suggest in this chapter is that how individuals construct and reconstruct identity may not be unique to two bankers from two of three main ethnic groups in Nigeria but could be typical of social beings irrespective of context. In essence, the *ethnicization of identity* may be applicable to those in both ethno-homogeneous and ethno-heterogeneous societies. I also hint that as globalization spans countries and workplaces, identities of employees in the global north and global south may tend to become increasingly intersecting, *multiplexic*, and *multisecting*. The world then may not just have become one global village but may be increasingly becoming one ethnicity. Lastly, those who have not yet thought of 'ethnicity' in this way (e.g., ethnic aspects of 'English,' 'French,' or 'U.S.-American' identity) might soon discover it in their own lives.

References

Ayida A (1960) *A Critical Analysis of Banking Trends in Nigeria*. Nigerian Institute of Social and Economic Research Conference Proceedings. Ibadan: Nigerian Institute of Social and Economic Research.

Bader V (2001) Culture and identity: Contesting constructivism. *Ethnicities* 1(2): 251–273.

Barth F (1994) Enduring and emerging issues in the analysis of ethnicity. In: Vermeulen H and Covers C (eds) *The Anthropology of Ethnicity: Beyond Ethnic Groups and Boundaries*. Amsterdam: Het Spinhuis, pp. 1–32.

Barth F (ed) (1998) *Ethnic Groups and Boundaries: The Social Organization of Culture Difference*. Prospect Heights: Waveland Press Inc.

Baumann G (2002) Collective identity as a dual discursive construction. In: Friese H (ed) *Identities: Time, Difference and Boundaries*. Oxford: Berghahn, pp. 189–200.

Bourdieu P (1984) *Distinction: A Social Critique of the Judgment of Taste*. Cambridge: Harvard University Press.

Cairns G and Sliwa M (2008) *A Very Short, Reasonably Cheap and Fairly Interesting Book about International Business*. London: SAGE.

Cohen AP (2013) *Symbolic Construction of Community*. New York: Routledge.

Department for International Development (DFID) (2006) *Policy Brief 15*. London: Overseas Development Institute.

Eriksen TH (2002) *Ethnicity and Nationalism: Anthropological Perspectives*. London: Pluto Press.

Fry R (1976) *Bankers in West Africa: The Story of the Bank of British West Africa Limited* (Vol. 3). London: Hutchinson Benham.

Hall S (1990) Cultural identity and diaspora. In: Rutherford J (ed) *Identity: Community, Culture, Difference*. London: Lawrence & Wishart, pp. 222–237.

Hofstede G (1980) *Culture's Consequences*. Beverly Hills: SAGE.

Holvino E (2012) Time, space and social justice in the age of globalization: Research and applications on the simultaneity of differences. *Practising Social Change* 5: 4–11.

House RJ, Hanges PJ, Javidan M, Dorfman PW and Gupta V (eds) (2004) *Culture, Leadership, and Organisations: The GLOBE Study of 62 Societies*. Thousand Oaks: SAGE.

Jackson T (2013) From human resources to human capital, and now cross-cultural capital. *International Journal of Cross Cultural Management* 13(3): 239–241.

Jackson T (2017) Mainstreaming cross-cultural management studies through inclusive scholarship. *International Journal of Cross Cultural Management* 17(2): 173–174.

Mahadevan J (2001) Engineering culture(s) across sites: Implications for cross-cultural management of emic meanings. In: Primecz H, Romani L and Sackmann S (eds) *Cross-Cultural Management in Practice: Culture and Negotiated Meanings*. Cheltenham: Edward Elgar Publishing, pp. 89–100.

Mahadevan J (2017) *A Very Short, Fairly Interesting and Reasonably Cheap Book about Cross-Cultural Management*. London: SAGE.

Mustapha AR (2006) *Ethnic Structure, Inequality and Governance of the Public Sector in Nigeria*. Programme Paper Number 24. United Nations Research Institute for Social Development (UNRISD).

Newlyn WT and Rowan DC (1954) *Money and Banking in British Colonial Africa*. Oxford: University Press.

Otite O (1975) Resource competition and inter-ethnic relations in Nigeria. In: Despres LA (ed) *Ethnicity and Resource Competition in Plural Societies*. Netherlands: Mouton Publishers, pp. 119–130.

Paton GD (1948) Report on Banks and Banking in Nigeria, Unpublished Bank of England File Copy (OV68/I, folio 165).

Primecz H, Romani L and Sackmann S (eds) (2011) *Cross-Cultural Management in Practice: Culture and Negotiated Meanings*. Cheltenham: Edward Elgar Publishing.

Sanusi SL (2011) Banking reform and its impact on the Nigerian economy. *CBN Journal of Applied Statistics* 2(2): 115–122.

Schwartz SH (2006) A theory of cultural value orientations: Explication and applications. *Comparative Sociology* 5(2): 137–182.

Tajfel H and Turner JC (1986) The social identity theory of intergroup behavior. In: Worchel S and Austin WG (eds) *Psychology of Intergroup Relations*. Chicago: Nelson-Hall, pp. 7–24.

Trompenaars F and Hampden-Turner C (2004) *Managing People across Cultures*. Chichester: Capstone.

Turner J, Reynolds KJ, Haslam A and Veenstra KE (2006) Reconceptualising personality: Producing individuality by defining the personal self. In: Postmes T and Jetten J (eds) *Individuality and the Group: Advances in Social Identity*. Thousand Oaks: SAGE, pp. 11–36.

Weedon C (2004) *Identity and Culture: Narratives of Difference and Belonging*. Maidenhead: McGraw-Hill Education.

12

UNEQUAL INTEGRATION

Skilled Migrants' Conditional Inclusion Along the Lines of Swedishness, Class and Ethnicity[1]

Elin Hunger, Miguel Morillas, Laurence Romani and Mohammed Mohsen

Introduction

This case chapter contributes to cross-cultural management (CCM) literature in its approach to 'culture' as a multifaceted and socially constructed notion formed by boundaries such as language, class or ethnicity. Most work in CCM approaches (national) culture as presenting a certain form, an entity; either as a combination of values (as in Hofstede, 2001; House et al., 2004), as a political culture (Chevrier, 2009; d'Iribarne, 2009) or as constructed socio-historical sense-making frameworks (Gertsen et al., 2012, see also the review by Adler and Aycan, 2018). In contrast, we emphasize the plurality, fluidity and boundary aspects encompassed by culture. The case presents 'Swedish culture' as interrelated with the social construction of 'Swedishness' and aims to shed light on the latter's implicit class and ethnic boundaries. The context of our study is the labour-market integration of highly educated professionals perceived as skilled migrants in their new home society: Sweden. All of the interviewed professionals were participants in an internship program at a Swedish organization. We find that the cultural environment ('Swedish culture') to which they needed to adapt is based on implicit norms that reflect the power structures of Swedish society.

An 'Integration' Initiative

This case study considers an initiative in a large Swedish multinational—'*The Organization*'—employing mostly university graduates from the business and economics, law and IT fields. '*The Initiative*' is an internship program for 'skilled migrants', that is, for foreigners with an academic degree or extensive equivalent experience (Iredale, 2001). To date, approximately two thirds of the roughly 300 participants have been offered employment after completing a three- to six-month unpaid internship. This employment is primarily temporary and often within *The Organization*.

Methodology

Our research is inspired by critical CCM studies (Romani et al., 2018). In other words, we approach intercultural situations as embedded in—often unconsciously reproduced—power inequalities. We adopt critical theories such as those found in the work of Bourdieu (e.g., 1980, 1984) and Lamont (2000), in particular, in our understanding of social classes, which are not only connected to economic privileges or academic degrees; social distinctions are also (re)produced by everyday actions that distinguish individuals (ways of talking, dressing) and by the importance given to some elements (e.g., school attended) over others (the degree itself). Looking at everyday practices in *The Organization*, we employ the notion of forms of capitals when considering individuals' positioning in the field. Economic capital can be seen, for example, as access to economic wealth; social capital as access to a social network (of resources) and cultural capital can, for example, be manifested in an academic degree. Likewise, we insist on distinction and boundaries in our understanding of ethnicity and, along with Barth (1998: 15), see that it is "the ethnic boundary that defines the group, not the cultural stuff it encloses". In other words, we treat ethnicity as a notion that lies in the eyes of the beholder: as dependent on social actors' contextually bound interpretations of what they see as distinctive markers (e.g., colour of skin, learned cultural behaviours, religion).

All of the authors were involved in the field study, either in conversation with HR representatives or with interns and mentors. This case furthers the work by Hunger and Mohsen (2017) and is an ongoing study currently building on 30 interviews in Swedish, Spanish, Arabic or English (depending on the researcher's common language with the interviewee), in which we asked open-ended questions about *The Initiative* (mostly with HR representatives) and about the interns' education, previous jobs and exposure to the Swedish labour market. The interviewees came from all continents, but Middle Eastern and Eastern European countries were overrepresented in the population of interns participating in *The Initiative*. All interns were university graduates and, with one exception, had working experience from their country of origin, third countries and sometimes also from Sweden.

Case Presentation

The interns had usually learnt about *The Initiative* through The Swedish Employment Services. Most had applied (sometimes without much hope) for hundreds of jobs before they were given information about, and access to, this initiative.

In the following sections, we detail the dimensions that intersect in the integration challenge met by the skilled migrants taking part in *The Initiative*.

'Swedishness'

At *The Organization*'s headquarters, most work is done in Swedish, although the official working language is English. From the organizational side, it is stated that the overarching goal of the internship program is to offer skilled migrants a Swedish reference from a well-known and respected company. During the interviews, though, most participants—irrespective of their current status as intern or employee—stated that the goal of the program was to learn Swedish at work. This may mirror the central role the Swedish language has played in the interns' previous encounters with the Swedish labour market, and that language, apart from being a communicative tool, has symbolic meaning. An example of an encounter underscoring the central role of speaking Swedish at work is given by Lucy, who understands but does not speak Swedish:

> Seriously, I went to [The Employment Services]: they told me to clean toilets. . . . I'm sure even if I don't use my [double MSc] degree I can help you photocopy something. Isn't it insulting asking a professional lawyer or surgeon to clean toilets?

Lucy is referring to a situation in which her inability to speak Swedish was seen as a legitimate reason to disregard her 16-year professional track record working in the Asia–Pacific region. Apart from the isolated nature of cleaning work, in which she would be unlikely to improve her language skills, she found the suggestion humiliating. The scenario occurred before she entered *The Initiative*, but Elias—originally from the Middle East and now permanently employed— tells a story that shows Swedish language capabilities affect life inside *The Organization* as well.

> I had a performance appraisal with my boss [during the internship]. I asked whether she could offer me employment, referring to my tasks being the same [as those of my colleagues]. She said that she could if I would learn to talk to customers [in Swedish].

Elias' example shows that even though he was already completing the same tasks as his colleagues, his Swedish language ability determined whether he would be employed. Paradoxically, the corporate language in *The Organization* is English, and most Swedish professionals are fluent in this language. In Sweden, it is not uncommon for university classes to be taught in English; citizens are exposed to English in their daily lives since international TV shows and movies are not dubbed but texted, and English is recognized, as in other places, as the lingua franca of international business. Hence, it is possible to argue that the condition placed on Elias had symbolic rather than strictly practical meaning.

However, working in a 'Swedish way' refers to constructs beyond language: the vast majority of current and former interns told us they had experienced external pressure to adjust to new social rules and norms in the Swedish working environment. Alina, who previously lived in Eastern Europe, develops her thoughts on the difference between social interaction in Sweden and Eastern Europe saying:

> [W]hen I came back [to work] after the weekend: 'Have you had a good weekend?' And I thought: 'Ok, so I'm supposed to tell them what I [did during] the weekend?' I'm not used to such questions. (. . .) It's so different. So very, very many new things for me.

The interviewees often referred to 'Swedish working culture' as a less formal way of socializing in the workplace. Many also related it to aspects that they value, such as flexibility (so that you can pick up your children from kindergarten, for example) and corporate acceptance of employees being on sick leave. Sabina, originally from Eastern Europe, perceives Swedish organizations as less hierarchical, and as places where bosses know the name of all employees. She adds: "I found it strange in the beginning, then I realized it simply *is* like this. People are nicer here". At the same time, this informality translates to ambiguity, and misinterpretation becomes a social liability for the individual who is new to—or deviates from—the norm. Samer (originally from a Middle Eastern country) explains how indirect communication made him question his common sense. He was new in his position and it was not clear to him whether others thought he was doing his job properly. He says:

> You feel insecure. Am I doing something wrong or am I doing it right? Because also here in Sweden, they don't tell you if you do something wrong: they ask you to try again, [they tell you] you can do it another way.

Nadyia is the only participant who explicitly underlines that she considers reciprocal cultural exchange central to her life in Sweden. She says: "[The Swedes] learn a little bit about us. Since we're many coming to Sweden [from a Middle Eastern country], it's important one knows a little bit about our traditions and thinking." In contrast to Nadyia's view, many other interns talk about one-way adaptation. Fardin (originally from a Middle Eastern country), says that "you have to be open-minded and secular and accept their views. You have to be really liberal—that is more important than knowledge [your competences]." Hence, in Fardin's experience, one has to be perceived as liberal and secular to fit in to Swedish society.

Class

The interns' participation in *The Initiative* is not compensated, but participants get about 400 Euros a month as an integration aid from the Swedish government if they participate in the program. In other words, only those who already have financial security can engage in the program. In terms of the length of the program, most participants consider six months as sensible—some refer to this as the typical length of a Swedish probation period. When it comes to (the lack of) payment though, the participants hold more polarized views. Lydia says:

> Not getting paid when having an internship is quite humiliating from an honest perspective . . . I know people with *kids* doing this, and I wonder how the hell do you actually finance looking after your family? And psychologically [a salary] makes you feel better . . . I'm not asking for a full salary, but at least [a thousand Euros] a month.

In her statement, Lydia highlights that the unpaid nature of the internship might hinder some people from attending the program, for example because of their financial responsibility to look after their family. She also explains how her positive experience of the internship was partially dependent on her former husband having a well-paid job and her having 'Swedish middle-class markers':

> My ex-husband and I have [a countryside residence], a boat, a flat in the [upper class district]. And, of course, then I'm seen to be [one of them]. But the refugee doesn't. The refugee lives in [a low-income district, heavily populated by immigrants] . . . You know you can't relate . . . because they have a different lifestyle.

Ana (from an Eastern European country) adds that she does not feel included in the corporate norm, because her life outside of work looks different, and that she still feels as though she is on a "trial period" when it comes to corporate life and living in Sweden. Elias (from a Middle Eastern country), expresses similar ambivalent feelings towards a future in Sweden:

> You have a little bit of high expectations when you have been studying for five years, have had a better job in your country, and then you get a job here which is a little bit less interesting. Then, you get the feeling that this is the highest I'll ever get here.

Elias' experience is supported by Victoria, who shares a story that illustrates how a *Swedish* university degree (rather than a degree as such) makes a significant difference in the labour market. She experienced the hierarchical segregation of Swedes and 'immigrants' when she was an intern in another Swedish organization. She recalls the situation:

> We were talking [about the] scarcity of doctors and nurses in Sweden. And another colleague was saying that she has a friend whose husband is a doctor from Italy and he cannot find a job. And then somebody says: 'Ah, that is another thing, you cannot compare it. We were saying that it is difficult to find *Swedish* doctors'.

Victoria's statement highlights that her colleagues had a specific notion of 'Swedishness' in mind when they implicitly referred to the higher status of "*Swedish* doctors": in Swedish society being a doctor is considered high-status, but that status is preconditioned by having a Swedish (educational) background.

Many interns share the view that their access to Swedish career opportunities is limited, perhaps mirroring the fact that most interns, if not all, entered at a lower hierarchical level than the positions they had occupied in the countries where they had previously worked—a view shared by *The Organization*'s HR department.

Ethnicity

Ethnicity can be seen as "a dichotomization of others as strangers, as members of another ethnic group, impl[ying] a recognition of limitations on shared understandings" (Barth, 1998: 15). In the following section, we focus on encounters where recognition of boundary markers has triggered ideas of (limited) shared understanding.

Reflecting upon others' perception of her ethnicity, as well as of her presumed skills, Lydia tells us that her contact person at The Employment Services first suggested she take a job in an "Asian restaurant", as he associated her supposed ethnicity with Asian restaurants. She recalls:

> Then he [told] me I should look into working as a tour guide at [the City Hall], like taking people around speaking Chinese. I was just like: have you even *looked* at my CV?

The contact person at The Swedish Employment Services seemed oblivious to Lydia's aspirations to continue her successful career, as well as her experience of his statement as both reifying (assuming she could speak Chinese based on her appearance) and derogatory (not placing value on her professional experiences, but rather associating her appearance with a specific form of service work).

The interviewees' experience of The Employment Services and labour market appears to vary depending on their alleged ethnicity. Tom, who grew up in and holds a master's degree from North America, moved to Sweden upon graduation and is the only participant who did not have any previous working experience before attending the program. He is also the only intern we met who presumably would be recognized as having a 'Western ethnicity'. What stands out in his story is that he evaluates the internship in terms of the benefits he thinks it could provide him—unlike the other participants, he seems never to have considered it his "only chance".

> When I came to Sweden I wanted to get into one of the accounting firms, like Deloitte or PWC or something like that, but I enjoy working here within [*The Organization*] and it fits my educational background. Like, as long as I get to learn stuff and develop it's all right.

In contrast, Amala, who grew up in South Asia and currently holds a temporary position in *The Organization*, repeatedly relates her own situation to that of the others, those she also considers foreigners. She connects the feeling of foreignness with vulnerability, which stems from a lack of social inclusion: she talks about how she was depressed at the beginning of her internship and how she struggled because she did not have a mentor. In fact, Amala had to learn many things on her own: "Like, [I] even *forced* myself. I don't want to give up as this is one of the best opportunities I have at hands. . . . Because I'm not in a situation to have a better time."

Tom's narrative, discussed previously, also lacks the element of adjustment, which, for example, is found in Elias' comments on the potential pitfalls of not fitting in—in the workplace as well as in society. Elias tells us about remarks he has heard, made by persons he perceives as 'Swedish', about persons perceived as 'non-Swedish':

> [They say] 'he comes from that place, [therefore] he thinks like that'. And then one instantly feels that there is a barrier, and that is pretty decisive for one's ability to advance in one's career.

The quote illustrates that such comments remind Elias that he is 'non-Swedish'; that there is a distance, a "barrier", and that he is dependent upon those he perceives as having a Swedish ethnicity. He describes his experience as follows: "It's mostly like you don't want to work with someone who thinks differently or acts differently".

Another participant, Sabina, explicitly emphasizes the importance of hard work, and her belief that it is the only way to get what one wants. But while she says the Swedish labour market is open for everyone who shows willingness and ability, she also makes some comments that indicate her experiences have been contradictory. "I know that my first name is a problem and I know that my accent causes trouble" and "it is *actually* only a strength of mine, that I speak an additional language". Hence, it seems as if Sabina herself has identified that ethnicity boundary markers put her at a disadvantage in Swedish society, although she is also aware of the contradiction it implies: knowing an additional language *is* an advantage, but not one necessarily valued in practice.

In a sense, the way of thinking given voice by Elias and Sabina indicates that they are, and have been, reflecting on how to make sense of themselves in the Swedish (organizational) context. The theme is found in other participants' stories as well and may mirror the fact that most participants—including those now employed by *The Organization*—were well positioned in terms of all forms of capitals in their respective countries of origin, that is, economic (e.g., access to economic wealth), social (e.g., access to a social network of resources) and cultural (e.g., academic degree). Indeed, their very presence in *The Organization* is filtered by preselection mechanisms along the lines discussed in the section on *class* (the internship being unpaid being the most prominent one). Organizational acknowledgement of some of this preselection is evident when talking to those holding managerial positions. Kerstin, a manager whose boundary markers connotate 'Swedishness', says:

> Here, we speak about skilled persons, [highly educated professionals] of different ethnic origin. There is already in place a form of selection when one works in [an organization like this]. . . . What is happening here is really nothing (. . .) compared to the integration challenges that exist in society as [a] whole. These are persons that already have a university degree from [a foregin country].

In her comment, Kerstin points to the impact of class (which she relates to education) but downplays ethnicity. However, because moving to Sweden for most participants has meant a shift from being perceived as 'a highly educated professional' to being perceived as 'a skilled migrant' (as the ethnic dimension acquired importance in the new, Swedish, organizational context), some participants tell stories of how their former class-related capital (e.g., linguistic ability, dress codes) have been made invisible to varying extents. Since the shift is involuntary, some participants seem to have developed differentiation strategies to counter the judgements of others by, for example, bringing the class privileges of their origin to the forefront in a conscious attempt to challenge implicit assumptions about migrants' backgrounds. As these attempts at seeking recognition are not necessarily always met, ambivalent feelings and self-assessments related to how one is perceived in Swedish society, as well as organizational contexts, are common. Tahmid develops this line of reasoning, saying:

> People are really nice to me, people are really nice. Of course, there are some people, I have the feeling . . . they don't know what kind of family I belong to, or what kind of status sort to say. [*Lowers tone*] So they go: 'Oh,

this kind of guy is from [a South Asian country]' you know . . . I can't blame them for thinking like that cause it's a poor country.

To counter such judgements, one differentiation strategy seems to be to distance oneself from one's co-nationals or those one perceives to be one's co-ethnics, seeking to highlight that co-nationals may have very different behavioural patterns and habits from one's own, despite coming from the same country. Cristina says that: "I decided to meet a few [people coming from my country in Eastern Europe] at the beginning, but I was disappointed, and I was like 'no'". Cristina's view is shared by Darya, who emphasizes the importance she ascribes to class over ethnicity:

> Sometimes [when walking] on the beach with my daughter, we hear [our native] language, and she goes: "Mom, that girl speaks [a language of Eastern Europe, too]". And they play with each other. [But people that we meet, they should] have appropriate . . . the same background, you know . . . [To] find new friends, and they should not be anybody, but they must have the same education, I think.

To conclude, being ethnicized as a skilled migrant in the Swedish (organizational) context seems to generate a search for social positioning that is not always fulfilled. Accordingly, the participants sometimes find themselves in a no man's land where their own, more complex, perception of their identities is neglected. In this new territory, their sense of class belongingness is constrained due to perceived ethnic boundary markers (that is, if they are not exhibiting the right 'Swedish' middle-class markers). As a result, they adopt strategies to counter other's perceptions of their identity and to draw class boundaries towards those who are recognized, by themselves or others, as their co-ethnics.

Power and CCM: Implications From This Case

This case illustrates the need to go beyond values and cultural dimensions in the understanding of intercultural interactions. A critical CCM approach is necessary because there are implicit power rules behind the experience of difference: people are judged in unequal terms and adaptation is usually only expected from some. In our understanding of cultural differences, we adopt the concept of *boundaries* from the studies of class and ethnicity (Barth, 1998; Bourdieu, 1984; Lamont, 2000). We show how these boundaries crystallize around perceived deviation from a normalized notion of class, ethnicity and 'Swedishness'. What is at stake is the inclusion of the program participants into the labour market: we show how boundaries are drawn to mark distinctions around different forms of capitals in this access to work.

The three main forms of boundaries considered in this case study are 'Swedishness', class and ethnicity—to which concepts such as language and status are closely related. They echo previous studies on management in Sweden (e.g., Holmberg and Åkerblom, 2006; Zander, 2000) that insist on the central importance of (Swedish) communication in management. In the case study, this 'Swedishness' (using Swedish language and working in a 'Swedish way') reveals how those who do not master these cultural norms are penalized, despite working in the headquarters of an organization operating internationally. The ('Swedish') cultural norm is imposed on the interns and eclipses their previous international working experience.

The interviewees reveal how the interns' cultural capital (for example, degrees) is concealed when it differs from that considered appropriate: a given lifestyle, or Swedish educational degrees. Employees perceived as members of ethnic minorities are implicitly associated with a modest social background, which triggers interns to engage in 'class work', that is, efforts to distinguish themselves from 'other' migrants (e.g., those living in modest suburbs). However, not all of them will have the same resources (capital) to succeed in conveying the right kind of class image. Yet, interns are selected on the basis of their existing economic capital, as the internship is not remunerated. This condition of integration is also documented by Aten et al. (2016). From the field studies, it transpires that the interns are deprived of their symbolic capital: their sources of capital do not seem to receive any form of acknowledgement, unless they echo the urban (white), 'Swedish' middle-class experience of the other employees, speaking Swedish at work.

This case at first appears to be about labour integration of interns because *The Initiative* is officially about socializing skilled migrants in a Swedish work environment. However, considering the boundaries pointed to by the interns, we can argue that this socialization occurs within conditions that do not value much of the interns' multiple sources of capital (e.g., linguistic, work experience, academic degree). In other words, the situation faced by the interns is one loaded with power: the power of the norm, of those who benefit from it and those who will prolong the status quo in which their position is dominant. The socialization in a Swedish environment is thus far beyond learning the 'Swedish' work style, but also about entering the struggle of positioning oneself in a social hierarchy.

Reflexive Considerations

The three dimensions that organize our chapter have emerged from the data. Reflecting upon the research process, and our interaction with field participants, we argue that Miguel and Laurence (who migrated to Sweden for work) were most likely seen as skilled migrants by HR representatives and, by the interns, probably as members of an ethnic group perceived as a minority in Sweden. For Elin and Mohammed, who both grew up in Sweden and who attended the same Swedish university, we believe that the interns related Elin to the privileged 'Swedishness' described in the case, while Mohammed probably was seen as belonging to an ethnic minority.

Both in data collection and analysis, we were aware of possible boundaries created around ethnicity and language, as well as an alleged 'Swedish' way of working. We were not especially sensitive to forms of discrimination based on sexual identity, age or ability, and we may very well have overlooked them. Boundaries of class and status became visible during the analysis using perspectives inspired by Bourdieu.

This case presentation aims to convey the voices of the interns, and we acknowledge that the voices of HR practitioners have been given less precedence. Our ambition from the start has been to study potential forms of oppression likely to be endured as a consequence of the vulnerable positions of (unpaid) interns. This study, however, reveals that ethnicity, combined with access to different forms of capital, seems to shape very different conditions for the interns navigating the different linguistic, cultural and social boundaries encountered in their integration.

Recommendations

Based on our case study, it appears that the integration of skilled migrants into the labour market is dependent on notions of class and perceived ethnicity. Though most practitioners would expect new employees to learn the local ('Swedish') way of working, this study shows that integration is not only dependent on migrants' efforts to learn about a different culture, or on their hard work, but is also conditioned by their capacity to recognize and navigate the power-laden dimensions of class and ethnicity.

In this case, 'Swedishness' intersects with ethnicity and class and, as a result, we question whether existing descriptions of Swedish national forms of work culture (e.g., Holmberg and Åkerblom, 2006; Zander, 2000, and even more general works such as House et al., 2004) actually portray Swedish culture as experienced by a given social class—most likely the middle class, as it is seen as the most desirable social positioning. We therefore invite further studies in CCM to investigate whether the advanced cultural preferences of, for example, forms of leadership and work cultures are not, in fact, portraying the preference of a given class and therefore possibly normalizing not only a cultural but also a social mode of action.

This case study invites all of us to reflect critically on how we draw boundaries. What makes us assign an 'ethnic minority status' to a group, and, in contrast, a 'nationality' (e.g., Canadian) to another? How do we assign class, and how is it (potentially) linked to perceived ethnicity or nationality?

Additionally, we encourage practitioners to reflect on the forms of labour market integration provided for executives coming from different countries. By unreflexively giving precedence to local forms of work (language and practices, for example), different forms of capital are not acknowledged and are even less valued. In consequence, the potential of cultural diversity is unlikely to be realized and the benefit of a multicultural workforce a lost opportunity. We recommend practitioners reflect on established norms of practice and systematically question them as follows:

- What do we mean by 'succesful' integration of, for example, skilled migrants in our organization? Is this integration dependent on dimensions other than the person's willingness to integrate? What are these dimensions? Why?
- Is our prefered language at work our official corporate language? If not, who benefits from use of this language and who does not? Is this advantage reproducing hierarchical privileges?
- What have we implemented to appreciate and take advantage of the diversity brought to the organization by our employees? Is this working? Why/ why not?
- How explicit are our promotion criteria? Do they (implicitly) ask for behaviour attached to a certain class and ethnicity, which happens to be that of most of our managers?

Note

1. The authors of this chapter have received financial support from the Ragnar Söderberg foundation and Jan Wallanders and Tom Hedelius foundation, as well as Tore Browaldhs foundation (Sweden).

References

Adler N and Aycan Z (2018) Cross-cultural interaction: What we know and what we need to know. *Annual Review of Organizational Psychology and Organizational Behavior* 5: 307–333.

Aten K, Nardon L and Isabelle D (2016) Making sense of foreign context: Skilled migrant's perceptions of contextual barriers and career options. *International Journal of Cross Cultural Management* 16(2): 191–214.

Barth F (ed) (1998) *Ethnic Groups and Boundaries: The Social Organization of Culture Difference* (2nd ed). Long Grove: Waveland Press.

Bourdieu P (1980) *Le Sens Pratique*. Paris: Editions de Minuit.

Bourdieu P (1984) *The Distinction: A Social Critique of the Judgement of Taste*. Cambridge: Harvard University Press.

Chevrier S (2009) Is national culture still relevant to management in a global context? The case of Switzerland. *International Journal of Cross Cultural Management* 9(2): 169–183.

d'Iribarne P (2009) National cultures and organisations in search of a theory: An interpretative approach. *International Journal of Cross Cultural Management* 9(3): 309–321.

Gertsen M, Søderberg AM and Zølner M (2012) *Global Collaboration: Intercultural Experiences and Learning.* Houndmills: Palgrave Macmillan.

Hofstede G (2001) *Culture's Consequences: Comparing Values, Behaviors, Institutions and Organizations across Nations* (2nd ed). London: SAGE.

Holmberg I and Åkerblom S (2006) Modelling leadership: Implicit leadership theories in Sweden. *Scandinavian Journal of Management* 22(4): 307–329.

House RJ, Hanges PJ, Javidan M, Dorfman PW and Gupta V (eds) (2004) *Culture, Leadership, and Organizations: The GLOBE Study of 62 Societies.* Thousand Oaks: SAGE.

Hunger E and Mohsen M (2017) *Im/Materiell praktik: Berättelser om etnicitet och klass i ett praktikprogram på ett svenskt företag.* Kandidatuppsats i företagsekonomi, Handelshögskolan i Stockholm.

Iredale R (2001) The migration of professionals: Theories and typologies. *International Migration* 39(5): 7–26.

Lamont M (2000) *The Dignity of Working Men: Morality and the Boundaries of Race, Class, and Immigration.* New York, NY: Russell SAGE.

Romani L, Mahadevan J and Primecz H (2018) Critical cross-cultural management: Outline and emerging contributions. *International Studies of Management and Organization* 48(4): 403–418.

Zander L (2000) Management in Sweden. In: Warner M and Joynt P (eds) *Management in Europe.* London: Thomson Learning.

13

GENDER INITIATIVES BETWEEN SUPPORT AND DENIAL

A Cross-Cultural Study of Two Automotive Companies in Germany and France

Mounia Utzeri, Beáta Nagy and Iuliana Ancuţa Ilie

Introduction

Despite the increased attention to promote gender equality, to fight discrimination and to raise awareness of gender issues in the corporate world, efforts have brought about only limited results (Catalyst, 2018). Our starting point to explain this paradox is Acker's contribution (2006) which argues that gender is a constitutive and organising principle of every organisation and reflects wider societal inequalities. This means that companies wishing to tackle gender inequality nonetheless continue to reproduce inequalities unconsciously because the whole organization of society is already 'gendered'. From the perspective of this model, gender must be analysed as more than yet another marker of difference. However, if *only* gender is taken into account, other intersections become invisible and lost. For instance, the experience of those who are both a gender minority and a minority in terms of nationality might not be fully understood if gender becomes the only analytical category. Moreover, nationality is relevant as there are often "country images" attached to how a certain nationality is perceived by others and these images might also intersect with gender images. Consequently, we need to move towards the analytic framework of intersectionality.

Holvino (2012) has strengthened the notion of intersectionality and highlighted the idea of the "simultaneity of social differences". She conceptualises "race, ethnicity, gender, class, sexuality, nationality . . . as simultaneous processes of individual identity, institutional/organizational practices and social/societal practices" (Holvino, 2012: 7). This approach is particularly useful because it underlines that multiple, contradictory and contextual identities are more likely to emerge when the lives of both men and women become increasingly transnational.

In our chapter, we show how a combination of both models might be helpful for analysing the complexity of the intersectionality of gender and nationality/country of origin in cross-cultural contexts. Starting from Wallerstein's (1974) world system theory, we consider that different countries possess different power positions based on their position in the world economy, e.g., core countries, semi-periphery countries, or periphery countries. A country's relative position might affect its citizens' valuation in various contexts as well (Wallerstein, 1974). In a world characterized by increased international mobility, where people come from or their nationality might influence how they are received and perceived in a host country. We also posit that uneven power distribution in wider society complicates situated identities by more firmly embedding some people at the centre and others at the semi-periphery. We assume that gender is part of the corporate inequality regime and that it intersects with the aforementioned kind of inequality.

With these insights we undertake the study of two automotive companies in France and Germany. Both have diversity policies that prioritize gender. We focus on the narrated experiences of those employees who are international managers in this gendered organizational context. From their experiences, the intersections across gender and nationality become visible. The contribution lies in providing an intersectional approach to gender diversity and diversity by national background in a cross-national context.

Methodology

This case draws on qualitative interviews, participant observation and documentary analysis. The actual research was conducted by the first author between 2012 and 2015. The material, which provides the empirical basis for this chapter, stems from interviews conducted with 10 participants: three male and seven female managers, with four respondents at the French site and six at the German site. Table 13.1 provides a brief description of the interviewees.

TABLE 13.1 Interviewees' Description

Country of Case Companies	Gender of Respondents	Country of Origin	Level of Management
France	Female	Spain	Middle
France	Female	Poland	Middle
France	Male	Bulgaria	Middle
France	Female	Germany	Upper
Germany	Male	Italy	Middle
Germany	Female	Turkey	Lower
Germany	Female	France	Middle
Germany	Female	Hungary	Lower
Germany	Female	China	Upper
Germany	Male	Turkey	Upper

The sample is composed of what we refer to throughout the chapter as "international managers". We refer to international managers as those individuals in the companies studied who are neither French, nor German citizens in the respective organizations. We also did not include the descendants of immigrants to Germany or to France who hold passports of these countries. They were not expatriates either, but professionals who opted for an international career, or, as they are often called in the management literature "self-initiated expatriates" (Cerdin and Selmer, 2014). The interviewees thus do not belong to the dominant (national) groups of the case companies. Beyond being of another nationality, other dimensions such as ethnicity might play a key role (e.g. Utzeri, 2018).

The aim of the interviews was to find out how international managers in these companies perceive the issue of gender equality and experience the related organisational interventions. Our methodological approach throughout the chapter is intersectional, for it utilises Acker's gender inequality perspective and Holvino's notion of simultaneity of social differences to interpret the narratives of the participants. The main questions were broken down into two major blocks and formulated as follows: 1) According to your own experience and career path, is the management in your company gendered? How may gender have influenced (or not) managerial careers and advancement? 2) How do you perceive and experience the equal opportunity policies and other voluntary programs aimed at increasing women's representation at management level in your company?

Case Presentation

Gender and Diversity in the Context of the Case Companies in France and Germany

As political, legal and institutional contexts are likely to account for various models of gender equality and diversity in organizations (Acker, 2006; Tatli et al., 2012), it is crucial to briefly present the attitudes and regulations regarding gender in France and Germany. Both countries have gender equality policies in place, ranging from antidiscrimination legal frameworks to gender quota in political and economic decision-making positions (DIW, 2018; Eurofound, 2011).

The Special Eurobarometer 465 (TNS opinion & social, 2017) offers a comprehensive picture of various gender-related issues, such as the perception of the share of housework and caring activities, the question whether men should promote gender equality, attitudes towards legal measures to ensure parity in politics, and more. When asked whether they think that gender equality has been achieved at work, 69 percent of the respondents in France answered "No", yet when asked whether they think gender equality was achieved in leadership positions in companies and other organizations, the percentage increased to 72

(TNS opinion & social, 2017: 9–10). In Germany, 50 percent of the respondents did not think gender equality was achieved at work, this percentage increasing to 55 with respect to gender equality in leadership positions (TNS opinion & social, 2017: 4).

In addition when asked whether the most important role for men is to earn money, 62 percent of the respondents in Germany and 68 percent in France disagreed (TNS opinion & social, 2017: 7). Likewise, opinions about whether the most important role of a woman is to take care of her home and her family did not vary across France and Germany, with 72 and 71 percent respectively of respondents disagreeing (TNS opinion & social, 2017: 7). These results point towards French and German social contexts which seem to be supportive of and promote gender equality between men and women.

However, the majority of the workforce in the automotive industry in Europe is male (Catalyst, 2018). This can also be connected with Moore's findings (2015: 225) which signalled the existence of powerful gender stereotypes regarding femininity and masculinity, which further affect whether a job is considered "suited" for a woman or a man. We understand masculinity and femininity not as inborne characteristics, but rather as learned images and perceptions which shape gender roles.

Despite various measures undertaken to tackle gender balance among employees since the early nineties, our case companies in France and Germany remain a male domain: both organizations are characterised by vertical segregation; at the time of the study in 2013, nearly 10 percent of the management positions were held by women in the German company and 16.2 percent in the French company. There is also a strong horizontal gender segregation within the companies studied. The representation of women in HR, finances, and in sales and marketing is relatively high, with up to 70 percent of the workforce being female, but women typically hold positions in first-line (lower) management or middle management. Men make up the majority of upper managers.

The automotive industry is a technically and technologically driven industry. The previously mentioned female-dominated HR and marketing departments rarely are a path to top positions, such as executive and supervisory boards. Research and development, technical engineering, design and, recently, IT (Hanappi-Egger, 2012; Gill et al., 2017), are the key pool from which candidates for top management positions are selected.

Promoting nationality diversity alongside disability and gender is part of greater-diversity projects implemented by both companies. The principle of diversity is governed by antidiscrimination law and civil rights anchored in the French and German legal framework. Both countries are bound to the EU anti-discrimination law. However, only gender diversity is combined with affirmative actions such as a voluntary or mandatory gender quota. Organizational measures labelled as "managing diversity" at the French and German company range from awareness training to policy-based instruments for ensuring neutrality in recruitment processes. Ethnic origin and nationality diversity in both companies often seem confined to the companies' official communication and corporate social responsibility messages and are less obviously expressed in actions.

Interview Statements

In this section we present the key insights that emerged from the interviews of international managers, highlighting the way gender and nationality intersect in cross-cultural contexts.

Legitimacy of the Male Norm: "This Is a Men's World . . ."

Although the various initiatives found at both companies attempted to tackle gender issues in the workplace, all interviewees clearly declared gender as irrelevant to their career paths. The underrepresentation of women at top levels both in the French and German companies triggered the introduction of programs and measures countering this situation; inequality was made visible, but the international female and male managers interviewed in both French and German contexts concealed and denied gender-based inequality.

When asked about the reasons behind the underrepresentation of women in management, the interviewees unanimously answered that this was due to the technical character of the automotive sector. In this way, it becomes apparent that gender affects the assumptions made about women's skills, abilities and interests. Moreover, the belief that "this is a men's world, it has always been like this"—which is left unquestioned—legitimizes a male-dominated industry. Furthermore, the international male managers reinforced the existing inequality by stating that this is normal and natural in their countries of origin as well (see Table 13.1), where women face similar situations. Past reality ("it has always been like this") becomes an explanation for the present state and even for the future; or, as an international male manager postulates: "Women are just not made for these jobs, the automotive industry is and will stay a male area".

Although the interviewed male managers failed to acknowledge existing gender-based discrimination, the female managers seemed to comply with the gendered structures of their companies by reproducing the discourse of their male colleagues: one international female manager explained the scarce representation of women in technical fields by stating that "girls are just not attracted [to this field]". More importantly, international female mangers considered gender (manifested in a certain form of behaviour) as accounting for the hierarchy at the management level. For example, a French female manager working for the German company stated: "We women are different, too soft and emotional, we are not made for management, and we go against our nature [if in management positions]". A Chinese female manager indicated that women "are not used to being ambitious and assertive like men", affirming stereotypical masculine patterns of expected managerial behaviour. Therefore, intentionally or unintentionally, both female and male international managers complied with and legitimized gender inequality.

A closer investigation suggested, however, that these perceptions, for instance the denial of any gender inequality, are rooted in meritocratic discourse (the idea that decisions are solely rooted in merit-based criteria) which seems to be well anchored in both companies. International female managers chose to underline their competence and dismiss both their nationality and their gender. According to their own statements, they are aware of the simultaneous interplay between gender and nationality; the two dimensions reinforce each other. Likewise, a Turkish female manager at the German company explains: "Because I am Turkish, they expect a submissive person, hence, probably wearing a headscarf and quiet . . . Well, I am not, and I am loud. In my eyes, I never had a problem because I am a woman, it is rather the fact that I am Turkish and all stereotypes around the issue". In the interviewee's perspective, her nationality is rather determinant with regard to how the others perceive her, and being a woman is less problematic. Moreover, by highlighting the stereotypes linked to the image of Turkish females in the German society (wearing a headscarf is met with strong rejection both in Germany and France—see El Hamel, 2002; Weichselbaumer, 2016), the interviewee clearly shows how gender, nationality and ethnicity can merge in a given setting to produce marginalization. Moreover, these quotes also signal that the image of the country of origin can negatively influence how international managers are perceived in a new context.

A Polish female manager working for the French company believes gender would not create a debate in a different national context: "In Poland it is normal that women work in science and engineering, they even hold high positions in these fields. This is a legacy of the USSR times, while here in France they are rather underrepresented". She explicitly criticises the masculine image of technology and engineering professions prevalent not only in the French company but in French society at large. Therefore, the interviewee points to the existence of cultural categories regarding gender and the world of work, and she also suggests a possible explanation: communist regimes encouraged women's emancipation, and for her, being a woman is not a disadvantage. Working now in a cross-cultural context, where other images and beliefs are in place, she might challenge them and support another view of gender and gender policies. For the Polish female manager, her identity is a cross-cultural asset which supports the achievement of organizational change towards higher gender equality. This also means that the processes of simultaneous social differences might be culture-specific.

In this complex web of affirming, denying and constructing their identity elements, international women managers suggested and revealed innovative ways of overcoming and subverting the power relations in place. For instance, they describe the intersection of gender and nationality as a "surprise effect" or as a "weapon" or even "strength". A Spanish female manager working for the French company reveals how her multiple identities not only coexist, but can cause discomfort among her colleagues: "My counterparts must be careful, because they cannot categorize me, I am not French and not a man while I am a mechanical engineer, they do not know which strategies they must use, so I have the advantage". A French female manager working for the German company underlines: "This is my strength, I can play with this when bargaining, I am neither a man nor German, I catch attention, people remember me, men lower their guards in front of a woman, and this is where I hit".

The international male managers we interviewed do not regard themselves as belonging to a minority due to their country of origin or nationality in their working context, and this is also not projected upon them by the others: "Apart from the fact that my French colleagues struggle with my name, I never experienced a negative situation linked to my nationality, otherwise I wouldn't be where I am now", explained the Bulgarian male manager. The image of his country of origin seems to be positive and he is not perceived as being negatively different. Therefore, in contrast to the experiences of the international female managers, the international male managers do not recount any jokes being made about their nationality or their country of origin at the workplace. Meritocracy is again brought forward though its effects when discussing gender inequalities were unclear: "Our Company ensures equal opportunity for all, being Turkish never played a role in my career", said the Turkish male manager. He seems to believe in the assumption of working for a merit-based organization, thus, the existence of women's career advancement programs contradicts the assumption of fairness.

Does the meritocratic discourse actually hide the practice of inequality? How can CCM dismantle this discourse which risks becoming dominant? These are some of the questions which are tackled in the following section.

Power and CCM

This case illustrates the intricacies of the relationship between affirmative action programs (here: initiatives aimed at increasing women representation at top management level), the way they are understood and experienced by both female and male international managers, and the collision with the discourse of meritocracy. We approached this from an intersectional perspective to show how the interlinking of dimensions such as gender, nationality, and country of origin may negatively influence how certain individuals are perceived. We combined the insights of intersectionality theory with Holvino's (2012) simultaneity model. It elaborates on how working abroad might have different effects on women's and men's lives and how the country of origin and the nationality of men and women abroad become relevant.

However, the experiences and perceptions of international female and male managers are greatly shaped by discourses of meritocracy, which deny any relevance of the markers of difference, as well as the fact that such markers may have power implications. The assumption of working for a merit-based organization renders any diversity programs unavailing in the eyes of the interviewees and grants merit an inviolable position.

Our case study reveals multiple power implications: first, implementing programs designed to support women's career advancement can be a double-edged sword. The two companies focus solely on one identity marker (gender) which ties women to a fixed and unidimensional identity. At the same time, under the umbrella of such diversity measures, women are put into an inferior group, as this group apparently requires support. Second, the companies seem to be unaware that by their equality measures, they interfere with the assumed meritocracy of their organizations. If meritocracy is in place (and all the respondents strongly adhered to this assumption), why do the companies advantage women over men? How should the interviewed female and male managers make sense of their experience, considering the tension created by the assumption of sameness and difference?

These observations point to the paradoxical nature of power as described by Mahadevan (2017): in any interaction, one can find manifestations of power; from this point of view, power is omnipresent but it is also subject to change and reconfiguration. All our respondents are exposed to the "flows of power" (Clegg, 1989), but nevertheless they have the ability to act upon such flows. The international female managers reject the unidimensional image of identity projected upon them and show how simultaneous identity markers, such as gender, nationality and country of origin empower them. Avoiding placement in one category is a source of strength for some of the international female managers. The power of being different is gained also by ascribing different meanings to certain categories, as in the case of the Polish female manager: for her, working in a technical field *is* something for women. The case reminds us that it might be misleading and exaggerating if we focus on one category only (Acker, 2006) and we can see how efforts to accomplish equality can be biased.

A critical CCM should direct its attention towards such interpenetrating realities and their outcomes in a given context. It should foster dialogue between organizations, scholars and society at large, and, more importantly, it should continuously challenge established (or in the process of becoming established) beliefs, norms and policies.

Reflexive Considerations

The first author's multilayered standpoint had significant implications in the overall research approach. Moroccan-born, with a French upbringing, originating from suburban areas of Paris, studying abroad and finally working abroad for various German automobile manufacturers over the last decades, the first author could reflectively bring forward the ways in which gender, ethnicity and nationality intersect, rendering thus the interviewees' experiences visible.

The second author's perspective is influenced by her specific embeddedness into the post-socialist legacy of state feminism in Hungary. Because the gender topic in Eastern European countries has been perceived both solved and exaggerated by the general public and business stakeholders alike (as also noted by the Polish female respondent), it is even harder to find evidence for gender inequalities in post-socialist reports. Still, with these experiences one learns to read between the lines and understand the unspoken words.

The third author joined the writing process examining the bases and the claims of the chapter and approaching the material through a CCM lens. Interested in the changes of paradigms and thought over time, she is aware of the influence of her own experiences on any of her attempts of meaning-making in a given context.

In our chapter, we aimed to question and destabilize the work of gender equality strategies and to show that strategic discourse and practice represent a set of power relations. We also recognise the subjectivist nature of the experiences of our interviewees. In practice, both female and male interviewees, enjoying a relative status of power, typically adopted composed and professional attitudes tainted by managerial discourse. Many times, we could sense how the questions addressed to female interviewees awakened counter reactions and resistance, how they tried to smooth rough spots or hide issues. This was even more striking among male interviewees; resentment and frustration with regard to gender-equality measures were omnipresent.

Recommendations to Researchers, Students and Practitioners

There are at least two intertwined aspects which should be at the forefront of researchers', students' and practitioners' minds, as shown by our case study. On the one hand, organizations themselves design diversity measures which might set off unforeseen effects (e.g., homogenizing the category of female employees). At the same time, such measures collide with discourses of meritocracy, which already stands for commitment to equality. On the other hand, organization members have their own sense of what it means to be female or male. For instance, some of the international female managers in our study seemed to believe that women are not born competitive and assertive, thus incorporating and reproducing gender bias. Conversely, the interviewed international male managers failed to recognize that they, too, are gendered subjects; for instance, when they implicitly assumed that flexible work arrangements are only targeting women.

Therefore, the role of those committed to CCM and critical CCM is not only 1) to identify the intersections of various levels of meaning-making within organizations and to expose taken for granted beliefs and organizational practices, but also 2) to bridge the divide between men's and women's interests in organizations without falling into the pitfall of reductionist and universalist approaches.

Dominant organisational practice can be challenged and current gender diversity programmes can be enhanced by giving a greater attention to the narratives of international female managers. For some of them, there is no conflict between being a female and working in a technical field. It is their understanding and their perspectives which should be integrated into organizational frameworks. HR departments and organizations might benefit more from incorporating the alternative views of managers holding various nationalities or having various cultural backgrounds, than holding to a specific national way of "doing gender diversity".

Moreover, gender is not a standalone dimension, and gender programs should take into account other possible intersecting dimensions if a consistent change is to take place. Gender inequality should not only be challenged in terms of numbers, but rather in terms of valuing multiple competencies instead of meritocratic values charged with gendered and cultural assumption of work and management. We recommend companies to incorporate these critical views into HRM practices (for instance, redefining competencies and developmental appraisal) to challenge the dominant group not only numerically but "culturally".

It is necessary that researchers dedicate efforts to understand distinct experiences and the effects of connected roles and situations. For instance, the chapter shows the intricacies of men's attitudes towards gender inequality, gender diversity and intersectionality at large.

Only a critical analysis of beliefs regarding gender, nationality, ethnicity or other diversity dimensions can stop reinforcing stereotypes, thus finding an equitable solution that respects the needs of various social actors. Holvino's (2012) model of simultaneity and Acker's (2006) idea of inequality regimes enhance a multifaceted approach to organizational structure and culture.

We recommend that our readers go beyond the proposed interpretations of our case and think of other possible evaluations. They should address and reflect upon the following prospects: what does an organization value and what is the place of meritocracy within it? What could be the unintended effects of a meritocratic discourse on the sense-making of the employees and their identity construction? How is diversity understood by the members of a specific organization? Are diversity initiatives tailored to this understanding or are they a result of current trends? How and in which context or role can we challenge and encourage female and male employees to call into question their own beliefs and assumptions?

References

Acker J (2006) Inequality regimes: Gender, class, and race in organizations. *Gender and Society* 20(4): 441–464.

Catalyst (2018) Quick Take: Women in the Automotive Industry. Available at: www.catalyst.org/research/women-in-the-automotive-industry/#footnote19_h0yrecc (accessed 24 February 2019).

Cerdin J-L and Selmer J (2014) Who is a self-initiated expatriate? Towards conceptual clarity of a common notion. *The International Journal of Human Resource Management* 25(9): 1281–1301.

Clegg SR (1989) *Frameworks of Power.* London: SAGE.

DIW (2018) DIW Women Executives Barometer 2018. Available at: www.diw.de/documents/publikationen/73/diw_01.c.575403.de/dwr-18-03.pdf (accessed 7 May 2019).

El Hamel C (2002) Muslim diaspora in Western Europe: The Islamic Headscarf (Hijab), the media and the Muslims' integration in France. *Citizenship Studies* 6(3): 293–308.

Eurofound (2011) French Law to Increase Number of Women Directors. Available at: www.eurofound.europa.eu/publications/article/2011/french-law-to-increase-number-of-women-directors (accessed 7 May 2019).

Gill R, Kelan EK and Scharff CM (2017) A postfeminist sensibility at work. *Gender, Work and Organization* 24(3): 226–244.

Hanappi-Egger E (2012) Shall I stay or shall I go? On the role of diversity management for women's retention in SET professions. *Equality, Diversity and Inclusion: An International Journal* 31(2): 144–157.

Holvino E (2012) Time, space and social justice in the age of globalization: Research and applications on the simultaneity of differences. *Practising Social Change* 5: 4–11.

Mahadevan J (2017) *A Very Short, Fairly Interesting and Reasonably Cheap Book about Cross-Cultural Management.* London: SAGE.

Moore F (2015) An unsuitable job for a woman: A "native category" approach to gender, diversity and cross-cultural management. *The International Journal of Human Resource Management* 26(2): 359–363.

Tatli A, Vassilopoulou J, Al Ariss A and Özbligin M (2012) The role of regulatory and temporal context in the construction of diversity discourses: The case of UK, France and Germany. *European Journal of Industrial Relations* 18(4): 293–308.

TNS opinion & social (2017) Special Eurobarometer 465. *Gender Equality.* Available at: http://ec.europa.eu/commfrontoffice/publicopinion/index.cfm/Survey/getSurveyDetail/instruments/SPECIAL/surveyKy/2154 (accessed 11 February 2019).

Utzeri M (2018) *A Chance or a Trap? Understanding Gender Equality Schemes in Management.* PhD dissertation, Corvinus University of Budapest, Doctoral School of Sociology. DOI 10.14267/phd.2018034.

Wallerstein I (1974) *The Modern World System: Capitalist Agriculture and the Origins of the European World Economy in the Sixteenth Century.* New York: Academic Press.

Weichselbaumer D (2016) Discrimination against Female Migrants Wearing Headscarves. Available at: http://ftp.iza.org/dp10217.pdf (accessed 6 May 2019).

14

GLOBAL NORTH AND GLOBAL SOUTH

Frameworks of Power in an International Development Project

Hamid Foroughi

Introduction

The international development sector is composed of institutions and policies that arose after the Second World War to alleviate poverty and improve the living conditions in 'developing countries'. In such projects, people from different countries work together. The international development sector is, thus, by default 'cross-cultural' and, therefore, relevant for Cross-cultural management (CCM) theory and practice. However, it is seldom considered how international development projects involve a *specific* cross-cultural configuration which, as this case suggests, creates hierarchies in terms of the interrelated aspects of power and knowledge.

Specifically, international development projects involve the cross-cultural cooperation between organizations and individuals from developed countries ('the Global North') and from developing countries ('the Global South'). The terms Global North and Global South refer to the observation that those countries that rate the highest on development indexes—e.g., education, income, life expectancy—are mostly located in the Northern Hemisphere, whereas those countries that rate lower, tend to be located in the Southern Hemisphere. However, there is more to these terms. For instance, the countries of the 'Global North' are often the former colonial powers, whereas the 'Global South' is comprised largely of former colonial territories. In terms of culture, there is also the idea that the countries of the Global North are implicitly 'Western', in contrast to the presumably 'non-Western' regions of the Global South (Mahadevan, 2017: 121). The aforementioned hierarchies are thus partly 'real' (economic indicators of development) and partly rooted in commonly held ideas about the world—for instance, the assumption that 'Western culture' as implicitly 'developed' (Jackson, 2013; Primecz et al., 2016).

From the aforementioned perspective, we should view certain aspects of the international development sector as problematic. Although many development projects can have an immediate impact on improving the livelihood of the beneficiary communities, scholars who are critical of the development sector highlight how development aid has its own perils. For instance, it is argued that the foreign aid is unsustainable since it creates a chain of dependencies (Cardoso, 1982). In particular, post-colonial research—the academic study of the cultural legacy of colonialism and imperialism—maintains that the discourse of development has depicted an image of the South as backward, and a part of an inferior culture 'whose deficit can only be compensated by taking over Western ideas of rationality, productivity and modernity' (Ziai, 2016: 31). This literature has also discussed that the discourse of development can and will recreate hierarchies between North and South which can be seen as the continuation of the colonial economic regime (Escobar, 2011; Ferguson, 1990).

These hierarchies between North and South can also be reproduced in development projects, as they are funded by powerful donor organizations in the North which have their own perspectives on development. This has implications on what is perceived as legitimate knowledge (Mahadevan, 2017), which in turn could reinforce existing hierarchies. Postmodern and post-colonial thinkers have discussed the close relationship between power and knowledge extensively (e.g. Foucault and Gordon, 1980; Bhabha, 1994; Frenkel, 2008). Their argument is that existing relations of power render certain discourses (e.g., the expression of a set of ideas) possible, which in turn support a certain regime of truth or a certain knowledge claim. They also argue that knowledge created within a dominant discourse is likely to engender and support relations of power (Foucault, 1978: 97). These scholars further maintain that such power imbalances are normalised through the working practices that are accepted as a part of the normal discourse and therefore often remain invisible and rarely addressed. Despite the crucial importance of these matters, we know little about how these structural power asymmetries are reproduced at the micro level in development projects and how it affects the work practices in multicultural teams or the difficulties of addressing these issues at the micro level. To help answer these questions, I present a case study of a rare incident in which such implicit power asymmetries were openly discussed in an international development project. I analyse this event with the help of Clegg's (1989) 'frameworks of power', which suggests that power effects and how they are experienced are shaped by intersecting flows of power, namely structure, rules of practices and agency.

Methodology

This chapter employs a case study approach (Yin, 2003) to the members of a funded research project in the area of international development. The divide between Global North and Global South is visible in this team on both organizational and individual level (see next section), and this made this team an ideal setting to study the interrelated effects of power on cross-cultural cooperation. My aim was to understand how team members make narrative sense out of how they experienced the Global North and Global South divide when working together. To this end, I conducted semistructured interviews with six researchers (three of them from the Global North and three of them from the Global South) between July and September 2018. The interviews were 60 minutes long on average. The interviews were audio-recorded and transcribed. Because the topic of divide between the Global North and Global South in terms of power and knowledge already had been raised by some researchers from the Global South during an internal team workshop, a reflection on this event and the topic itself became a major focus of the interviews. Also, I got access to internal documents and memos which were exchanged by the researchers on this topic. Out of this information, I reconstructed the actual events during the workshop.

Case Presentation

The Governance and Development Research Consortium was a research project funded by a European donor agency. It involved North–South collaboration for research on themes related to governance in developing countries. The project was led by Worldwise (pseudonym), a reputable UK-based research organization with the experience of producing evidence to support international development policy. Partner organizations were based in four countries in the Global South (South Asia and East Africa). Together, this team should come up with 'scientific' evidence of what it takes to improve upon governance in these countries of the Global South.

What is notable about this setting is that countries of the Global South involved in the project are former British colonial territories. Furthermore, the researchers representing Worldwise in this project originate from the Global North (most of them were in fact Anglo-Saxon or Anglo-American). In the following, I use the term "UK-based" to indicate this group of people who are internally diverse in terms of their nationality but nonetheless similar in the sense that all originated from privileged Western European or North American contexts. Finally, the researchers representing the partner organizations in the Global South originated from these countries of the Global South (either in South Asia or East Africa). So, when I use the term "East African" or "South Asian researcher" in the following, I do it to indicate their individual country of origin but also their organizational affiliation and, thus, their current place of work.

Nonetheless, the team members were quite diverse in terms of gender, social class, age, work experience, internationality, nationality, country of origin and societal culture. Worldwise and partner organizations had been collaborating on this research project for several years. The research focused on understanding the difficulties of improving governance and development indexes in developing countries. The donor organization in the United Kingdom was pleased with the progress of the work and granted Worldwise additional funding to extend the work of the consortium by conducting complementary research to investigate the validity of the previous findings and shed light on some of the unanswered questions.

In preparation for this new phase of the research project, Worldwise organized a research workshop where researchers from all parties involved could come together to reflect on the previous findings, discuss how to present the research, and plan how to proceed. To facilitate the participation of partners from the Global South, it was decided to hold the meeting in a non-European country where it is easier to obtain an entry visa for team members with a non-European passport. A conference centre in the outskirts of an East African capital was chosen, as it offered competitive prices and a secluded place where the team could spend a full week working together. The chosen conference centre was in an old heritage state, surrounded by lush tea fields. The consortium leaders at Worldwise thought that what they perceived as "the natural surroundings" of the conference centre would provide a peaceful environment, in which team members could work on the project and plan their future work in a relaxing environment, away from the hustle and bustle of the city. The rural location of the site was also deemed advantageous to an effective use of the limited time available, so that participants would not be distracted by side activities. Participants were encouraged to stay onsite to maximise the amount of time the team members spent together, hoping it would forge a more collaborative work environment.

When the Worldwise staff arrived at the hotel, they were pleased to have found the old historic hotel in its beautiful surroundings. The complex consisted of many classic heritage bungalows in an early colonial pavilion built in the early 20th century. They were all quite excited to meet their partners, with whom they had been in regular Skype conversation but had not met in person for some time. In fact, since many Worldwise staff members had recently joined the project, it was going to be their first time meeting their research partners from the other organizations.

In the first two days, the project team gathered and started to work on various issues. The team made good progress, and the discussion was generally unruffled, if not uneventful. However, some tensions were slowly building up as the meetings progressed. It turned out that some of the team members from South Asia and East Africa were unimpressed with the venue and expressed their discontent about being restricted to the insulated hotel. They started planning on how to leave the conference centre to enjoy the evening elsewhere in a more relaxed environment. On the third day, they organized a taxi which then transported some of East African and South Asian researchers to a bar near the conference centre. Meanwhile, the UK-based team members worked on their research designs or caught up with other projects that they were working on. The next evening, when a minibus parked outside the hotel, the UK-based researchers learned that most of the partner researchers had arranged to visit the city centre, while none of "them" (UK-based researchers) were told about this.

Because of this, tensions rose which were interpreted along the lines of Global South and Global North by the researchers themselves. It seemed that, somehow, the idea of an identifiable group of researchers 'from the Global South' emerged, as opposed to a group of 'White Western' researchers who represented United Kingdom -HQ and 'the Global North'. This happened despite alternative differences in terms of class, gender, age, experience, country and nationality which were also present in this team.

The perceived rift between members from the Global South and the Global North escalated on the fourth day of the workshop. Although previously the split was most apparent in the ways in which team members spent their time after the work hours, the division became more noticeable during work meetings. In their retrospective reflections during the interview, Worldwise staff stated that they did not expect this level of tension in their relationship with partner researchers. At times, even what they thought would be a simple technical decision about modifying the deliverables provoked strong resistance from members of the Global South partners and resulted in a polarised debate. One of the UK-based members recalled the growing tensions in the work meetings:

> I can think of one example now. Our team leader had made a decision that because of the limited budget for the second phase of the project, instead of doing a country report that summarises the report for each country, we can produce three thematic reports that look at the findings across all different countries. We did not think that this was going to be a contentious issue [at the time], as the decision was made purely based on the budget and time limitations. But when she brought this up with our partners, one of the partner researchers strongly questioned why she was making this decision. A couple of other researchers from partner organizations backed her [the partner researcher] up and questioned why Worldwise was taking the power away from the local countries. They felt that we were somewhat manipulating the process so that the analysis can be made by Worldwise staff rather than the local country experts.

The discussions at times got polarised, as project members started to pick a side in the debates according to whether they were positioned as 'Global North' or 'Global South' team members. In several discussions, UK-based researchers backed up the Worldwise project leaders, while several other researchers, based in partner organizations in the Global South, questioned the rationale for the decision made by the project leaders. One of the UK-based researchers retro-spectively recalled how the meetings became polarised:

> You know some of the discussion got much more emotional than expected. Some issues did not get resolved at that point. When I think back about the dynamics of the disagreement, it [must have] felt like Worldwise white researchers are arguing against coloured southern researchers.

Nonetheless, it appeared that the project team had made some progress in dis-cussing their approach to research and planning the project. As experienced managers who had worked in several North–South collaborative projects in the past, Worldwise project leaders were not unfamiliar with such workplace disagreements. They understood the discussions as a typical disagreement that could arise between HQ and operations staff in any complex project involving multiple parties. Yet, as they had sensed a growing sense of discontent among the partner researchers, they thought it would be good to discuss this more openly and directly, hoping that it could help mend the relations.

Consequently, the Worldwise project leaders addressed the group in the last few hours of the workshop and asked whether there were any substan-tial issues that the partner researchers wanted to discuss before they all left the conference centre. After a few seconds of uncomfortable silence, a South Asian researcher responded by criticising Worldwise management practices for a relative lack of transparency. She also spoke about excessive control, and about how Worldwise staff (in particular, project leaders) imposed their will on the partner organizations. This was backed up by some of researchers from South Asia and East Africa, who questioned existing power imbalances in the project. Another South Asian researcher based in partner organizations resisted what she described as an existent "*knowledge hierarchy*" among the project members. She described this as a context wherein Western employees and their (Western-based) theoretical knowledge is deemed superior to an inside (emic) perspective to development, based on the contextual knowledge of local project members.

Some of the criticism that was directed towards Worldwise went beyond the work practices within the particular consortium and referred to a general "extractive" nature of research in the international development sector. While the researchers of the Global South stated that this was not the case in the latest phase of the project, they also argued that in many instances local staff are pro-viding the raw material—that is, the data collected from local respondents—while the processing and generation of valuable goods—that is, the analysis of the data and producing the reports—is done elsewhere (the Global North). They suggested that such practices create and entrench a hierarchy of knowl-edge, as the conceptual work, in which the intellectual and reputation rewards lies, is left in the hands of UK-based researchers. As such, they argued that the existing practices in the industry do little to foster the intellectual advancement of researchers in the partner organizations in the Global South.

In particular, one of the researchers based in a partner organization interpreted such power imbalances within the industry as the remnants of the colonial system. This analogy with the colonial process was partly inspired by the colonial heritage of the site of the workshop. In particular, a few of the researchers perceived the choice of the venue as an affront to them and as a sign of insensitivity of Worldwise staff members about such power imbalances. A researcher from East Africa pointed out that she was uncomfortable in the venue as she found it a blunt reminder of the colonial history in her own country. Another researcher from South Asia also made similar remarks, suggesting that the venue reminded her of upsetting memories of her grandparents who had worked as indentured labourers in a British colonial tea plantation.

Another researcher from South Asia then argued that existing work practices based on the stated knowledge hierarchies between Global North and Global South have real implications for the delivery of the developmental projects and weaken their overall impact on the host countries too. He reasoned that the general consensus that the Global North needs to develop the Global South is flawed: "This means that development projects often builds on Western theories; as a result they are often implemented with little understanding of the local context and the structure of the society". In his view, the project structure and practices which sustain this knowledge hierarchy between North and South made it more difficult for researchers in the Global South to use their knowledge effectively to influence the development goals.

> The imposition from the North towards the South makes it more complicated to give leverage, or room to manoeuvre, to local development partners [so that they can] use their understanding of the local context and their knowledge for tackling a particular development issue in the best possible way. This knowledge hierarchy creates more discrepancy between what are *real* outcomes of the research and [between] the *expected* outcomes which are being driven from the North.

This direct and harsh tone of criticism was quite surprising for most UK-based researchers. They understood the rationale behind some of the issues raised by partner researchers and were sympathetic to their concerns about the power imbalances in the international development world. Like their partners in the Global South, UK-based staff had joined the international development sector with the ambitions to help empower developing countries to tackle their developmental difficulties and ameliorate some of the unjust practices in the world.

The UK-based researchers acknowledged that they often drew on Western theories rather than emic development perspectives, as the former was more readily available to them. More broadly speaking, they maintained that comparatively fewer substantial frameworks are developed from an indigenous point of view as so much of the 'Southern' work still draws on 'Northern' frameworks. They understood that this could create some power imbalances in the research projects. They were, however, also aware that they had to work with the requirements of the donors, who often brought in their own perspectives and required the delivery of the project in a tight timeframe. This meant that the structure of the work, agreed deliverables and time limitations often restricted their ability to engage with alternative sources of knowledge. One of the UK-based researchers explained it like this:

> In theory, each researcher can bring their own framework and perspectives. There are always alternatives. You could say there is a hierarchy and criticise it, but you have to have a pretty robust and well-defined framework before you start collecting data and analysing data. In the end, we are limited by the structure of the project. *There are always alternatives, and, yes, you technically could have an enormous report to include all these perspective. It is philosophically possible.*

The discussion about this 'knowledge hierarchy' continued for over an hour. As the initial antagonizing discussions subsided, different researchers, both from the Global North and the Global South, pushed for a constructive and collaborative approach to address the issue. The Worldwise project leaders accepted that some of the adopted practices might have caused a continuation of a certain knowledge hierarchy and vowed to find ways to tackle this issue. But they also highlighted that power imbalances are not only limited to the hierarchies between the Global North and Global South. For instance, they suggested that, at times, younger female researchers might be disadvantaged due to certain norms that associate expertise and authority to masculinity and seniority. They called for ways to tackle all sort of dysfunctional power imbalances. To make this more official, the project team agreed to assign a 'knowledge hierarchy whistleblower' who should try to act as an arbitrator if and when future issues arise.

Power and CCM

Working in a cross-country setting involves dealing with different implicit forms of power asymmetries. We therefore need to carefully reflect upon how power and the categories of difference that seem to prevail at work intersect. This is important because such hierarchies could have implications for the participation of different actors in the process of knowledge creation. Knowledge hierarchies can be understood as the result of ongoing 'flows of power' at three different levels: structure, practice and agency (Clegg, 1989). In his classic work, 'Frameworks of Power', Clegg suggests these flows of power are interconnected and shape the experience of power (see also Mahadevan, 2017). Analysing a phenomenon like 'knowledge hierarchy' thus requires understanding the relations of power at all above levels.

Analysing structural aspects of power means that we need to look at social structures, discourses, norms and regulations that sustain certain hierarchies. For instance, as discussed in the previous section, the dependency of development projects on funds from the donor organizations, based in the Global North, have implications for the nature of the relationship between the lead organizations, based in the Global North, and partner organizations in the Global South.

First, this creates asymmetric power relations within international development projects which are typically conceived and directed by staff members from the Global North while staff members from the Global South implement and manage the projects on a day to day basis. These power asymmetries are normalised and legitimated—and, to some extent, compounded—through staff members from the Global North having higher perceived cultural capital—that is, the social assets of a person—such as degrees from well-known universities and being affiliated with prestigious organisations and influential people (see also Goxe and Paris, 2016). As such, staff members based in the Global North are seen as having the 'right' education and contacts, and are perceived as fluent in using the language, the vocabulary and the theoretical frameworks that donors are drawing upon and that they can provide the type of analysis that donors are looking for. The dependency of the development project on funds from the Global North thus works as a structural factor which can feed into the knowledge hierarchies that were discussed in the case study.

Second, it can be also argued that such knowledge hierarchies are recreated by the international development discourse which is closely affiliated with the discourse of 'help' which depicts 'non-Western countries or 'the Global South' as undeveloped and in need of Western help and education (Ziai, 2016). This dichotomy often presupposes that it is only 'the non-West' or 'the Global South' that can learn from 'the developed West', which implicitly undermines the idea that 'the non-Western Global South' might also contribute to the process of knowledge creation its own right (Mahadevan, 2017).

We should also analyse practices that might contribute to knowledge hierarchies. Practices are procedures adopted by organisations which can strengthen or reduce power imbalances and knowledge hierarchies. In this case study, I discussed that the division of labour in the project could significantly influence power hierarchies and enable or limit the contribution of the Global South in the process of knowledge creation. For instance, when the research design and conceptual frameworks are finalised by researchers in the lead organization based in the Global North, the role of researchers in the Global South will be restricted to data collection which can significantly limit the scope of their participation in knowledge creation. The practices surrounding the process of data analysis, that is who writes the report and which people will be named (e.g., as authors) on the produced outputs (e.g., reports), will also have implications on power asymmetries in the international development projects. People and organizations who are named on the reports will often gain the intellectual credit for the work and can use them as reputational assets to further their career and organisational brand.

Finally, knowledge hierarchies can be analysed at the 'agency' level; that is, the extent to which individuals by their own capacity can overcome, influence or, in fact, strengthen systems of power. Individual researchers have some degrees of freedom in influencing knowledge hierarchies. For instance, in the meeting in East Africa, researchers based in the Global South attempted to appropriate the power asymmetries by raising the issue directly with their other colleagues in the consortium. Worldwise consortium leaders also made an impact by allowing the discussion to take place. They also attempted to involve partner researchers—based in the Global South—in the process of research earlier, so they can contribute to the project design. As such, individuals can influence (albeit to a limited degree) the dynamics of production of knowledge hierarchies by amending the practices that were upholding a certain knowledge hierarchy. Although in this case, Worldwise consortium leaders acted to reduce knowledge hierarchies, we can imagine a scenario in which a manager takes the opposite direction by initiating practices which further entrench power asymmetries.

In summary, this case suggests that structure, rules of practice and agency come together in shaping actual power effects and how they are experienced. I suggest that cross-country collaborations in general and international development projects in particular should create a space for to the discussion of knowledge hierarchies, so that project teams can empirically negotiate their work processes to deal with different perceptions and biases.

Reflexive Considerations

As a researcher originally from the Global South, I sympathised with the viewpoints put forwards by researchers from South Asia and West Africa. I tend to share their view that overlooking local knowledge has contributed in the failure of some of the progressive and developmental programmes in these parts of the world. However, having worked and currently being employed in the Global North context (United Kingdom), I also understood the challenges faced by Worldwise researchers which limited their capacity to delve deeper in these issues. Writing this manuscript made me think about the role of hybrid actors like myself in bridging these gaps. Although structural issues exist, hybrid actors with awareness of different viewpoints can use their fluency in both cultural domains to shape a constructive dialogue between different parties involved to generate new insights. In what follows, I briefly outline the recommendations that I draw from this case study.

Recommendations to Students, Researchers and Practitioners

Working with the assumption that any cross-cultural experience can be analysed from traditional etic theories of culture—that is, study of cultures from a generalised, predefined and universal set of cultural dimensions—is problematic and could backfire. Based on this case, it is recommended that when one is involved in a cross-country project, one should be attentive to the dominant discourses that could marginalise or silence alternative interpretations and practices. In other words, we need to problematize the common or dominant understanding that has been taken for granted or has remained unchallenged, despite existing evidence that suggests otherwise. As emphasised by Mahadevan (2017), we need power-sensitive tools to establish a non-discriminatory and non-stereotyping CCM practice. As such, I suggest we should sensitise ourselves to different forms of knowledge hierarchies by asking the following questions:

- What are the dominant discourses that shape attitudes and values in a particular industry?
- How do such dominant discourses produce discontent or grievance among those who are disadvantaged by them?
- How do existing social structures, norms and regulations negatively affect an equal participation of a group of workers in a cross-country project?
- How can the adopted work practices impact the participation of different groups in knowledge creation?
- How can our individual actions and attitudes appropriate the practices and structures which are restricting the participation of certain groups of workers in knowledge creation?
- What are other knowledge hierarchies or power imbalances—besides Global North versus Global South—which might restrict workers participation in the creation of knowledge?
- What is the role of hybrid actors—that is, those individuals who can bring in alternative perspectives—in the reduction of knowledge hierarchies?

Conclusion

This case study shows that structural power asymmetries contribute to how knowledge hierarchies are produced and maintained by different actors and in different contexts. As they are normalised in everyday practice, they often remain hidden, but it does not mean that they are not experienced by individuals or have no impact on the outcome of work processes. Recognising them as substantial forces at work is the first step in paving the way to addressing them. Future research should look into the difficulties of addressing knowledge hierarchies in more depth, in particular, it is important to explore how the existence of multiple relations of power and hierarchies of knowledge (not only Global North vs. Global South) can complicate this matter further.

More specifically, this case study shows that practitioners in the international development sector in particular should be attentive to such hierarchies. One of the main challenges in overcoming cross-cultural differences is making them explicit (Di Stefano and Maznevski, 2000). This is because team members might have diverging perspectives of the risks of an open conflict or might presume that nothing can be done about it given the systematic nature of such hierarchies. The time constraints set by donor agencies also means that discussing power asymmetries is not a priority. This can be reversed if donors pay specific attention to how a project tackles global knowledge hierarchies as one of their criteria for assessing development projects.

References

Bhabha HK (1994) *The Location of Culture*. London: Routledge.

Cardoso FH (1982) Dependency and development in Latin America. In: Alavi H and Shanin T (eds) *Introduction to the Sociology of "Developing Societies"*. London: Palgrave, pp. 112–127.

Clegg SR (1989) *Frameworks of Power*. London: SAGE.

Di Stefano JJ and Maznevski ML (2000) Creating value with diverse teams in global management. *Organizational Dynamics* 29(1): 49–63.

Escobar A (2011) *Encountering Development: The Making and Unmaking of the Third World*. Princeton: Princeton University Press.

Ferguson J (1990) *The Anti-Politics Machine: "Development", Depoliticization and Bureaucratic Power in Lesotho*. Cambridge: Cambridge University Press.

Foucault M (1978) *The History of Sexuality: An Introduction*. New York: Vintage.

Foucault M and Gordon C (1980) *Power/Knowledge: Selected Interviews and Other Writings 1972–1977*. New York: Pantheon.

Frenkel M (2008) The multinational corporation as a third space: Rethinking international management discourse on knowledge transfer through Homi Bhabha. *Academy of Management Review* 33(4): 924–942.

Goxe F and Paris M (2016) Travelling through the class ceiling? Social mobility of "traditional" and "new" expatriates. *International Journal of Cross Cultural Management* 16(2): 171–189.

Jackson T (2013) Reconstructing the indigenous in African management research: Implications for international management studies in a globalized world. *Management International Review* 53(1): 13–38.

Mahadevan J (2017) *A Very Short, Fairly Interesting and Reasonably Cheap Book about Cross-Cultural Management*. London: SAGE.

Primecz H, Mahadevan J and Romani L (2016) Why is cross-cultural management scholarship blind to power relations? Investigating ethnicity, language, gender and religion in power-laden contexts. *International Journal of Cross Cultural Management* 16(2): 127–136.

Yin RK (2003) *Case Study Research Design and Methods*. London: SAGE.

Ziai A (2016) *Development Discourse and Global History: From Colonialism to the Sustainable Development Goals*. London: Routledge.

15

EXPLORING OUTSIDER/ INSIDER DYNAMICS AND INTERSECTIONALITIES

Perspectives and Reflections From Management Researchers in Sub-Saharan Africa

Emanuela Girei and Loice Natukunda[1]

Introduction

In this chapter, we aim to contribute to the development of an intersectional approach to culture in cross-cultural management (CCM) studies by exploring the experience of insider and outsider ethnographers.

Our particular focus lies in ethnographic research, which can be understood as a 'frame of mind', informing both research and practice (Mahadevan, 2017, chapters 1 and 2). In this sense, managers can also act as 'ethnographers' if they wish to better understand how the people around them understand and interpret their realities and daily events.

Simply put, ethnographers seek to understand how groups of people make sense of their world. The underlying perspective adopted is informed by social constructivism, which suggests that reality is not objective but constructed via social contacts and interactions.

Critical ethnography, to which we refer, pays attention to and actively engages with the power dynamics shaping how reality is constructed. The underlying assumption is that the social construction of reality is not a neutral process, but it is rather affected by historic and structural inequalities and privileges that inform individual sense-making, performance and positioning. This means that no researcher, ethnographer, student or manager (nor their colleagues) can have a neutral, objective or detached position on how they try to make sense of their own and others' experience. In this regard, it is important to consider that most CCM knowledge originates from what is commonly termed the 'developed Western' world or the 'Global North'. More widely, it has been argued that management knowledge is firmly rooted in "Westocentric assumptions" (Prasad, 2009), as it has been predominantly produced in North America and the United Kingdom, ignoring non-Western organisations.

It is widely recognised that being an insider ethnographer (e.g., sharing key characteristics with the participants, such as skin colour or national/ethnic identity) or an outsider has a significant impact on the research process (Roger et al., 2018) and more generally upon management practice. However, in management studies, including mainstream CCM, insider and outsider identities have been predominantly conceived on the basis of nationality or national culture or both. This might lead to an understanding of cultures and identities as fixed and stable. Conversely, intersectionality invites us to consider two important caveats.

One is that culture (and identity) can and should be conceptualised beyond, across or within mere national borders. It is, therefore, possible to conceptualise culture (and identity) in the form of professional culture, organisational culture, gender culture and so on. Additionally, Mahadevan (2011) argues that all these levels of culture might be as equally powerful as the assumedly most important national culture. Thus, identities can go beyond nationality and geographical classification to cover a range of identities including age, caste, ethnicity, religious belief, sexuality, physical ability, personality and even class (Tinker and Armstrong, 2008: 53).

Secondly, we should recognise that our identities and affiliations are also positioned, framed and shaped by those around us (such as research participants and colleagues). Thus, we understand 'insider' and 'outsider' status as social and situational and continuously intersecting with other axes of identity; related, for instance, to skin colour, ethnicity, gender and class. However, intersectionality, as we understand it in this chapter, is not simply about adding identity markers, such as gender or race, to each other. Rather, it is about understanding how these markers interact among themselves and how such processes reinforce or potentially challenge existing inequalities and asymmetries. So, our chapter is not about the researchers' identities 'as they are' but rather about the processes and systems through which they are constructed ('made') and performed ('done').

Starting from this background, we also acknowledge that intersectionality has been often used (especially in management studies) as "a tool for collating and commodifying 'differences'" (Liu, 2018: 83), eschewing exploring interlocked systems of power and oppression, such as those dominating the academia and knowledge production more widely. In this sense, previous research has shown how an instrumental adoption of the notion of intersectionality, which positions race along with other axes of identities, can undermine efforts to address racism and marginalisation, while simultaneously reinforcing white privilege and domination (Rodriguez and Freeman, 2016).

Thus, although this chapter aims to explore how a focus on intersectionality might help supersede an understanding of identity and culture as fixed and stable and thus a rigid divide between insider and outsider researchers (looking specifically at sub-Saharan Africa), we shall do so acknowledging the relevance of issues of race and racism, whiteness and blackness and wider asymmetries that have historically framed the relations between indigenous African populations and outsiders, and between African scholars and outsider scholars in academic knowledge production. Thus, as it will be discussed in the following pages, we do embrace the epistemological and political value of intersectionality, but we are also cautious and attentive not to obscure historically rooted and still existing asymmetries including those shaped by race and skin colour.

Thus, the twofold argument we develop in this chapter on one side explores how a focus on intersectionality helps CCM scholars and practitioners working in sub-Saharan Africa to supersede rigid understandings of insiders and outsiders. On the other side, it emphasises the importance of recognising our own different positioning in the wider context, and in the wider systems of domination and oppression, such as those that have shaped academic knowledge production so far.

The chapter is divided into four further sections. In the next section, we introduce some key methodological issues that lie at the foundation of this research. Then, we present the case studies and the empirical material, reflecting on how identity is continuously constructed along with the research process and on its role in the knowledge production processes. This is followed by a section that highlights some key issues regarding power dynamics, identity and CCM knowledge. The final section highlights some recommendations for colleagues, students and practitioners engaging in CCM in the Global South.

Methodology

This case draws on two kinds of sources, namely our own experience and qualitative interviews. More specifically, we had several reflexive meetings, which focused on our experience as insider (Loice) and outsider ethnographers (Emanuela) with organisations in sub-Saharan Africa. They attribute meaning to their working contexts and guide their actions and decisions.

In addition to the authors' reflexive meetings, this research also draws on in-depth interviews with five insider and five outsider researchers selected through snowball sampling. These 10 researchers all have experience of doing research in sub-Saharan Africa with national organisations, including nongovernmental organisations, primary schools, social enterprises and local government. Organisations were located in rural areas, small town centres as well as major cities in sub-Saharan Africa. During the interviews, participants were encouraged to, as much as possible, reflect and share their experiences of doing research in an Africa-based organisation. Interviews lasted approximately one hour; they were all recorded and transcribed verbatim.

Case Presentation and Reflexive Considerations

In this section, we first explore the authors' research context and introduce some key reflections. We then analyse further some key issues, also drawing on participants' views, which we discussed during in-depth qualitative interviews.

Emanuela

I worked as a management advisor and researcher in Uganda with different nonprofit organisations, mainly working in rural and semirural settings. For instance, one of them was based and operated in a rural setting, with a minimum level of infrastructure (e.g., there was no electricity and no running water) and worked especially with farmers. The other two organisations I worked with were based in semirural small towns and operated in rural areas with a variety of groups (such as women, farmers, schools). All these organisations had less than 10 members of staff and were entirely dependent on foreign donors' funds.

As an organisational psychologist with 15 years of experience in a similar role in Europe, I saw these assignments as an opportunity to reflect more systematically and widely on my practice, as they evoked a number of questions regarding the appropriateness of my background in such a role, and the impact of my own identity and positionalities. More specifically, since the beginning of my work with them, I had to constantly take into account my identities, for several reasons. For instance, my whiteness was a clear identity marker, which was constantly emphasised in several ways by the people I met and with whom I worked, which compelled me to continuously investigate my whiteness, not as a physical marker, but as a 'performative identity' (Liu, 2018: 88) which shapes power dynamics and the relational constellation of the research context. In addition, I was a management advisor and researcher and I was expected to provide guidance on management and organisational issues. However, although I was committed to challenging the Westocentric nature of management knowledge, I often perceived the ambiguity in my position, caught between being committed to critiques on the Western gaze on the Other and sensitive to the marginalisation of African voices and scholars on the one hand, and, on the other hand, being a white Western woman studying Ugandan organisation.

Loice

I did ethnographic research with one of the Ugandan agricultural research organisations which had slightly over 500 employees. The employees came from all over the country and thus had varied cultural backgrounds, since Uganda is comprised of over 50 ethnic groups. Besides, some projects were internationally funded and controlled, with both national and international staff.

Along this research, I experienced what could be called a double insider positionality. I am black Ugandan and have been raised in Uganda, and I also had worked at the case organisation prior to returning there as a researcher.

However, although it could be assumed that my nationality and previous experience with the organisation were an advantage in negotiating what would be naturally considered to be cultural boundaries, my experience was more complicated than this. Because I had worked in the organisation as a line manager, participants were, in some instances, looking at me as a top management representative. In addition, despite being black Ugandan, I had been educated abroad and my education and exposure to foreign culture somehow disqualified me from the insider positionality. And I was often reminded: "You've changed, remember this is Kampala, it's not Europe". In other terms, my old identity as manager and my foreign education seemed to prevail on my national/ethnic identity and this supports the notion that categorisation of culture goes beyond nationality, as discussed previously.

Towards an Intersectional Approach to Insiderness and Outsiderness

Starting from quotes taken from our reflective meetings and the interviews with our colleagues, in this section we discuss two key issues that emerged from our data related to researcher's identities and intersectionalities, namely precarious identity's boundaries, and endogenous/indigenous knowledge.

Importantly, and in line with our commitment to acknowledging historically rooted asymmetries between indigenous and outsider scholars in the production of knowledge about sub-Saharan Africa, we shall use the 'insider' and 'outsider' labels when referring to the research participants.

Precarious Boundaries

With precarious boundaries, we intend to highlight how our identities are not fixed and stable, but rather are continuously shaped and negotiated through the encounters we make, and such processes can hardly fit rigid categorisation along national, colour and ethnic boundaries.

For instance, although researchers working in sub-Saharan Africa can, to some extent, be distinctively labelled using the insider/outsider markers due to skin colour and nationality, one clear aspect that emerges from our data is the complexity and diversification of national culture, which makes the 'insider' label particularly precarious or unstable. For example, from our data it emerges that, although the 'insider' label may presumably fit a black national born and raised in sub-Saharan Africa, it often happened that researchers were positioned as nationals and yet as outsiders, as discussed by Diane:

I am of the same nationality with them but I was a total foreigner among them. So, when you are talking about a foreigner doing research among natives; I was typically that among native Ks.

(Diane, Insider Participant)

This quote shows that sharing the national cultural background does not ensure neither familiarity nor higher ability or possibility to understand the local context. Previous research has explored the distinctiveness of doing research in Africa from an insider status (e.g., Natukunda et al., 2016), highlighting a set of distinctive dimensions, including those related to the impact of Western knowledge systems but also regarding a set of specific challenges faced by native researchers along the research process, from access to participants to the politics of representation (Natukunda et al., 2016).

In addition, both insider and outsider researchers highlight how their role and their status are profoundly unstable and continuously shifting, as discussed in the following quotes:

Yes, I felt that I was not trusted especially at the beginning of the study. At times, I would be speaking to them and then they switch to their local language which I did not understand. That would happen when I was not with the interpreter. That died off over time and they got free with me.

(Clare, Insider)

But along the research, it happened that I was in a situation where I was an insider . . . Or if I was in a meeting or workshop with different organizations, if I was there with my colleagues, I felt an insider with the organisation even if there were other people from Europe, I felt closer with the organization [I was working with] than with other [white] people.

(Sarah, Outsider)

These quotes not only highlight the plural, constructed and shifting nature of our identities, but also emphasise the need to acknowledge that our identities and affiliations are positioned, framed and shaped by the research participants and the research context more widely. This supports those critiques toward a homogenised and simplified conceptualisation of national culture (common in mainstream CCM studies) and invites us to embrace notions such as 'multiple cultures' and 'cultural complexity' (Mahadevan, 2011), which frame culture as a fluid, in-progress, multifaced, context-bound system, and recognise that within the same national borders a plurality of cultures coexists.

This does not mean that insider and outsider researchers share the same experience. For instance, outsider researchers discussed at length their own subject position, especially with regard to their whiteness. From our research, it emerges that virtually all white researchers and practitioners with experience of empirical work in sub-Saharan Africa are, sooner or later, compelled to deal with their whiteness, here understood not as a physical attribute, but rather as performative identity resulting from historically rooted asymmetries and privileges, that, as shall be discussed in the following sections, can and should be challenged.

Indigenous/Endogenous Knowledge

Another key issue that emerges from our data are the categories of indigenous and endogenous perspectives. This relates to the quality, depth and authenticity of the knowledge produced by insiders and outsiders and their abilities or possibilities to further and strengthen what is usually called 'indigenous knowledge'.

In general, there is no guarantee that 'insiders' or native African researchers would be better positioned than Western native researchers for indigenous knowledge generation. For instance, one of our participants expressed the following:

> There is a debate about how African scholars should engage a lot with African issues because they may understand them better; that's the assumption. A lot of literature on management in Africa is produced by Europeans and all the other people. Some people are advocating for Africans to study Africa. But your experience and mine as well shows that we are actually not 100% conversant with our own society.
>
> *(Maria, Insider)*

However, while many of our participants agreed that, in itself, the insider/outsider identity does not necessarily ensure either better relations or easiness to understand the local contexts, it also clearly emerged that the lack of empirical research in sub-African contexts hampers the research process and the production of knowledge responsive to the local context, as outlined here:

> I am also doing a literature review on the same area and I have got more than 1000 papers of research work done and less than 20 are from researchers based here. It is a serious issue. When these [Western-based researchers] people write, they push their own perspective and interpretations. It doesn't help us. So, we need people who are based here who can generate knowledge that has that flavour of here.
>
> *(Grace, Insider)*

> We are quite limited sometimes as Western researchers because we are theoretically sensitized and the whole theories and concepts that we are basing our study on are Western to start with. So, it's about challenging those things, it's about seeing everything from a different point of view which I think is absolutely essential and most studies should be carried out from the African perspective to start with instead of the Western as a

point of reference unfold. And for that, I think it's very important to have African researchers doing that. But that's why I think that there is a synergy or at least a symbiosis if we combine two researchers from different backgrounds. I think that could lead to very valuable research.

(Claire, Outsider)

Her (a Ugandan colleague) supervisor happened to come and he was white. When he was there, people started to talk, to participate actively in the research . . . People think that when someone of a different colour comes to study about your community, in the back of their mind maybe this person has some projects or interventions that will help. [. . .] also, there will be some persons that will want to be associated with a white researcher, just for a question of status, and thus they are willing to volunteer information.

(Rob, Insider)

Thus, because of the multiple intersecting identities and positionalities, including multiple outsider and insider status, the assumption that an insider may be better positioned in the process of indigenous knowledge generation about Africa may need to be reconsidered. Good research practices and good data are often the results of insiders' and outsiders' collaboration, as well as of reflections on identity-making and knowledge-production processes and the relations among them. These reflections cannot eschew acknowledging the domination of Western perspectives in management studies, including in CCM, and the simultaneous neglect of alternative views, which we discuss in the following section.

Power and CCM

From the previous sections, there emerge two key issues that are particularly important for CCM researchers and practitioners. One refers to how power dynamics shape our identities and those of the persons around us, and the other refers to knowledge and the process through which it is developed and used.

Starting with the latter, in the previous pages we have highlighted that when undertaking management research and work in cross-cultural contexts, one of the challenges that needs to be addressed is the dominance of Western perspectives and the simultaneous neglect of alternative views.

To this regard, several pieces of research have exposed that management knowledge, despite its universalistic pretentions, has been developed mainly by Western (especially Anglo-American) scholars and has focused especially on organisations located in the United Kingdom and North America (Girei, 2017; Jack and Westwood, 2009). Importantly, this is true also for the field of CCM, which despite being focused on management "within, across, between and beyond cultures" (Mahadevan, 2011: 3), not only has been broadly developed for and within Western circles, but also significantly neglected issues of power and inequalities, and contributed to nurturing Eurocentric understandings of management and organisations (Romani and Höök, 2010). Mainstream CCM is often underpinned by assumptions about the superiority and universality of the Western canon, which, in turn, wittingly or unwittingly contributes to promoting or justifying derogatory representations of management knowledge and practices coming from the rest of the world.

Thus, several scholars have called for stronger engagement within the field with issues of power and inequalities (Primecz et al., 2016), with endogenous knowledge and with historically marginalised voices (Jackson, 2013). In this regard, Jackson argues that we "need to look further to the way knowledge is created within the global context, the dynamics involved in this and the way these changing dynamics may construct different ways of interpreting these realities" (Jackson, 2014: 4).

However, this should not be unreflectively translated into a call for indigenous knowledge, as often happens, and this for two reasons. One is that the notion of indigenous knowledge is often embedded in a romanticised aura, but lacks clear definitions (Jackson, 2013). The second is that the common understanding of the term (which usually refers to what is local against what is global and from outside) is highly problematic because it neglects intersections of cultures and ways of knowing. For instance, it has been argued that Africa and the West are much more intermingled and internally diversified than assumed by binary thinking about local and global or Africa and the West (Appiah, 2007; Zeleza, 2005). Other scholars have pointed out that African and Western ways of knowing are both tainted by their encounter and neither of them can claim to be completely pure (Quayson, 1997). As we saw in the previous pages, this view is also shared by our interviewees, which openly discussed the inaccuracy of the assumption that Africa-based researchers are most suited for knowledge generation about the continent. In this sense, we find the notion of 'radical contextuality' (Escobar, 2008: 200) to be more productive. This notion calls for a stronger embodiment and embedment of context(s) (human, cultural, symbolic, economic and so on) in research and managerial practices and processes. In this sense, the priority for cross-cultural researchers and practitioners is to closely engage with the context where they are working, so to understand what is meaningful and what is relevant, thus expanding and diversifying CCM knowledge.

This leads us to the second key issue emerging from the previous quotes, related to identity and power dynamics. Although the previous pages invite us to go beyond rigid categorisation about insiders and outsiders, we think it is important to recognise different roles for researchers that come from abroad and researchers that live where the research takes place but also the histories they come from and with. We thus acknowledge that an incautious emphasis on intersectionality might obscure historically rooted asymmetries and existing systems of oppression and privilege (Liu, 2018). For instance, it could be said that virtually all white researchers with experience of empirical work in sub-Saharan Africa are, sooner or later, compelled to deal with their whiteness, as it clearly emerged from the authors' and research participants' experiences. Here, whiteness is understood not as a physical attribute, but rather as performative identity resulting from historically rooted asymmetries and privileges. Thus, when we do research or managerial work in cross-cultural contexts or both, it is particularly important to position ourselves in the global context and reflect on how wider inequalities might impact in the specific context where we are working. For those committed to decolonising CCM research and practice, it becomes imperative to recognise and question these dynamics of privilege and power and open up possibilities for alternative ways of understanding, interpreting and interacting. In practice, this can be translated, in continuous self-reflective practices accompanied by a wiliness to learn new lenses to interpret the world around us and new ways of working.

Recommendations to Students, Researchers and Practitioners

In this concluding section, we summarise three key implications derived from our study. For each of them, we offer some questions to reflect on and recommendations.

Beyond Rigid Categorisation

A key point that emerges from our study is the need for students, researchers and practitioners to go beyond rigid categorisation of insider and outsider and to develop sensitivity and awareness of the continuous making and unmaking of our identities along the research process. The different encounters that we make and the different events that occur in how we make sense of CCM situations, as researchers and practitioners, continuously construct the relational settings we are involved in. This makes it possible for insider and outsider subjectivities to be simultaneously present or to move from one to the other several times. Another intertwined implication of our study is the centrality of an intersectional approach to identity, which requires not only to be aware of the different intersecting axes that make up our identities, but also to acknowledge how they together shape dynamics of power, privilege and oppression. It is thus important to ask: how is the insider/outsider boundary shifting in the specific relational context I am in? Which axes of identities are shaping the relational contexts and how? How are such intersecting identities shaping power dynamics? And are these power dynamics reproducing or contesting wider rooted asymmetries?

Beyond Indigenous/Endogenous, Towards Radical Contextuality

Our case suggests that rather than speaking of indigenous and endogenous knowledge, it might be more productive to focus toward a radical contextuality, so to privilege knowledge that makes sense in and is relevant to the specific context where we are working. This leads us away from romantic or exotic ideas of authentic knowledge, as well as abstract management ideas, which might not apply or be relevant in many CCM contexts.

Thus it is important as researchers and practitioners to ask: what do I know about the historical, political, economic and cultural context in which I am now involved? How does this knowledge guide how I interpret what is happening around me? How does my work here have an impact on these contexts?

Outsider/Insider Differentiation

Our case cautions against the dangers of an unreflective embracement of the notion of intersectionality, especially when it serves to conceal or overlook white privilege and wider asymmetries. In this regard, it is crucial for those engaged in CCM research or practice, and sensitive to the call for decolonising management knowledge, to position their own work in the wider context. This includes starting from the acknowledgment of the domination of Anglo-American perspectives in management and organisation studies and thus taking the specificities and dilemmas of working and doing research in the Global South into serious consideration. Crucial questions are thus: whose voices am I echoing? Who is benefiting from my research or practice? How does my research or practice contribute to decolonising management knowledge with regard to both its process and outcome?

Note

1. Alphabetical order; both authors contributed equally to the chapter.

References

Appiah KA (2007) *The Ethics of Identity.* Woodstock: Princeton University Press.
Escobar A (2008) Afterword. In Dar S and Cook B (eds) *The New Development Management: Critiquing the Dual Modernization.* London: Zed Books, pp. 198–203.
Girei E (2017) Decolonising management knowledge: A reflexive journey as practitioner and researcher in Uganda. *Management Learning* 48(4): 453–470.
Jack G and Westwood R (2009) *International and Cross-Cultural Management Structures: A Postcolonial Reading.* London: Palgrave MacMillan.
Jackson T (2013) Reconstructing the indigenous in African management research. *Management International Review* 53(1): 13–38.

Jackson T (2014) Cross-cultural management from the South: What a difference global dynamics make. *International Journal Cross Cultural Management* 14(1): 3–5.

Liu H (2018) Re-radicalising intersectionality in organisation studies. *Ephemera* 18(1): 81–101.

Mahadevan J (2011) Engineering culture(s) cross sites: Implications for cross-cultural management of emic meanings. In: Primecz H, Romani L and Sackmann S (eds) *Cross-Cultural Management in Practice*. Cheltenham: Edward Elgar Publishing, pp. 89–100.

Mahadevan J (2018) *A Very Short, Fairly Interesting and Resonably Cheap Book about Cross-Cultural Management*. London: SAGE.

Natukunda L, Johnson P and Dibben P (2016) A tale from the field: Reflexivity during management research in an African based development organisation. *Africa Journal of Management* 2(4): 422–437.

Prasad A (2009) Contesting hegemony through genealogy: Foucault and cross cultural management research. *International Journal of Cross Cultural Management* 9(3): 359–369.

Primecz, H, Mahadevan, J and Romani, L (2016) Why is cross-cultural management scholarship blind to power relations? Investigating ethnicity, language, gender and religion in power-laden contexts. *International Journal of Cross Cultural Management* 16(2): 127–136.

Quayson A (1997) Protocols of representation and the problems of constituting an African "Gnosis": Achebe and Okri. *The Yearbook of English Studies: The Politics of Postcolonial Criticism* 27: 137–149.

Rodriguez J and Freeman, KJ (2016) "Your focus on race is narrow and exclusive": The derailment of anti-racist work through discourses of intersectionality and diversity. *Whiteness and Education* 1(1): 69–82.

Roger K, Bone AT, Heinonen T, Schwartz K and Slater J (2018) Exploring identity: What we do as qualitative researchers. *The Qualitative report* 23(3): 532–546.

Romani L and Höök P (2010) The hidden side of cross-cultural management: A study agenda on absent perspectives in cross-cultural management research, education and management training. In: *2010 IACCM Conference*, UCLAN, Preston, UK, 22–25 June.

Tinker C and Armstrong N (2008) From the outside looking in: How an awareness of difference can benefit the Qualitative Research process. *The Qualitative Report* 13(1): 53–69.

Zeleza, TP (2005) Transnational education and African universities. *Journal of Higher Education in Africa* 3(1): 1–8.

16

HOW AND WHY AN ACADEMIC EXPERT LEGITIMATIZED SOCIAL MARGINALIZATION

The Case of Making and Shaping a Corporate Language Policy

Anders Klitmøller

Introduction

The juncture between corporate language policies and power has attracted increased attention within cross-cultural management (CCM) studies (e.g., Wilmot, 2017). However, little is known of how intersecting categories and their power effects are reproduced and academically legitimatized when working on corporate language policies in the multinational corporation (MNC). In this case I critically explore the three stages—pre-workshop, workshop and post-workshop—that where central for the making and shaping of a corporate language policy in the Danish MNC 'DanXY'. Here, I zoom in on the relationship between a manager, and myself, as an academic expert, as it unfolded in the making and shaping of the policy. I find that our pre-reflexive actions aided rather than critically challenged the power effects of the policy. I show how and why I, as an academic expert, came to legitimatize the reproduction of intersecting categories that excluded a certain grouping from getting access to English education. My motivation for making my pre-reflexive actions in this policy process explicit, is to invite students, researchers and practitioners to reflect upon their choice of categories and their reasons for using them when engaging in industry–university collaboration.

Methodology

In this case, I rely on data in the form of a formal and an informal interview, a business case, PowerPoint presentations, and e-mails. The data was gathered in the Danish owned MNC, DanXY. In 2015 the manager invited me to participate in a workshop. This workshop, which was executed in 2016, was central to making the company's global corporate language policy.[1] The corporate language policy consisted of two parts. One part of the policy entailed the possibility for employees to assess their English language proficiency online. They could then choose an online English language "training package" according to their level of proficiency (e-mail quote). Another part of the policy entailed that English language proficiency demands was associated with job roles and included in appraisal interviews.

In retrospect, it became clear that the manager had reproduced, and I had academically legitimatized, intersecting categories associated with four groupings in DanXY. These groupings were differently situated in the organizational hierarchy and the global economy. There were two central categorical divisions which made up the four groupings.

The first categorical division is related to the groups power position in the organizational hierarchy. "Salaried employees"[2] had a relatively higher position compared to "hourly paid" workers in DanXY. The second categorical division relates to the socioeconomic progression, and economic growth potential, of a group of countries. Developing countries is a category I use to encompass the following groupings of countries which are represented in the case; "emergent economies", "emerging countries", "new growth markets", "stake countries", "BRIC countries" and "growth regions".[3] Developing countries, are positioned relatively lower in terms of power in the global economy compared to developed countries. The four groupings represented by the intersections between the two sets of categorical divisions, are shown in Table 16.1:

TABLE 16.1 The Four Groupings and Their Power Positions in the Organizational Hierarchy and the Global Economy

	Developed Countries	*Developing Countries*	*Power Position in the DanXY Hierarchy*
"Salaried employee"	"Salaried employee"— developed countries	"Salaried employee"— developing countries	*High*
"Hourly paid" worker	"Hourly paid" worker—developed countries	"Hourly paid" worker—developing countries	*Low*
Power position in the global economy	*High*	*Low*	

In my approach to reflexivity I am inspired by Pierre Bourdieu (2003). He invites students and researchers to study themselves in the same way that we study others. By doing so, we can get a clearer understanding of how and why our pre-reflexive actions, as academics, make and shape the different social processes we are involved in. In my understanding pre-reflexivity means that there are aspects of our social actions and their consequences that we do not reflect upon. Here reflexivity does not merely mean that we reflect on what we do. It is also the ability to understand *how* and *why* we do the things we do; an ability that makes us likely to acknowledge the social consequences of our actions. This, in turn, makes it easier to change our actions when we engage with others. Bourdieu (1977) finds that social relations and social recognition is central for understanding the activities we partake in (Wacquant and Akçaoğlu, 2017). So, it is by reflecting on our pre-reflexive actions, in this case our use of categories, when we relate to others in search of recognition, that we may gain a deeper understanding of our social actions.

Case Presentation

In the following sections I showcase how the manager and I, in the making and shaping of the corporate language policy, focused on the category "salaried employee" as intersecting with the category from developing countries. I also display, that by having this focus, how the manager reproduced, and I pre-reflexively legitimatized, that the category "hourly paid" workers were excluded from English education. I argue that this exclusion from educational resources was particularly problematic for "hourly paid" workers from developing countries. This was so, because this grouping was marginalized *both* in the organizational hierarchy and in the global economy. After showing *how* I came to academically legitimatize this exclusion, I reflexively consider *why* I, in search for recognition, did so.

Pre-Workshop: Reproducing Intersecting Categories

In the pre-workshop stage of making and shaping the corporate language policy, two actions were central for the reproduction of intersecting categories in DanXY. First, the manager used an established corporate initiative to motivate the need for increasing English language proficiency. Second, the manager argued for the need of English education in a business case and a PowerPoint presentation. Here he focused on the grouping "salaried employees" from developing countries, and their lack of English language proficiency.

The manager linked the necessity for increasing English language proficiency in DanXY to a corporate initiative which entailed some desirable behaviours. The initiative entailed a set of behaviours which the CEO had emphasized in " . . . *flaming letters . . . as . . . enablers for our strategy*" (interview quote). One of these behaviours was "collaboration". It was the perceived link between English language proficiency and "collaboration" on a global level— or rather a lack thereof—which encouraged the manager to work with a corporate language policy in DanXY:

... So that was it [collaboration] which triggered me. It was the collaboration part because through my work ... I was very ... aware ... that it was a limited amount of our employees ... who spoke [English] on a level which would make them able to do collaboration.

(Interview quote)

The manager also developed a business case and a PowerPoint presentation. In the business case he emphasized the category "salaried employee". He focused on "salaried employees" inability to "collaborate", because of a lack of English language proficiency:

An internal survey in DanXY ... documented that a large proportion of our DanXY colleagues don't speak or understand English at a level that allows them to collaborate across language borders. Not only is this a problem in some of our growth regions like S[outh] America, Russia and China but [it is] even so in ... European markets like Germany, France and Italy.

(Quote from business case)

Here, the manager includes both "salaried employees" from developing and developed countries, and their inability to act in concordance with the desirable behavior of "collaboration". However, it became clear, in a PowerPoint presentation for the Human Resources Senior Vice President, that his focus was on the intersection between "salaried employee" and developing countries:

The fact is however that a large part of our employees is excluded from collaboration due to missing [English] proficiency. . . . The background [is that on] average 26% of DanXY white collar employees [across 30 countries] will ... *not be able* to attend an English spoken class due to language difficulties ... It is noteworthy that a number of new growth markets are to be found on the right-hand side of the graphic ["right-hand side of the graphic" refers to countries with high English non-proficiency level].

(Quote from PowerPoint Presentation)

In a subsequent interview, it became clear why the manager had focused on the intersection between the categories of "salaried employees" and developing countries:

... We have some countries that are particularly bad, and that actually helped me in my argumentation because for example China and Brazil were bad ... [and] had a very low level ... [of] English proficiency ...

and that coincided with that exactly these two countries were at that time BRIC countries, and it were also some of our stake countries. So, that also sharpened the argumentation . . . that exactly those countries in which we . . . wished to do a whole lot, there they spoke miserable English, right.

(Interview quote)

In sum, the manager used the initiative of desirable behaviours, and "collaboration" in particular, to emphasize the need for English education. To push the corporate language policy forward he used the intersection "salaried employees" from developing countries since this group of countries was of strategic interest to DanXY. However, by explicating this group in his policy work, he also implicitly and pre-reflexively omitted "hourly paid" workers. An omission which I, as an academic expert, came to legitimatize in the making and shaping of the policy.

Workshop: The Academic Legitimization of Intersecting Categories

The second stage of the corporate language policy process was characterized by the preparation and execution of a workshop. Here the efforts of the manager centred in on the academic legitimization of the business rationale behind the corporate language policy. He wanted me, as an academic expert, to legitimatize his pre-workshop actions.

In the first part of a PowerPoint presentation I delivered at the workshop I confirmed that language differences could have detrimental impact on "collaboration", due to lack of "trust", problems with "knowledge sharing" and "communication" and increase in "conflict". Thereby I legitimatized academically that low English language proficiency was detrimental to collaboration. Thus, I established a research-based link between the corporate language policy and the corporate initiative, so central for the managers' policy efforts.

In the second part of my presentation, I legitimatized the intersection between the category "salaried employee" and developing countries. I had supported this partition in an e-mail correspondence before the workshop in which I stated that:

It also seems like you have instigated some important initiatives, so you raise the general language level. Of course, this is particularly important in relation to the groupings which have a lot of communication in English.

(E-mail quote)

In underscoring that English education on a global level should be reserved to groupings with a high degree of interaction in English, I had pre-reflexively legitimatized that the resources central to the corporate language policy should be reserved to specific employment categories. In this case that of "salaried employee". Also, in my PowerPoint presentation at the workshop, I explicitly related the category "salaried employee" to developing countries. Indeed, the manager had, in an e-mail, up to the workshop pushed the importance of academically substantiating the intersection between the categories:

> Hi again—I forgot to mention but I am personally convinced that language training is potentially a motivating factor thereby also potentially a retention factor for employees. I believe this goes . . . for young people in emerging countries. I will be happy if this can be substantiated.
>
> *(E-mail quote)*

Hence, I included fieldwork data in my presentation, containing a story of a Mexican white-collar worker who had been enrolled in a language training program in a Danish MNC. On my PowerPoint slide, I concluded the following: "In emergent economies, such as the Mexican, English language programs are central for the retention of white-collar employees. English is viewed a[s] crucial for career development and social mobility" (quote from PowerPoint presentation).

Perhaps not surprisingly, the workshop, to which I was invited, was not primarily aimed at developing new ideas concerning the corporate language policy, but rather, to do something else:

> . . . One thing is what I postulate another thing is to actually hear it from one in an academic research environment tell some things. It is . . . always interesting and thought-provoking. I think that maybe legitimization might not be the right word either but being a part of enhancing my argumentation about it.
>
> *(Interview quote)*

Although in this statement he is reluctant to use the word legitimization, he centres his prior argumentation around the notion, and states that the workshop was politically motivated:

> . . . But I thought . . . quite simply that it was interesting to get that voice with [an academic]; I myself can do a bit of basic research on the things, but I thought it was interesting to get another voice in who could say something about some of the experiences one had from a research point of view. So, for me it was also a question of like legitimatize the whole project. So, it is also a bit political, I would say.
>
> *(Interview quote)*

Thus, the purpose of the workshop was to create legitimacy to the policy process; an action of which he seemed reflexive about. So, his aim with me was to reinforce the trustworthiness of his line of reasoning: "There the academics, you see, also created a credibility around the whole argumentation"(interview quote). In line with this, I legitimatized the need for a corporate language policy, by arguing that low English language proficiency is a hindrance to "collaboration". I also legitimatized the intersection between the category of "salaried employee" and developing countries. In doing so I pre-reflexively excluded "hourly paid" workers from the policy process. This was particularly problematic for the grouping who was dually excluded from obtaining resources, namely "hourly paid" workers from developing countries.

Post-Workshop: Explicating the Reproduction and Legitimization of Social Marginalization

It was not until the post-workshop stage of making and shaping the corporate language policy that the manager and I together, made explicit the categories which he had reproduced, and I had academically legitimatized. Here the categories of "salaried employee" and its opposition, namely that of "hourly paid" worker became clearer to me. So, did the power effects of those categorizations, and their intersections with developed and developing countries. The manager, and I, contributed, on a pre-reflexive level, to a social division that was deeply rooted in the organization and the global economy. Thereby we aided in the continuous socio-economic marginalization of "hourly paid" workers.

The category "employee" in DanXY, was contextually determined. So, at times it meant "salaried employee", rather than all persons working in DanXY. The latter category was in the post-workshop reflections of the manager contrasted to that of "hourly paid" workers: "Yes, so . . . in many regards we have this . . . cleavage between the things we do when we talk hourly paid [workers] and salaried employees. Because there are different premises" (interview quote). Per the manager, the difference between the two groupings, associated with the two categories, was that the "hourly paid" workers were more educationally and electronically marginalized:

> Yes, generally we have a huge cleavage between the two employee groupings with us. It is a part of what can you say more traditional contractual differences. . . . You see, it varies from country to country. It is about the hourly paid are somewhat more in and out. It is more a workforce which you regulate up and down according to need. It is typically people, dare I say which are on a lower educational level compared to the salaried employee group. It is typically people where we due to occupational politics do not allow ourselves to push content over, which demands IT equipment.
>
> *(Interview quote)*

For the manager, including the "hourly paid" workers in the English education, was not an immediate option, especially since the learning modules where
based on digital technology: "We cannot presume that these people have com-
puters or for that matter mobile telephones. Quite simply it is not politically
permissible" (interview quote). So, the fact that "hourly paid" workers were
already technologically marginalized compared with their "salaried employee"
counterparts, led to further marginalization, since it became comparatively
more difficult for them to participate in online English education. It also led to
the hierarchization of "hourly paid" workers from developed versus developing countries. For while, the manager would not force "hourly paid" workers
to participate in English education and would not forbid it either. Arguably,
"hourly paid" workers in developed countries have more experience, time and
access to the Internet and communication technologies than the latter group.
Thereby "hourly paid" workers in developed countries had grander possibilities of raising their English proficiency level, central for career mobility, compared to "hourly paid" workers in developing countries.

Power and CCM

In this case, I have centred on the relationship between the manager and
myself as an academic expert. This relationship proved fundamental for the
reproduction and academic legitimization of the intersecting categorizations
characterizing the making and shaping of a corporate language policy in an
MNC. Central to intersectionality is an interest in understanding how categories intersects and shapes social marginalization (Boogaard and Roggeband,
2010), and the role of academics in constructing and reproducing inequality in
organizations (McCall, 2005; Villesèche et al., 2018). Here I have drawn on a
Bourdieu-inspired take on intersectionality and reflexivity (Tatli and Özbilgin,
2012; Bourdieu, 2003).

I have highlighted how both managers and academics are cultural producers
(Bohman, 1997). Hence culture, and its context-specific categories, is generated through our actions when we engage in social relations. Importantly,
cultural categories are never neutral. Rather categories are infused with power
effects. This is so, since categories are central for the division of resources; in this
case, English education. Therefore categorizations, in effect, shape English
language skills or the lack thereof, and thus are decisive for power positions
in the global capitalist order (Wilmot, 2017; Vaara et al., 2005). Indeed,
Bourdieu argues that the form of power most pivotal for understanding social
reproduction is the ability to categorize. This is because categorization, often
in an unnoticeable manner, allows one to impose one's view on the world,
thereby shaping the world to one's advantage (Wacquant and Akçaoğlu, 2017).
Here, both students and researchers alike might, albeit perhaps pre-reflexively,

legitimatize certain categorizations and consequently inavertedly aid in the reproduction of social marginalization.

Reflexive Considerations

Thus far, this case has highlighted *how* rather than *why* I, as an academic expert, legitimatized categorical intersections in the making and shaping of the corporate language policy. So, in the following section I will, in a reflexive manner, consider why I acted like I did. In line with Bourdieu (1977), I am of the opinion that every social relation entails a negotiation of power. The ability to exercise power is only possible, however, when we are recognized as being powerful (Wacquant and Akçaoğlu, 2017). To gain recognition, one must present oneself as knowledgeable and skilled in the eyes of the person from which one wants to be recognized. In this case, I wanted the manager to recognize my abilities. To do so, I pr-reflexively used his categories when we worked together. However, because of my background and job position at a Danish university I, by adopting his categorizations, also academically legitimatized his categories and their intersections. Presently, in Denmark, academics are experiencing increased pressure towards industry–university collaboration. Here one can, as I did in search for recognition, become too focused on presenting aspects of one's research and data, which legitimatizes practitioners' existing worldviews. I believe that one should rather, in the role of an academic expert, challenge practitioners' common-sense categories. For a while, the first point of departure tends to reproduce and enforce existing social divisions in the organization, the latter focal point allows for an extension of the practitioners' understanding and use of categorizations. So, it is important to acknowledge that our embeddedness in academia, as either student or researcher grants us power—power which can be used to reproduce existing modes of action, as explicated in the present case, or be used to critically reflect upon culturally embedded power effects.

I also came to learn that pre-reflexive actions characterize the whole research project, even when taking a more critical approach. Hence, in the final stages of writing the chapter, I came to realize that I had misinterpreted a part of the policy. This was the part which entailed that English-language proficiency demands were associated with job roles and included in appraisal interviews. In the first reading(s) of the data related to the corporate language policy, I became convinced that the "salaried employees" at the lower end of the organization would become more marginalized by this initiative, compared with "salaried employees" in more elevated positions. I was of the understanding that I had played a legitimizing role in this. However, through a critical reassessment of my pre-reflexive theoretical understanding of the material, and an informal follow-up interview, I found that the opposite was true. Indeed, this policy action levelled the power differentials within the group of "salaried employees". When I told the manager this he laughed and said: "*Now your whole theory collapses*" (interview quote). This experience taught me that one must be continuously reflexive, even when engaging in and applying a more critical approach to organizational policies. Another yet similar problem holds for the writing phase. Indeed, in the process of writing the present case I pre-reflexively used, and perhaps still do, overly complex academic language, relative to the target audience of the book. This shows how language in academia is also used to gain power (Bourdieu, 1991). In turn, this might then exclude students and practitioners from obtaining insights into a more reflexive way of grasping social life in organizations.

We might again ask, *why* I do so? My answer would be the same. My too-critical and theory-laden interpretation of the case and my too-complex academic writing was aimed at gaining recognition—this time, not from the manager in an MNC, but from the editors of the book and senior researchers at universities. And again, my pre-reflexive actions would, had I not reflected upon the way I interpreted the data through working on this case, have reproduced a certain theoretical worldview. It would also have legitimatized the exclusion of students and practitioners with lower academic English language proficiency level from understanding the case and its conclusions. Thereby I would have pre-reflexively excluded them from critically assessing their involvement in policy processes. In sum, the first step towards reflexivity is to acknowledge that the social use of language is not power free (Bourdieu, 1991). Here we, as academics, also act pre-reflexively, and we do so for the same reasons that practitioners do: namely, to be recognized as competent and skilled professionals.

Recommendations to Students, Researchers and Practitioners

Taking this into consideration, it is central that we as practitioners in industry or academics at universities acknowledge our pre-reflexive need for recognition. This is important because we pre-reflexively use social categories to obtain that recognition. Categories that can have marginalizing consequences for certain groupings. I believe that reflecting on our pre-reflexive inclinations to act in a certain way is an ongoing work.

One way of creating reflexivity is to continuously ask how and why we act a certain way when we engage in social relations. To do so, one can take a critical theoretical approach when engaging with industry as an academic. This is because, by using a theoretical standpoint that differs from the worldviews dominating the organization, we can disrupt and make explicit practitioners' pre-reflexive use of categories. This also goes for students who strive to become practitioners. Hence practitioners can use critical theory obtained at universities to challenge common-sense categories guiding the ascription of recognition and the division of resources within a given organization. Conversely, it is equally important that we as academics are sensitive towards the categorizations used in industry. This is because we can use practitioners' categories to disrupt our own inclination to reproduce a certain theoretical worldview. Furthermore, as academics, we can use each other and our diverse experience with communication to different audiences, to make explicit for each other our pre-reflexive ways of writing. In line with this, I invite students, researchers and practitioners to explore the following questions:

- Which categories, and intersections thereof, characterize the policy processes in the organization, and which social divisions do they create?
- How do I as a student and researcher use critical theory to disrupt, and thus make explicit, the pre-reflexive categories used by practitioners in industry?
- How do I as a student and researcher use empirical categories to critically disrupt, and thus make explicit, pre-reflexive and theoretically laden ways of interpreting data?
- How do I as a student and researcher use my fellow students or research colleagues to disrupt marginalizing ways of writing?
- How can I as a practitioner in industry, use a critical approach that makes explicit dominant pre-reflexive categories and their social consequences?

So, I believe through a critical engagement with organizational categories, the theories we use to decipher them, and the way we communicate, we can continuously find new possibilities for social action in organizations.

Notes

1. Although the manager labelled the initiative a "strategy" (e-mail quote), I use the term "corporate language policy" when describing the making and shaping of the initiative. This is because I view the initiative as an aid for the corporate strategy, rather than the strategy itself.
2. In this case, the category "salaried employee" includes the groupings "white-collar employee" and "colleagues". The category "employee" is more ambiguous. In some instances, it refers to "salaried employees" and in others to all persons employed by DanXY.
3. By using the category: "developing countries", I take the common denominator between "emergent economies", "emerging countries", "new growth markets", "stake countries", "BRIC countries" and "growth regions" to be different from that of developed countries. Therefore, developing and developed countries are an ideal type and nonexplicated categorical division that I use to present the case.

References

Bohman J (1997) Reflexivity, agency and constraint: The paradoxes of Bourdieu's sociology of knowledge. *Social Epistemology* 11(2): 971–1186.

Boogaard B and Roggeband C (2010) Paradoxes of intersectionality: Theorizing inequality in the Dutch police force through structure and agency. *Organization* 17(1): 53–75.

Bourdieu P (1977) *Outline of a Theory of Practice*. Cambridge: Cambridge University Press.

Bourdieu P (1991) *Language and Symbolic Power*. Cambridge: Polity Press.

Bourdieu P (2003) Participant objectivation. *The Journal of the Royal Anthropological Institute* 9(2): 281–294.

McCall L (2005) The complexity of intersectionality. *Signs* 30(3): 1771–1800.

Tatli A and Özbilgin MF (2012) An emic approach to intersectional study of diversity at work: A Bourdieuan framing. *International Journal of Management Reviews* 14(2): 180–200.

Vaara E, Tienari J, Piekkari R and Säntti, R (2005) Language and the circuits of power in a merging multinational corporation. *Journal of Management Studies* 42(3): 595–623.

Villesèche F, Muhr SL and Holck L (2018) *Diversity and Identity in the Workplace: Connections and Perspectives*. Cham: Palgrave MacMillan.

Wacquant L and Akçaoğlu A (2017) Practice and symbolic power in Bourdieu: The view from Berkeley. *Journal of Classical Sociology* 17(1): 55–69.

Wilmot NV (2017) Language and the faces of power: A theoretical approach. *International Journal of Cross Cultural Management* 17(1): 85–100.

INDEX